NOBODY TOLD US WE ARE DEFEATED

Nobody Told Us We Are Defeated

Stories from the New Iraq

Rory McCarthy

Chatto & Windus
LONDON

Published by Chatto & Windus 2006

2 4 6 8 10 9 7 5 3

This book is published in association with Guardian Books.
Guardian Books is an imprint of Guardian Newspapers Limited.
The Guardian is a registered trademark of Guardian Media Group plc.

theguardian

First published in Great Britain in 2006 by
Chatto & Windus
Random House, 20 Vauxhall Bridge Road,
London SW1V 2SA

Random House Australia (Pty) Limited
20 Alfred Street, Milsons Point, Sydney,
New South Wales 2061, Australia

Random House New Zealand Limited
18 Poland Road, Glenfield, Auckland 10, New Zealand

Random House (Pty) Limited
Isle of Houghton, Corner of Boundary Road & Carse O'Gowrie,
Houghton, 2198, South Africa

Random House Publishers India Private Limited
301 World Trade Tower, Hotel Intercontinental Grand Complex
Barakhamba Lane, New Delhi 110 001, India

The Random House Group Limited Reg. No. 954009
www.randomhouse.co.uk

A CIP catalogue record for this book
is available from the British Library

ISBN 9780701180560 (from Jan 2007)
ISBN 0701180560

Papers used by Random House are natural,
recyclable products made from wood grown in sustainable forests.
The manufacturing processes conform to the environmental
regulations of the country of origin

Printed and bound in Great Britain by
Mackays of Chatham PLC

For my parents

War happens to people, one by one. That is really all I have to say and it seems to me I have been saying it for ever. Unless they are immediate victims, the majority of mankind behaves as if war was an act of God which could not be prevented; or they behave as if war elsewhere was none of their business. It would be a bitter cosmic joke if we destroy ourselves due to atrophy of the imagination.

Martha Gellhorn, *The Face of War*, 1967

Contents

Preface

I didn't know it would turn out the way it has in Iraq, nobody did. Nor can I say with any authority what will happen there in the years to come, except that it seems to me the violent reaction unleashed by the invasion of 2003 still has a long, long way to run. All I can tell you is that I lived in Baghdad for nearly two years as a reporter for the *Guardian* and I witnessed the war for myself. I didn't live in the fortified bubble that the Americans called the Green Zone and, apart from a week at most, I wasn't embedded with a military unit. For most of the time I lived in a house on an ordinary street.

The time after the invasion was a passing moment when it was still safe enough to move around the country independently and to speak to Iraqis on their own terms. Too quickly that changed. In the last few months I spent in Iraq I couldn't leave Baghdad without travelling with the military and there were even parts of the city that were too dangerous to enter. I returned again in October 2005, just after the *Guardian* journalist Rory Carroll, who replaced me in Iraq, had been kidnapped. After thirty-six hours he was released unharmed and we flew home together, leaving behind a country that was becoming ever more closed off to the outside world. A few weeks later, two suicide car bombers attacked the hotel where we had been staying, killing at least eight Iraqis, whose apartment block was flattened, and wrecking the room in which I had spent my final months in Baghdad.

Early on I realised that of all the thousands of words written and spoken about this war across the world each day, most came from our generals, our diplomats and our politicians in the West and very few came from the Iraqis themselves. A war silences a people and obscures the truth and the war in Iraq has done so more than most. The least journalists can do is to record what we have seen and heard so it cannot be forgotten or denied: not the official version of events but real experiences captured on the ground.

I have on my desk in front of me now a pile of thirty-two notebooks from those days, filled with the words of Iraqis. These are some of their stories.

R.M.
Beirut, April 2006

1

Out of the Graves

Qais was sitting in the front seat of the car and talking again about fear. He believed there was a policeman who patrolled inside your mind, scrutinising every thought even before it was formed. The policeman in your head was bigger than the policeman on the street, he said. You knew not to let your mind think for itself. It was the secret cog in the machine of dictatorship. He said it wouldn't be easy to dislodge the policeman even now the regime had fallen.

Qais was my guide. He had a round face, a day's growth of beard and a pair of small, circular spectacles. It was impossible not to be charmed by him. In private he was a poet consumed by grand imagined romances. In public he had spent many years working at the front desk of the Ishtar Sheraton, a concrete-heavy but once luxurious riverside hotel in Baghdad. In the last years before the war he worked as a guide for state archaeological tours and he delighted in stories about the ancient lords of Mesopotamia, men like Hammurabi and Nebuchadnezzar. At night he would get drunk and then we argued.

It was a warm afternoon in May 2003 and we had left Baghdad to drive south. The road was narrow and choked at first and then gradually it broadened out, following the path of the Euphrates into the clay-red farmland of southern Iraq. To the side of the highway, just a few miles outside the capital, we passed a walled compound piled with dozens of wrecked

3

military vehicles. Broken olive-painted armoured personnel carriers and upturned tanks lay side by side or on top of one another. Each still bore the white Arabic numerals that identified division and regiment. A month before, thousands of American soldiers had fought their way up this road, blasting through the Iraqi army emplacements in the push towards Baghdad. The remains of the routed army had already been swept up and tidied away. Later they would be stripped for scrap.

As the road widened, fields stretched out on either side. Small mud ridges divided the land and thick groves of date palms sheltered modest brick farmhouses. A queue of eucalyptus trees, the bark peeling off their trunks, stood along the verge. A car passed with a roughly hewn wooden coffin strapped to the roof. It was heading for burial in the cemetery of the Valley of Peace in Najaf, a holy city for the Shia Muslims who make up more than half Iraq's population. Our driver raised his hands from the wheel for a moment, turning his palms upwards in prayer as we overtook the convoy of mourners. After an hour or so the road passed at a distance the ruins of Babylon, the deathbed of Alexander the Great and perhaps the most glorious of the ancient cities to which Qais had led his tours. Now they were occupied by American troops and almost completely out of bounds.

At the village of Mahawil there was a narrow dirt trail on the left. There was no signpost but rutted tracks showed many cars had already passed this way so we followed and skirted round a barren hillock. Before us was a large expanse of mud, an abandoned field. Crowds of people were crouched down poring over the soil. A sour smell rose up. Dozens of broad, shallow craters had been carved out of the earth, and between them were narrow, connecting ridges that had been trodden down into walkways. To one side were rows of large, clear plastic

4

bags. The bags were spaced neatly a few feet apart and each was filled with old clothes and beneath the clothes, human bones. Next to one bag was a broken pair of crutches. A prosthetic leg emerged from another. Some of the skulls still had rags tied around the eye-sockets, others were small enough to have belonged to children. A few of the bags contained identity cards with faded photographs. Scores of men and women were walking from one bag to the next looking at the identity cards and trying to recognise the pictures. If they couldn't find a picture there were other pieces of evidence to cling to: a shirt they recognised, a pair of shoes, a piece of jewellery maybe. In one case someone produced a crumpled cigarette packet and swore it had belonged to his missing relative. It was several minutes before I noticed here and there small tufts of what was unmistakably human hair protruding from the caked ground beneath me. I began to look out for them and to tiptoe carefully round them.

The first person I spoke to at the gravesite was a farmer. Today was his fourth day searching for the bodies of his three brothers. Like all the victims here, they were Shia Muslims taken away by Saddam's security forces and summarily executed in March 1991. The killings were the regime's response to the *intifada*, the brief moment in the wake of the first Gulf War when the Shia in the south and the Kurds in the north rose up in violent and chaotic rebellion against Saddam. The farmer was detached. I thought it was odd that he didn't cry. Instead his eyes stared straight ahead as if he didn't want to acknowledge the clamour around him. He had already found the remains of the youngest of his brothers: an identity card wrapped in a bundle of bones and rags, nothing more. Now he was looking for the remains of the elder two.

The second man I met was looking for his two cousins. One had been a soldier aged twenty-two when he went missing and the second was still at school and aged only seventeen. The man described how Republican Guardsmen, part of Saddam's loyal security elite and mostly Sunni Muslims from further north, came to his home and asked for food that March. He was afraid and stayed at the back of the house, but his two young cousins brought them out bread and dates. Then another Republican Guard officer joined them and said he needed two more prisoners to complete the quota that had been set for him and so the two young men were arrested. They never returned. A total of thirty-three people from this man's street alone were missing and thought to be in the grave.

By now the undertakers had arrived, offering wooden coffins priced at 15,000 dinars, around £7. The families knew in their hearts that the missing were dead, but few had held proper funerals or mourned for the customary forty days. They had had no bodies to bury. Now their grief had been released again by the fall of the regime. I walked over to the far side of the field where a crowd had gathered. Half a dozen men wearing orange kitchen gloves had hired a large, yellow mechanical digger and were tearing their way through the earth. I joined the crowd that pushed forward greedily to watch. At first they removed layers of topsoil, then after half a metre or so came the bodies, many already crumbled, others sliced apart by the machine itself. I say bodies, but they were hardly that. They were bones, grey and stripped of flesh. 'Give us space to dig,' one of the men in gloves shouted at us. 'We have to find them.'

In their haste there was no forensic analysis and no summoning of specialists to seal off the site or record the evidence, even though it was by now obvious what lay before us. This one field near the village of Mahawil, sixty miles south of Baghdad, was by far the largest gravesite uncovered in Iraq and evidence of a startling crime. Later it was determined there were 3,000 bodies buried in the field.

On the side of the hillock, away from the crowd and surrounded by half a dozen heavily armed American troops, US Marine Lieutenant-General James Conway, commander of the 15th Marine Expeditionary Unit, was talking in English to a small group of Iraqis. He was tall and wore the distinct mottled camouflage uniform of the Marines and a small peaked cloth cap to keep the burning sun from his skin. 'Our feeling is that you would rather do this yourselves,' he told them. 'The proper thing is for these people to be able to bury their families. We have the evidence we need.' And then he walked away.

Thirteen years earlier, in August 1990, Saddam had sent his army to invade Kuwait. Iraq was reeling from the cost of an eight-year war with Iran and the Iraqi dictator coveted the rich Kuwaiti oilfields, a desire he disguised in ageing notions of pan-Arab unity. He seized the little emirate swiftly but it was a huge political miscalculation. Neighbouring governments saw it not as a triumph of pan-Arabism, but as a threat to their own security and stability. Within six months the United States brought together a broad coalition of nations, including many in the Arab world, to stand against Iraq and its ruling Ba'ath party. The US military then led a war against Saddam's ill-equipped, conscript army, killing thousands of Iraqi soldiers and sending the rest retreating home. On the last day in February 1991, Saddam ordered a general to go down to the Kuwaiti border to sign a ceasefire. The next day the Iraqi people began a rebellion. The *intifada* spread rapidly across the country. As soon as the extent of the revolt was clear US President George Bush senior encouraged all Iraqis to resist and to topple his enemy in Baghdad.[1] But this time there was to be no Western military assistance, even though American troops were still deployed deep into southern Iraq.

The uprising began in Basra, when a tank driver fired a shell straight through a vast portrait of Saddam. Crowds quickly poured onto the street in defiance of the regime. Three days later Kurds living in the north also began a revolt. Thousands of soldiers disillusioned by war and defeat deserted their regiments and joined the uprising. Within days the rebels controlled fourteen of Iraq's eighteen governorates and nearly every major city in the south and north, leaving Baghdad almost isolated. Many of Saddam's officials and military officers were killed in the rioting. Even without the help of the US, it was the biggest challenge his rule had ever faced.[2] For a few days his regime seemed in grave danger. Then he dealt the rebels a swift and severe blow. The grave I saw was just one of many left from the crushing of the 1991 spring *intifada*.

When I first went to Iraq I was thirty-one. I had a degree in history and had been a journalist for nearly ten years, but I had no experience of the Middle East. I had been working for some time as a reporter with a French news agency in Hong Kong and Tokyo and in 1999 had been sent to Pakistan. Two weeks before I arrived in Islamabad, General Musharraf had taken power in a coup and pushed the country into the headlines, which, at least as far as I was concerned, was fortuitous. I quit my job and started to send stories to the *Guardian*. I wrote about the new military regime in Pakistan, human rights abuses, political corruption and Islamic militancy. I travelled in the Afghanistan of the Taliban and then returned after September 11 when their regime fell. I saw some fighting and took some risks but, still, I was only a freelancer on a modest retainer. Some days if my story didn't make the paper my translator earned more than me. I felt junior compared to some of the well-known reporters who flocked to Kabul with their bullet-proof jackets and testy egos and I certainly didn't consider myself a war correspondent. A year later I was still in Pakistan, but now on staff with the *Guardian*. They sent me to Iraq to cover the presidential referendum.

This was the first of two visits I would make to Baghdad before the American invasion. It proved easy to get a press visa, which was a sure sign that something was being stage-managed. Seven years earlier, Saddam had won a 99.96 per cent Yes vote. Now officials hinted the result would be even better. We were packed into coaches and driven to Tikrit, Saddam's hometown, where we saw nobody on the streets or at the shops. The only crowd was at the one polling station we had been taken to see, where people ran up to the cameras and pricked their fingers so they could mark their Yes vote in blood. The next day the government said every eligible voter had cast a ballot for the president, describing the 100 per cent result as a 'quantum leap' in democracy. It took much longer to get a visa for the second trip two months later. I went back to follow the UN inspectors as they drove around the country searching in vain for signs of a chemical-, biological- or nuclear-weapons programme. I followed them to several factories and warehouses which stored barrels of toxic-looking chemicals with names like Chemo-rat, though none proved to be anything more deadly than industrial pesticide.

It was a particularly difficult place to work. The regime controlled every aspect of life and dragged us journalists through its impossibly corrupt bureaucracy. As soon as I walked off the plane (every other step on the gangway was marked 'Down USA') I had to pay a bribe to avoid an impromptu AIDS test at the airport, where the doctors re-used a single steel needle. I had to have my satellite telephone sealed with tape at the airport, and another unofficial payment was demanded. I had to pay again when I had it formally unsealed at the Ministry of Information later that day. As a journalist I had to have an official Iraqi minder at my shoulder, ostensibly to translate and guide me through the country, but quite clearly also to report back on my activities and curb my inquisitiveness. I had only a little Arabic so I was more

9

reliant than I wanted to be on my minder. One day I had heard a rumour of a demonstration outside the headquarters of the intelligence service and I asked to be taken there. My minder, a precious man who always clutched a large leather purse in his hand, spoke to the driver and we headed off. Some time later we arrived in the middle of a busy market. There was nothing in sight that looked remotely like an intelligence agency headquarters. 'Perhaps you might like to buy a leather jacket?' he said. When I asked why we were there he said I was forbidden from visiting the intelligence building. On another day I was assigned a more junior and open-minded young bureaucrat. I asked if he could help me meet a political prisoner. A few days later he introduced me to a neighbour of his, a dentist, and we sat together on a sofa in the lobby of the Mansour Melia hotel. He had just been freed as part of a sweeping prison amnesty a few months before the war. I asked him to tell me about his arrest. He looked at me and began to tremble. 'They told us: "If you talk we will arrest you again and this time we will kill you,"' he said and he drew his finger slowly across his throat. I said I no longer needed to hear his story.

After the regime fell, the *Guardian* sent me back to Iraq, this time to live there as a correspondent. I flew to Amman and found a travel agent who arranged for me to take a $500 taxi ride in a large, GMC four-wheel drive across twelve hours of desert and into Baghdad. I left at midnight and the next morning I checked into the Hamra Hotel near Baghdad University. The rooms were in two dun-coloured towers, separated by an open-air swimming pool. Nearly every window was marked with a large cross in long stretches of masking tape, a largely symbolic precaution against the American bombing raids. The beds were narrow and hard.

The grave at Mahawil was discovered a couple of weeks later, at a time when no one could say precisely what was happening, or what was about to. There were only a few certainties. First, there had been a tremendous wave of looting immediately after the fall of the regime, which had now largely subsided of its own accord. Second, Shia clerics and their armed followers were taking over large parts of eastern Baghdad. And third, the Americans were here but they didn't seem to have much idea what to do next.

The grave, of course, was an old certainty. Many people had been killed in the Saddam years. Now here were the bodies. It was easy enough to report on the horror of what I saw, the grief of the relatives and the anger of those who wanted the Americans to conduct a proper survey. But I also thought how transfixing I found the graveyard, how other-worldly the place was. As I sat in the car writing up my notes, the graves just a dozen yards away, the sun was setting over the fields in the distance. Many of the families and most of the other journalists had left and it was quiet. I had stopped registering the foul smell. The heat had been sapped out of the day and the sky glowed.

A few feet in front of me an American man, who I supposed was with a television crew, laid out a rug by the side of his car and began to pray. A couple of Iraqis chatting nearby stopped to watch and their eyes widened. By the way the American folded his hands across his stomach they saw at once he was a Sunni Muslim. They began to talk loudly and gesture at him as if he had offered them some terrible insult. I went over with Qais. The American continued to pray silently.

'Don't be angry with him,' I said.

'He's a Sunni,' one of the men said.

'He's a Muslim. Shouldn't you respect him for that?'

'But he's a Sunni. Why is he here?'

Originally the difference between the two schools of Islam was a straightforward if bitter historical dispute. When the Prophet Mohammad died, there was a disagreement about who

11

should be recognised as his successor to lead the Muslim community. A meeting was held, which many attended, and it was decided that the role should pass to Abu Bakr, the Prophet's father-in-law, and so he became the first caliph. But another, smaller group complained about the decision and said the position should have gone to Ali, the Prophet's cousin and son-in-law. They were the Shi'at Ali, the partisans of Ali, or the Shia. The Sunni saw themselves as the orthodox, the Shia felt unfairly passed over.

After Abu Bakr there were two other leaders who ruled before Ali was finally made caliph. Then just five years after he was appointed, Ali was assassinated as he prayed at Kufa, a town in southern Iraq. After Ali's death his family lost the caliphate. His son Hassan thought about going off to battle the new caliph, Muawiyah, to retrieve the title for the Shia, but eventually decided to submit without a fight. Then Hassan's younger brother, Hussain, decided to pursue the family's claim to the caliphate. He was, after all, the Prophet's grandson. But Muawiyah refused to strike a deal and, before he died, appointed his son, Yazid, as heir. What had been a position appointed after consultation became an inheritance.

Most accepted Yazid, though the Shia did not. Hussain marched to reclaim the title. He had only a small group of loyal soldiers but nonetheless he set out from his home in Mecca heading for Kufa to begin the revolt. The Caliph Yazid in Damascus had heard rumours of his plan and sent down his troops to crush it. In 680, Hussain and his small force were surrounded at Kerbala, about forty miles from Kufa, and for several days they were besieged, their water supply cut off. Finally they were slaughtered in a desperate fight in the desert. Hussain, like many of his warriors, was beheaded. He was buried at Kerbala as the great martyr who died fighting injustice.

I have a poster that I bought once in a town near Kerbala, which depicts Hussain's death. It is a stylised picture, just like many I saw on the walls of Shia homes in Iraq. Hussain, wearing a golden helmet, lies dead in the arms of one of his fellow soldiers. His thick leather breastplate is pierced by three arrows and a single tear runs down his cheek. His white charger stands by him, its head raised high but with a tear also running down its cheek. Behind them the sky is a dark, blood red.

The Shia, in defiance of the Sunni caliphs, continued to recognise the imams who followed after Hussain. Across the Shia world, Hussain's death is re-enacted every year at the ceremony of Ashurah, where his martyrdom is felt as keenly as if he had died only yesterday. In Iraq, such was the potency of this ceremony as a symbol of the Shia faith and of resistance against tyranny that Saddam had it banned. Although the Shia are in the majority in Iraq, until the fall of Saddam they had never ruled their country and felt as unfairly excluded as their Imams Ali and Hussain. The seat of power in Baghdad, they said, was their rightful inheritance. The Mahawil grave, as they saw it, was another in a long line of betrayals, persecutions and martyrdoms.

It was true that when you stood in that field and peered into the hastily dug holes you saw an undeniable horror, something that was clearly a great crime. The problem with the grave only came when you were far away from it. Because, like dozens of similar sites across the country, it told different stories of Iraq, as many stories as you wanted to find.

For the advocates of the American invasion here was a justification: evidence of an extraordinary cruelty, an elimination of large numbers of an already persecuted population. It was forceful evidence of crimes against humanity and genocide. It was Saddam's regime at its most brutal and its most

13

exposed, a 'wonderland of terror' as one Iraqi dissident in exile described his era.[3]

Here too, though, was early evidence of America's failure to manage the peace. After other wars in other countries, in Bosnia and in Kosovo, graves like these had been sealed off. There, forensic scientists had carefully removed the remains, recorded the evidence and tried to identify the bodies before returning them to their families. Here the process of exhumation was chaotic and American generals stood by and watched. There is no forensic evidence collected from the Mahawil grave that would now stand up in court. If this had been a justification for war, why was there to be no accountability? What did the general mean when he said he had all the evidence he needed?

For the critics of Western foreign policy this was cruel evidence of how Washington and London had turned a blind eye in 1991 when it suited them. Thousands of Iraqi civilians were summarily executed over a period of several weeks even while Western troops were deployed nearby. When the revolt that an American president had encouraged was crushed and the protestors shot dead in mass graves, the governments of the West stood back and chose not to intervene. Although there was a near-nationwide uprising, they chose not to press onwards to Baghdad and topple Saddam. Under the terms of the ceasefire, they did not even stop the regime flying its military helicopters, which were to prove so vital a few weeks later when Saddam suppressed the *intifada*. They preferred a contained and sanctioned Saddam to no Saddam at all. He had a part to play in their foreign policy strategies and was still needed as a bulwark to the Shia theocracy next door, in Iran.

For the Ba'ath faithful, however, and there was no question that there were many still around in these early weeks, the graves showed a quite different Iraq: a nation that had been under threat from an anarchic rebellion. The rebels were

14

law-breakers, they were killing government officials and attacking government property and it had needed an iron fist to subdue them. I later met many people who supported Saddam and insisted Iraq had needed its strong man.

So in the graves lay the victims of Saddam's dictatorship, evidence of his crimes against humanity, the true legacy of his rule. If at some distant point in the future there was ever to be a reckoning with the past, here was a starting point. But any reckoning would be fraught with difficulty. Saddam and most of the senior party figures were Sunnis, as were most of the powerful security forces. It was true that they had persecuted the Shia, but they had not done this alone. Among the Shia in the south there were powerful figures who were also loyal Ba'athists. They had helped crush the uprising. They arrested or informed on their neighbours and in many cases at the time of this war they still lived near families of the missing. They were teachers, judges, policemen or local government administrators. Saddam had created an extraordinary state, something akin to Soviet Russia or Communist East Germany. It wasn't just a small leadership that was guilty of crimes. The guilt trickled down to the very bottom of society. What did it mean to bear guilt? It wasn't that everyone had murdered. It was that some had provided information, knowingly or unknowingly, that others had informed, others deceived, others made compromises. That was at the crux of Saddam's Iraq: he had tried to taint everyone with guilt. It was what had kept the regime going for so long, and it was what would make rebuilding the country so difficult.

A month later the story had moved on. Everyone in Baghdad was talking about what new government might emerge, or what the Americans were up to in the palace they had requisitioned in the centre of town. But I was still drawn back to the graves. I had heard rumours that there were men who had remarkably

15

survived the killings and I wanted to hear their stories. I wanted to know exactly what had happened here twelve years before. This time the site at Mahawil was almost deserted. Most of the bodies had been removed and several that had not been identified had already been reburied in small mounds of earth. Tied to each grave was the clear plastic bag that still held scraps of clothes. A large trench had been dug around the site and a barbed-wire fence set up to protect it, though from what was unclear. The stench had faded.

We went to Hilla, a large town a few miles further on, and asked at the newly established human rights office. It was true, they said, there were one or two men who had escaped from the graves and who were still here. They directed us to a small computer shop a few streets away. There a man was sitting at a desk editing an amateur film he had shot about the discovery of the Mahawil site. He had a friend who had seen the killings. He told us to wait and we sat watching his documentary with its shaky close-ups of skulls and sobbing mothers. Half an hour later the filmmaker returned with his friend, a taxi driver named Ali Abid Hassan. Hassan was thirty-nine and agreed to tell his story. He took me back to Mahawil and led me to a spot near a canal a little way off from the main gravesite. This, he said, was where he had been taken and almost killed.

It had begun in March, some days after the 1991 uprising had taken hold. Small groups of armed rebels and much larger crowds of civilians had come onto the streets in several south-ern towns and attacked government buildings, particularly police stations and offices of the several security organisations. Prisons and interrogation centres had been opened and their inmates freed. Hassan, like most young men, was in the army, a sergeant, although he had not been sent to fight in Kuwait. His brother Haider had fought in the invasion and had walked all the way home through Basra and up to Hilla. Once the rebellion

16

took hold they both deserted and went home. Though Hassan didn't say so, it seemed likely that they had both taken part in some of the rioting, which was largely unorganised and had no clear leadership. Hassan later spoke of how he had wanted 'revenge' against some of the most brutal of the military and security officials. But despite its initial strength, the uprising proved short-lived. Within days the Republican Guard, which had survived the Gulf War remarkably unscathed, began to re-assert control. A volunteer force drawn from the Sunni tribes north and west of Baghdad that had played a key role in the Iranian war and in the invasion of Kuwait, the Guard was a force to be feared.[4] As the crackdown began Hassan had already watched Guardsmen shoot down a woman in front of him at a checkpoint. She had walked through with her three sons and then returned to pick up a slipper one of her children had dropped. Inexplicably, one soldier pointed his rifle and shot her dead. These soldiers were the most ruthless force in the army, men 'chosen from those who had a heavy heart of hatred,' Hassan said. They were the most loyal to Saddam.

Four days after the woman was killed, Saddam's forces had virtually regained control of Hilla and Hassan decided to leave. He got in the car with Haider, who was then nineteen, and headed to the bridge that leads out of the city onto the road to Baghdad. At the bridge was a checkpoint manned by a group of men with guns, some soldiers, others wearing the olive-green safari suit of Ba'ath Party officials or dressed simply in dishdashas – the long, Arab robe. With no explanation, they ordered the pair out of the car and took them directly to the military base at Mahawil, one of the largest in the region. It had become a collection point for suspected rebels. There they were made to crouch on the floor surrounded by dozens of others until the early morning. There was no water, no food and occasionally a guard would walk past and beat them with a length of cable. Finally they were pushed into a large hall, crowded with what Hassan estimated were hundreds of other prisoners. He could see through a window into the courtyard where some of the prisoners were being brutally beaten. He saw one man he recognised, a man named Ibrahim. The guards took a bulldozer tyre and forced it over this man Ibrahim's head. He shouted and screamed and then they set fire to the tyre and Hassan watched as he burnt to death. He saw at least two others killed in the same way. For another day and an evening Hassan and the others were held at the camp. At midnight on the second day they were ordered outside.

'We were all in the army then and they told us we were returning to our units. Soon we started to get a feeling of what would really happen,' he said.

Their hands were tied behind their backs and a strip of cloth was torn off each of their shirts for a blindfold. They were divided into three or four groups and forced into five or six waiting buses. Hassan was split up from his brother Haider and was not even sure if they were on the same bus. They drove for fifteen minutes and then he felt the bus leave the main road and take an unpaved track. It was the same dirt road I had taken.

'We all started to get the feeling we would be dead soon,' he said.

They were led off the buses and told to sit on the ground. Somehow in the confusion Hassan found his brother Haider again and they sat next to each other, waiting.

'I felt the hand of my own brother and I felt safe for a time. I thought maybe we wouldn't be killed,' he said. 'And then they started shooting us.'

The gunfire was just a few metres away from where the two brothers were sitting, blindfolded in the field. Men were being led from the crowd in small groups and made to stand next to trenches that had already been dug into the soil and then they

18

were shot. But it quickly became disorganised. Several of the men tried to run away so the guards began forcing prisoners into the trench while they were still alive. Then they were shot where they lay. A man in a mechanical digger threw mud on top of the dead, burying them in the soil. Hassan said he believed the driver was later killed as well.

Hassan was taken away from his brother and, with two other prisoners, he was led to a path by the side of a canal. This was where, twelve years later, I was now standing with Hassan, surrounded by tall, green reeds. We were alone and the hot sun enveloped us in its warmth. Along the pathway we began to find evidence of what happened that night: some vertebrae, a rib bone, one button and eleven long, creamy-brown teeth collected in a little line. It could have been a display in a museum.

I am looking now at a black and white photograph of Hassan taken on the day we stood by the canal. His hair is dark, short and thinning and he has a closely-trimmed beard in the Shia style. He wears a patterned short-sleeved shirt and cheap, dark trousers. Behind him are the reeds, bent under the weight of the wind, and, beyond them, farmland rises into the horizon. Hassan is holding his hands up to his face, palms closed together as if in prayer and I can see the dark rings under his eyes. He seems to be swallowing his own words, words he cannot bear to let out. But he looks composed, still in control. I know that a few minutes after the picture was taken we had to stop talking. He was sobbing into his hands.

Hassan and the two men with him were made to sit by the canal and the guard began to shoot. He felt the guard's hand on his shoulder. 'I could feel that he didn't want to kill me,' he said. The guard fired his Kalashnikov and hit Hassan four times in his right leg. It shattered the bone and he fell forward into the trench, badly injured but alive. As far as he was concerned, an

19

act of divine providence had spared him from death. Later he would say: 'I was saved by God for a reason I will never know.'

He lay in the trench and waited. 'I was feeling the pain and I just kept it inside. I didn't want them to hear me.' The other two men with him had been killed. A mechanical digger drove over and covered them in a layer of dirt, but Hassan could still breathe. The killings continued for several minutes, until the canal was filled with bodies. 'After half an hour I heard the sound of a prisoner crying from the pain. I said to him: "Don't make any sound. Stay calm." I thought we were the only two alive.'

The second man, he later learnt, was an Egyptian named Mohammad al-Arabi.[5] They helped each other untie the cuffs binding their hands and then removed their blindfolds. With difficulty they climbed out of the trench and away into the darkness. For three days they walked through the fields until they found a farmer who took them in and dressed their wounds. Hassan sent a message to another of his brothers who collected him by car and drove him to the house of one of their relatives. The family treated his wound and pulled out three bullets. They had no anaesthetic to give him so instead they pushed a pillow into his mouth and told him to bite on it. They couldn't reach the fourth bullet, which even now was still lodged in his upper thigh. His brother told him his name was on a wanted list as a deserter and a suspected rebel. But remarkably, instead of staying hidden, Hassan went back to his military unit in the town of Amara, about an hour's drive away, and rejoined the ranks. He told his superiors that he had been shot by looters during the uprising. Some of his fellow soldiers had heard he was dead, others that he had fled to the refugee camps in Saudi Arabia where many other rebels had gone. It was an astonishing decision and even now it is difficult to grasp the enormity of the risk he was taking by giving himself up to the authorities who had tried so hard to kill him. Was he hoping to hide in the open? Did he think nobody would notice? Or that nobody would know what had happened?

Hassan judged the situation well, for these were chaotic times. On 5 April the regime made an announcement declaring the uprising over and later that month it issued the first of a series of amnesties. Those involved in the uprising, but not wanted for crimes of murder or rape, would be excused and allowed back to their jobs. There had been amnesties in previous years so they were not unknown, but they had often been used by the regime to round up suspected dissidents. Many times those trying to take advantage of the amnesty were simply arrested and taken away. Perhaps at this stage Saddam needed desperately to get the military back on its feet and under his control once more. Perhaps he could not afford to lose all the disillusioned and defeated young soldiers who had just deserted so spectacularly. For a second time Hassan survived. He was accepted back under the amnesty and was sent to the military hospital where his wounds were treated and three months later he was released from military service. He moved to Baghdad to live with his sister for several months. There he found work on a building site, helping, ironically, to reconstruct the headquarters of the Ba'ath Party, which had been badly damaged during the US and British bombing of the first Gulf War. Of course Hassan was anxious that he might be re-arrested, but no one in Baghdad knew his past, not even the friend who had found him the job. When the work at the party headquarters finished, he found another job buying and selling flour. He was earning a reasonable living.

One day in 1994, as he was at work in the wealthy Baghdad suburb of Mansour, four armed men from the National Security directorate approached him. 'Welcome,' they said, and slapped handcuffs on his wrists and shoved him into the back of the car.

They hit him three times on the back of his head with a pistol and sat him between two men on the back seat with his head between his legs. They drove him down to the National Security office in Hilla and put him in solitary confinement, occasionally bringing him out for interrogation.

'Where do you come from? Which party do you work for? What is your assignment?' they asked him, again and again. 'Which countries have you been to?' Hassan thought someone from his hometown had informed on him but not once did they ask about the graves. He was sure that the security officers didn't know the truth of his past.

However, the officers did ask if he had taken part in the *intifada*. Hassan remembered there had been an amnesty so he told them he had been involved: that he had fought, but not killed, a Ba'athist; that he had stolen from a supermarket; that he had helped loot the police headquarters. It was better to give them something, rather than nothing, he thought. Then they asked about the bullet scars on his leg. He told them he had been injured while fighting in the army. The questioning went on for eighteen days and then eventually he was released. From that day on he went from one job to the next, working as a daily labourer. Several times in the next nine years he was followed, re-arrested, questioned and then released by security officials. He was never convicted of a crime. It was just to remind him how closely he was being watched, as if they were telling him they knew his story. After dark came the nightmares and he would imagine security officials at his door waiting to arrest him. 'Even in my dreams I saw them,' he said. 'Every single minute I felt they would take me away for execution. No one can imagine what it was like.' His brother Haider was executed that night in March 1991. The family never found the body.

Then came the fall of the regime. Not surprisingly, Hassan welcomed the invasion and the collapse of the rule of Saddam and the tyranny of his many security forces. But it unleashed an anger that had been brewing for twelve years. Hassan was a quiet man, not particularly well-built and he still carried terrible scars on his right leg and a bullet embedded deep in his flesh. He was now married and had two young daughters, Rania, who was two, and Miriam, who was just a year old. When he spoke of them his voice was so gentle and loving that it was hard to imagine him in a violent rage. However, a few days after the collapse of the regime, Hassan and a group of other young men in Hilla had cornered one of the Ba'ath Party officials who had played a part in the executions of 1991. His name was Hamza Abu Shawab and he had held the rank of 'Udw Firqah, or group member, one of the top four ranks in the party only given to those regarded as extremely loyal if not complicit themselves. He wore a big moustache, in the Ba'athist style, and, formerly a shopkeeper, he had grown conspicuously wealthy through his devotion to the party.

'We chased him and we caught him,' Hassan said. 'We were very angry. "What am I supposed to do with you after what you have done to us?" I said to him. He was sitting on the ground and crying and asking for forgiveness and mercy.'

Hassan recognised him as one of those who had placed the burning tyres around the three men at the Mahawil camp. For a moment they thought of doing the same to him, Hassan said. They would place a tyre round his body, set it alight and leave him to die. In the end they could not. 'We really were about to kill him but I stopped and I changed my mind. I looked at him and I felt pity. We just couldn't. We decided to let him go.' The man got up, ran off and left the city never to return.

2

In Order Not to Forget

In his top pocket Hassan had a piece of paper with a list of names of local Ba'ath Party officials who he believed had taken part in the killings of March 1991. He said he was hoping to meet an American general and then he would ceremoniously hand over the list. He went through the names. 'I want these people punished,' Hassan said. 'I don't want anyone to forget what happened to us.'

Hassan wasn't by any means the only witness to the killings who wanted justice. There was the farmer, Syed Jabbar Syed Mohsin, who originally owned the land. On another day he described to me in detail how he had hidden in the fields and watched the executions. He saw prisoners brought for execution in three batches each day: in the morning, after lunch and late into the night. They came day after day. Once the grave was uncovered and the bodies removed he was one of several villagers who had tried to preserve the site. 'This is the place where sorrow grows,' he said. 'We want this sadness to be remembered again and again because we are not going to forget these people.' He spoke of building a garden or a mosque nearby in an act of remembrance. He also said he had given his evidence to a small group of Iraqi lawyers who were working at the newly established Human Rights Association office in Hilla.

I drove into the town to find these lawyers. There was fresh Arabic graffiti on the wall of the governor's office championing a popular Shia cleric called Moqtada al-Sadr, who had just emerged onto the political scene brandishing an ugly, hardline rhetoric. 'Yes, yes, yes to al-Sadr,' it said. In front of the court-house was a noisy crowd of petitioners and a little further down the road was the Human Rights office, in what once must have been a comfortable villa. There were still flowers in the large front garden and vines rambling over the wall, although they looked parched and untended. Inside there was little furniture, and what was there was either old and barely usable or so new it was still encased in plastic wrapping. The rooms were whitewashed and shabby. I was led in to a back room where I met Ahmed al-Barrak. Despite the heat he wore a suit in dark brown and a tie. He was thirty-nine years old and had short, neat hair. He was animated that day but every time I saw him afterwards he always struck me as a privately unhappy man. His shoulders would slouch with weariness and each time he was smaller than I remembered him. We sat in his office and talked about the graves, the witnesses and the suspects. Already an investigating judge from Hilla had taken sworn statements from three witnesses. So worried were the lawyers about the sensitivity of the case that Barrak kept the statements in his safe at home. 'We will keep them locked up until we find a procedure to put these people on trial,' he said. The issues were not the broader questions of whether or how to go about a process of accountability. For now it was too early. The talk about procedure was a way to delay, to calm calls for retribution. Dozens of people had come to his offices offering names of Ba'athists and demanding revenge be taken against them. The lawyers insisted any trials should be carried out under Iraqi law but beyond that they were still waiting for instructions on how to handle the cases. Nothing like this had been done before. They thought they should start with the most senior figures.

'If you want to kill a snake, you must cut off the head,' Barrak said. 'These Ba'ath Party members are still in our community and we must find a way to deal with them. Everyone who has killed must be brought to court.' Some arrest warrants had been issued but most of the senior Ba'athists had already fled town. The American commanders deployed nearby had little advice to offer the lawyers. They had to find their own way.

Like nearly all those in Hilla, Barrak was a Shia and like most others he too had lost relatives in the 1991 uprising: one of his uncles was executed, probably at the Mahawil gravesite although the family never found his body. A second uncle was arrested and sent to jail for two months. He became extremely ill and within a few months of his release he was dead. Barrak insisted he himself didn't take part in the rebellion. He told me later: 'It's now history but I am telling you the truth, I didn't participate.' But he said his family had long been targets for Ba'athists in the town.

His father joined the police force in 1952, when Iraq's last king, Faisal II, was still on the throne. After the Ba'ath took power in 1968 his father was made to join the party but because he did not attend the regular meetings he was kicked out of the police force four years later. He went back to the University of Babil, the provincial university in Hilla, studied at the college of law and found work at the courts. He was still working in Hilla as a lawyer. But the encounter with the party had not been forgotten. 'My family had a very bad political reputation in the eyes of Mr Saddam and his colleagues,' said Barrak, wearing their difficult past now as a badge of honour.

Theirs was a large family, like many in Iraq at the time: two boys and nine girls. They ran into trouble again in 1981 when two of the youngest girls were teenagers: Alann, fifteen, and Afra, sixteen, were overheard in school one day chanting slogans against Saddam. 'Down, down, Saddam Hussein,' they'd said. I could imagine them as children in the playground making this their little rebellion. Not a major act of political defiance, just a moment's excitement. Those four words changed their lives. The school teachers were loyal Ba'athists and reported what they had heard to the local security office. The two girls were arrested. Alann, the younger of the two, was jailed for six months. Her sister, Afra, spent six years in jail. This was the time of the war with Iran when there was the broad crackdown against Shia opposition parties, which the regime thought were working secretly with Tehran and had briefly looked like they might mount a serious challenge to the regime. Thousands of young men and women were arrested and disappeared on the slightest whim or rumour or reprisal. Perhaps the schoolteachers thought reporting the two girls was in line with this crackdown. Perhaps the family was already marked out because of Barrak's father. Eventually the two girls were released, but they never got jobs and still lived with their parents after all their brothers and sisters had moved away from the family home.

The other sisters grew into strong characters and followed successful professional careers: one ran a branch of an Iraqi bank in Cairo, another was an English professor in the city of Najaf, another was a pharmacist, another was a chemical engineer, another worked in the tax office in the Hilla local administration and the youngest was a kindergarten teacher. Barrak himself was accepted into Baghdad University, the best in the country. He studied economics but couldn't find work as an economist and so went back to the University of Babil in Hilla and took a second degree, this time in law. He later married a lawyer: when I was there his wife was still working as the town's deputy prosecutor. It was a respectable and I suppose largely apolitical profession. During the 1991 uprising, the family hid on a farm they owned among the palm trees south of Hilla and kept away from the uprising and the crackdown. A year later Barrak managed to obtain a visa for Jordan and spent three months there visiting one embassy after another trying to apply to emigrate abroad. He tried the Canadians, the Australians and the Americans but each proved too expensive and too difficult. In the end he returned to Hilla and continued to work as a lawyer until the fall of the regime. He was clearly well known in the town and came from what was now regarded as an honourable family in a country where perceptions of honour were a lifeblood.

Barrak showed me a book in Arabic that had been retrieved from a party office in Hilla. He said it was secretly produced by the regime. It was printed by the local Ba'ath Party Military Bureau and titled 'In Order Not To Forget' and it heaped praise on the men responsible for ending the uprising in 1991. It contained the names of several men from Hilla who took part in 'repressing the rebellion in the chapter of treason and betrayal'. On page 19 was the name of Mohammad Jawad an-Neifus, a leader of a branch of the large al-Bu Alwan tribe to which Barrak's family also belonged, who lived not far from Mahawil. The book reported that he had been 'distinguished' for his work in 'purification' and 'eliminating the rebellion'. The language was bold and defiant and it mirrored the regime's attitude at the time and subsequently. Barrak told other stories about Neifus: that he had appeared on state television after the uprising with the local military governor talking about how they had put down the rebellion, and that he had received a new Mercedes Benz and a gold-plated pistol for his trouble. The book made no attempt to deny that the uprising had been brutally crushed. Rather there was the sense that suppressing the revolt had been a proud duty. It was a sign of how remarkably confident the regime had been even at its moment of greatest weakness.

The book reminded me of a museum I had visited in the port

city of Basra six months before the American invasion. It was known as the Museum of the Martyrs of Hostile Persian Shelling and was originally established as a propagandist memorial to those killed in the Iran-Iraq war that raged through the 1980s. Since then exhibits describing the effects of the Gulf War and subsequent Western bombing raids had also been included: harrowing photographs showing dead children retrieved from the ruins of bombed buildings. Basra was a city devastated by war and few had not been touched by death's reach. Walking between two rooms of exhibits I found myself in a narrow corridor. On the wall hung sixty-eight certificates, each with a small photograph in its centre. They were there to mark some of the local loyalists from Saddam's regime who had been killed by the rebels in the 1991 uprising. One was a printer, another a teacher, others security officers. The certificates gave their date of birth, occupation and the date of their deaths, mostly in early March 1991. Occasionally there was a little more. 'Died when he was attacking the rebels,' said one. Several were pictured in uniform, often the olive-green safari suit of the party. There was no mention of the fate of the rebels or the executions. In the same grandiose tone the dead party men were described as 'Martyrs from the Page of Conspiracy and Betrayal'.

A few weeks after our meeting, Barrak was chosen by the American administrators in Baghdad to be one of twenty-five Iraqis who would sit on the Governing Council. Immediately after the war, the Americans had promised an Iraqi government within weeks. But the planning was haphazard. Some worried the government would be made up of the small group of exiles, some secular, some much more religious, who had spent the previous years pushing for war from the comfort of their homes in Washington, London and Tehran. However, it was already clear they had only limited popular support inside Iraq and couldn't easily fill the huge power vacuum created by the fall of the regime. The plan was scrapped. The next idea was to hold a large meeting in Baghdad to which hundreds of respected Iraqis from across the country would be invited and where they would then elect a council to rule alongside the Americans. That proved too complicated. In the end the Americans decided to prolong the occupation and allow the Iraqis only an advisory council. For this they simply handpicked twenty-five Iraqis, a mixture of exiles and men like Barrak who had spent the Saddam years living inside Iraq. Most Iraqis hardly knew them. Besides, it turned out, they were to have little power. It wasn't very far removed from what the British had done in 1920 – a different time but an equally troubled occupation – when Percy Cox, the Civil Commissioner running Baghdad, had set up a Cabinet of Notables to appease the Iraqis after they led a violent revolt against the occupying British army. The similarities were too striking to overlook. The British had drawn the borders of post-Ottoman Iraq and ruled it as occupiers. Within three years they had faced a violent rebellion. Now, less than a century later, the Americans were occupying Iraq and they too were soon to face a violent rebellion. After all the promises that this time round was different, that this was a liberation and the beginning of a new order in the Arab world, here was an early warning that there is rarely anything new about invasion and occupation.

The Governing Council was so divided by personal rivalries that for weeks it was locked in a stalemate, unable to take any meaningful decisions. It was supposed to appoint government ministers as a first step but even that was taking months. The failures of the council seemed only to mirror a broader change in atmosphere that was palpable across the country by the end of the first summer, a gradual but marked sense of ill ease. It

30

started with what was most obvious. Power cuts were now more frequent than before the war, not less. The electricity would cut off across Baghdad several times a day for three or four hours at a time. The four tall chimneys of the al-Dora power station, which rose up above the city, became an indicator of how much electricity to expect. Most days only one of the chimneys worked. On the occasional day, two would puff thick black smoke into the sky which, although it choked the horizon in a dark smudge, meant the brief respite of a day of near-continuous electricity – lights, a working fridge and the blessed air conditioner. The third and fourth chimneys never worked.

The water flowing from the taps became brackish and undrinkable. Power cuts meant water treatment plants were failing and the old system of underground pipes was rusting and poisoning the supply. Paul Bremer, the American administrator of Iraq, had insisted a few weeks earlier that there was more electricity being supplied than under Saddam. The Iraqis scoffed at his exaggeration. American officials then promised a pre-war level of electricity supply would be up and running by September. Few believed them. Petrol generators were for sale on every street corner, though a machine large enough to power a family house cost thousands of dollars.

There were suicide car bombs at the Jordanian embassy and then the UN headquarters. Aid organisations left in droves. Along with the bombs, the number of attacks against the US military was already rising, to more than a dozen incidents a day. American officers in these early days were paying $250 for tips about the fedayeen, the paramilitary fighters who had put up so much unexpected resistance during the invasion, but it did little to staunch the violence. British diplomats, who at first talked proudly of working from the grassy lawns of their old embassy with its wonderful views over the bank of the Tigris, were forced to retreat inside what was then called the Secure

Zone, a vast and heavily-guarded complex in the centre of the city hidden behind rows of razor wire and concrete blast walls. The zone enclosed an area that contained Saddam's former Republican Palace and the al-Rashid Hotel, where I'd stayed before the war. Embedded in the floor of the hotel lobby was a mosaic that showed a grinning George Bush senior above the words 'Bush is criminal.' It disappeared mysteriously almost immediately after the regime fell.

Security at the American military bases tightened dramatically. I saw a sign outside a recruiting station for the new Iraqi army that warned passers-by not to stop, stand or park near the entrance. 'VIOLATORS ARE SUBJECT TO DEADLY FORCE,' it said. Staff at the Coalition Provisional Authority, as the occupying administration was now known, stopped leaving the Secure Zone as often as they had before. They needed permission from their superiors, an escort of several close-protection bodyguards and at least two armoured four-wheel drives. Few bothered taking the risk.

It wasn't all bad at first. Internet cafés, once heavily restricted under Saddam, had sprung up everywhere and now charged less than a pound an hour to surf the web. Satellite television dishes rose from the rooftops for the first time. As I drove around Baghdad in the mornings I would listen to the BBC World Service broadcasting in English a daily reading from *Animal Farm*, a book banned in the Saddam days. Some shopkeepers and Iraqi businessmen were making quick profits. Parts of the telephone networks destroyed during the war were up and working again and old signposts had been replaced with freshly painted noticeboards. Some people, particularly teachers, were getting paid much more now than they ever had under Saddam, and they were spending their new wages. The main high street in outer Karrada, a shopping district round the corner from the hotel, was lined with shops selling fridges, televisions, cookers and washing machines stacked several rows deep across the pavement. More Iraqi policemen appeared to be on the streets, directing traffic or standing at busy junctions, but richer families were already employing squads of heavily armed bodyguards outside their villas. Some neighbours, anticipating the worst, had simply cordoned off their streets with lumps of concrete or fallen tree trunks. Almost every home still had a gun.

I was intrigued by a name that kept cropping up in my note-book: Mohammad Jawad an-Neifus, the tribal leader praised by Barrak's secret Ba'ath Party book for his part in the killings. He had been at the top of Hassan the survivor's list of perpetrators, along with others who were in some way linked to him (one had married his daughter; another was regarded as his local informant). What was more, other witnesses at the grave had also spoken of him as a ringleader. Neifus had been arrested near Hilla shortly after the fall of the regime but was acci-dentally released from American military custody a few days later and was still on the run. US Central Command admitted that the elderly tribal sheikh had duped a young American army legal officer who had no idea who he was and had cleared him for release. Now the Americans were offering $25,000 for information that would lead to his capture.[6]

Not long after I met Hassan I visited Neifus's village. It was a quick drive from the gravesite, across the main highway to Baghdad and on to a paved road that led past small farmhouses shaded by palm trees. At a small roadside store I asked a taxi driver for directions. The name of Neifus was widely known. I was already close to the house and he pointed out the rest of the way, then he turned and spoke of the tribal leader.

'I am not from the al-Bu Alwan tribe,' he said, 'and I am not going to defend him but he is not responsible. There was a military camp at Mahawil and that was the centre of the operation. As he was one of the senior sheikhs in this region so he worked with them. Honestly, I don't know what should happen to him. If he is really guilty he should be punished but only God knows the truth. This whole area was full of soldiers and Ba'athists. Educated people know what has happened. They know a single person can't make an entire mass grave. It needs help from others.'

I thought: but wasn't that exactly the point? The single person was all it had needed: a tribal leader, a policeman, a party functionary, an army officer. The individuals made up the institutions, they carried a responsibility. Saddam had understood it only too well. By making so many people complicit in the state's crimes he ensured their loyalty and in turn the survival of his system.

Neifus's house looked recently built. It was a large, two-storey brick building adorned with red columns. A young man came out, Qais explained to him who we were and after only a moment's hesitation we were invited in to sit on the carpeted floor of a room off the internal courtyard. Some minutes later, Khadum Jasim Jawad, the forty-one-year-old nephew of Neifus joined us. His hair was grey and he wore a moustache and a long dishdasha. His version of what had happened to his uncle was very different. He admitted Neifus had been arrested and said it had happened at around 9.30 one morning several weeks earlier and that his thirteen Kalashnikov rifles and three pistols had been confiscated. But he insisted the Americans had held a trial and found his uncle innocent before releasing him. He blamed the original arrest on a rivalry with the local governor and in indignation pointed out the bullet holes in the front wall of the house that had come from the gunfire that accompanied his uncle's arrest. What he said wasn't correct: there hadn't been a trial, let alone an acquittal. It was a half-truth but one that suited the family for now.

He said he had seen Neifus in Baghdad after he was released. 'Yes, I met him. He was in good health and good condition. The Americans had told him he was innocent,' he said.

He talked about Neifus, an old man aged about eighty-five who he said could neither read nor write. He was chief of the tribe but hadn't been a member of the party, Jawad insisted, and he was widely respected, someone who would resolve local disputes, and 'like water, he was straightforward'. Even in jail the Americans had called him 'Emir' or prince, he claimed. Neifus had seven daughters and four sons, three of whom, Saleem, Zaed and Basim, were still with the American military under arrest, he said. His wife had left for Baghdad to be with him on the run. No one knew where they were now.

They brought thin glasses of heavily sweetened tea and I asked about the killings of 1991. Jawad told me it had been a violent time and their main duty had been to protect the village and the families living there from 'intruders'. He said Taha Yassin Ramadan, Saddam's vice president who was now on the run himself from the Americans, had visited Neifus during the uprising and had tea with him and had helped protect the village. 'It was a very difficult situation and dangerous. There was raping, and looting and killing of people,' said Jawad. The family had been in trouble with the regime before. In 1979 another of Jawad's uncles, his mother's brother, was executed in one of Saddam's paranoid purges. He had been a military intelligence officer and had somehow fallen foul of the party leadership. They showed me a black and white photograph of him dressed in uniform and speaking on the telephone, a young man with cleanly-parted, thick dark hair. 'Saddam used repression with us and we were afraid,' said Jawad. That story was almost certainly true. Few were the families who emerged completely unscathed from Saddam's Iraq, even those who had vice-presidents round for tea.

I pressed him again about the mass grave. I wanted some acknowledgement of what had happened. 'We didn't know anything about the mass grave,' Jawad said. 'We heard the news only in the last month. My uncle is an old man and completely innocent. All the people here know my uncle and they want him to return to his home. It is only the Americans who can solve this problem.' I thanked him for the tea and left.

3

Progressive, Revolutionary and Triumphant

In those first weeks after the war anything was possible and everyone had a story to tell. I began each day sitting on the round, moulded plastic chairs in the hotel coffee shop downstairs with Qais. Each table was laid with plastic red mats that shone under the fluorescent lights. We flicked through the newspapers, looking for leads and then we drove off into Baghdad or some other part of the country. I hoped that the more people I spoke to, the more I would make sense of it all. I was never turned away. I drank sweet tea and ate in people's homes, sitting on the floor, scooping up balls of rice in my hand. In the evening I went to restaurants by the river where they roasted fish at the fire. I bought bottles of Lebanese wine from a Christian supermarket in my neighbourhood and drank them with Iraqi businessmen by my hotel swimming pool. I went to the Shia slums on the other side of town to meet a conservative young cleric who was forcing off-licences to close and ordering women to wear the veil. I saw thousands of Shia faithful pour into Najaf to welcome the return of an ayatollah who had spent the last twenty years living in exile in Iran and who was now demanding quick elections. Two weeks later I drove to Falluja to listen to a Sunni cleric encourage his congregation to rise up against the US military. Later that same day I met a couple of young American soldiers buying crates of Coca-Cola at a roadside stall on the outskirts of Falluja. I stopped to chat with them and soon they were boasting of how quickly they would

37

defeat the rebels holed up in the city. I met doctors in rural hospitals who had run out of medicines and who complained that dirty tap water was causing record cases of malnourishment and severe stomach illnesses. I spoke to Iraqi journalists who for the first time were able to set up their own papers and publish what they wanted, even if most of what they wrote was partisan, exaggerated or sometimes wholly wrong. And I met others who refused to write a word, including one elderly columnist who had spent time in Saddam's cells and who said to me: 'If my country is occupied then my pen is occupied too.'

In the lobby of my hotel, near the glass front door, was a small shop that sold unexceptional carpets, trinkets of silver and a handful of books. One day I was looking through the pile when I found a copy of the Iraqi state tourist guide from 1982. It was a small, orange book printed in Yugoslavia in the days of earlier strategic international alliances and it was written with such seductive innocence that it hardly seemed to describe the same Ba'athist Iraq I was trying to uncover. 'There is so much to see, so much you may want to take home with you, dear visitor,' the guide said. 'We'll try and help you a little. Of course, it all depends on how long you intend to stay.'[7]

Before the war, on my brief visits to Iraq, I had struggled to grasp the mechanics of the Ba'ath Party. After the war it disappeared into a fog of disputed history and vitriolic propaganda. Yet at the beginning the Ba'ath had been an ideology that was popularly supported. Several of the opposition exiles who had only just returned to Baghdad had been members of the party in its infancy. It was a secular movement that captured an aspiration at a time of great political upheaval. But somewhere it had become rotten. As it grew more powerful the party had turned in upon itself and became consumed by violence and paranoia.

In my guidebook there were photographs of the southern

marshes: men knee-deep in water, fishing by their narrow dug-out canoes and tribal elders gathered on carpets inside intricately woven floating reed houses. There were pictures and descriptions of the golden-domed holy Shia shrines in Kerbala and Najaf and, a few pages on, a photograph of two dozen Kurdish women, dressed in bright robes of reds, yellows, greens and pinks, dancing with linked arms against the backdrop of the broad green mountains of the north. One chapter showed reddening Western tourists in tight swimsuits lounging by an outdoor pool at the Habbaniya Tourist Village, in the deserts of western Iraq. This was then the largest tourist village in the Middle East and boasted a six-storey four-star hotel, three restaurants, bars, a night club, 500 chalets, two large swimming pools, a sailing club, a horse-riding turf, four tennis courts, a supermarket, an open-air theatre and an Arab tent casino. I tried to imagine Iraq as a major tourist destination. I knew the British diplomat and explorer Gertrude Bell once camped outside Falluja, but so many years later did tourists really ride horses through the western deserts?

The images suggested an Iraq that was relaxed but well ordered, welcoming to visitors and confident of its diverse identities. What a deceit. How could you sense, looking at this, that within a few years the marshes of the south would be drained, the villages bulldozed and most of the population chased into hiding as punishment for sheltering rebel forces? Or that a major campaign of ethnic cleansing would be launched against the Kurds in the north, culminating in chemical gas attacks on entire villages? Or that the seminary in Najaf, then the most respected in the Shia world, would be almost completely closed down and many of its clerics arrested or forced into exile, and that the Habbaniya Tourist Village would soon empty and be left to rot in the desert?

This was an Iraq, the guidebook insisted, that was in the

midst of a bold new social and political revolution that would throw off the dark legacy of centuries of Ottoman and British imperial rule and recapture the glories of its ancients whose names echoed through these pages: the Akkadians, the Babylonians, the Assyrians, the Greeks, the Umayyads, the Abbasids. The ideals of this movement were so broad and all-encompassing that even a simple guide to tourist sites was laden with their rhetoric. The book opened with a photograph of the omnipresent leader: 'Field Marshal Saddam Hussein, Hero of National Liberation'. Dressed in a suit, with head and shoulders facing the camera, he stood with a toothy, excited grin. The skin on his face was loose, jowly, creased in folds across his cheeks. He seemed on the verge of laughter. After his picture, came the musical score for the new hymn that would accompany the revolution, which, the guide said, had been adopted in accordance with Decision Number 851 of the Revolutionary Command Council of 3 June 1981 as the national anthem. The song, a heavy dirge with an oompah-oompah beat, was called 'The Land of the Two Rivers'.

The guide talked of a 'progressive, revolutionary and triumphant Iraq' and spent time recalling the ancient civilisations that founded their capitals in the cities of Babylon, Nineveh and Baghdad. The years of invasion and occupation that followed were dealt with summarily as one long, thankless episode: the Mongol sacking of Baghdad in 1258 (when the Tigris reputedly ran black with the ink from the thousands of books thrown into its waters), four centuries of Ottoman rule and decades as a British colony. 'The people of Iraq have worked hard to rid themselves of the effects of centuries of stagnation,' the guide said. 'Their achievements have been truly spectacular.' Now was the time of a new Iraq, with a national, democratic, socialist system, a 'pioneering experiment in the Arab revolutionary movement'.

But even in this little book were hints of the authoritarianism that in fact ruled in Baghdad. It admitted that, under the terms of this pioneering experiment, although Iraqis were in general to be treated equally, that would not include anyone who opposed the regime: 'The National Assembly is based on certain principles, such as the absolute equality of all citizens, with the exception of those who take a hostile stand against the Revolution and revolutionary transformations.'

It said that although democracy as an ideal was embraced, the revolution actually stood for 'the rejection of formalistic practices of democracy, with emphasis on the serious content of democratic practices which express the principles of the Revolution and the seriousness of its method'. In other words, opposition political parties were persecuted and chased into exile and the few elections held were tightly controlled, heavily rigged affairs. So here already was the catch. Although the Ba'ath revolution spoke of equality, democracy and socialism and promised to transform society, in fact it was another regime of the powerful, led and imposed by a small clique intent on overwhelming any opposition it might face. And so, as with many other revolutions before, the door to dictatorship was nudged open from the start. The regime's continued hold on power lay not with its original ideals, but with its acolytes, the rational men and women who in their daily work propped up the state in all its sickness. They were the key. At first I found it easy to judge these people. Surely they were guilty of something. I knew my attitude was vengeful, but it was so easy. Only much later did I decide that, not having lived under the regime, I didn't have the right to make such assumptions. What choices would I have made if I had lived their lives? Can I say truthfully that I wouldn't have given in to compromise?

One morning, a few weeks after the Ba'athist regime had fallen, I drove over the River Tigris and past the blackened shell

41

of the Ministry of Information. It had been abandoned and burnt out several weeks earlier and was just about to be permanently closed under the American occupying authority's new orders. Dozens of the ministry staff were gathered outside, meeting and filling out forms hoping for a job in another department or at least for a pension or some payout to compensate for the loss of their livelihoods. The ministry employed several thousand people to uphold the revolution and protect it from the mass of ordinary people for fear they might see through the lies and deceits. They controlled state television, radio and the handful of authorised newspapers, they provided a state news service that controlled the news, they censored Iraqi writers and poets, they spread the principles of the party and they controlled all visiting journalists, keeping them under tight scrutiny and extracting from them hundreds of dollars in bribes every day. It was these grey men who had made my life so difficult when I came to Iraq before the war. In the centre of the crowd was Uday al-Taie, the director general of the ministry, its most senior civil servant and a man we journalists had all met before the war. He was now excluded permanently from public office. I got out of the car, made my way over to him and introduced myself again. For the next two hours we talked in the forecourt of the ministry over which he had once presided.

Taie was an intelligent product of the elite, with trim dark hair and moustache and a handsome, well-oiled face. He was educated in Baghdad at a college run by American Jesuits and later in Paris. He spoke English, French and Spanish fluently. At the age of twenty-two he had joined the Ministry of Planning, later switching to the Ministry of Information. Immediately after the war with Iran, at the end of the 1980s, he spent two years in Paris as press attaché, some suggesting when he left that he had been expelled by the French for spying. In the months before the war it was rumoured that he was desperately hoping for another posting in Paris, but he appeared to have been passed over and did not hide his disappointment. Instead, aged fifty-five, he continued to work in the ministry, descending occasionally from his upstairs office to lecture foreign journalists late into the night on the double standards of Western foreign policy and the integrity and honesty of Saddam's regime. Always a step behind him was Mohsin, his assistant, his file-carrier: a short, shy and deeply anxious man. Taie had been more careful than his underlings not to take bribes openly but he was conceited and easy to dislike. He had the power to approve or deny visas for journalists and it only added to his hauteur. He liked to chide us for an inherent bias against his regime. As though lecturing a class of badly behaved schoolchildren he would point at the phone on his desk and say: 'If this is a telephone, and you tried it and you know it is, then please you should say it is a telephone. Don't make it out to be something that it's not.' He repeated his lesson for me now, almost word for word.

It was a warm morning and we walked through the crowd as we spoke. He began by talking about his anger at the new American-led occupation, particularly, of course, the policy of de-Ba'athification, which had left him and many of his staff out of work. The words tumbled out of his mouth in a torrent of frustration.

'There are 6,800 employees at the ministry. We don't know what will happen to us now. All the professors of the university are in the party, ninety-nine per cent of the director generals, their deputies and undersecretaries of the ministries, and 90 per cent of the departments are members of the party. There are about four million people in different levels of the party hierarchy. How can you dismiss all these people? You think that is going to work? I am not talking about the army and the police, nobody could continue that. But who are to be the

43

people who run this country, its universities, schools, the education system?'

Mohsin the file-carrier appeared silently by his side, as in the old days. It was odd talking to them now. Before Taie had had the power to order me out of the country, or deny me another visa and so I had listened politely to what he said, ignored his posturing and avoided confronting him. Now he had lost all of that power. He was still posturing and self-confident, but this time it didn't matter. Most of what he said was simply an unbending defence of his actions, but at other moments he seemed to imply he had been a reluctant victim of pressure to conform. He even seemed to hint that he didn't wholly regret the fall of the regime. 'OK,' he said, 'no one is denying that we needed this change in the system. But don't tell me about the way it was done. If you are talking about international law, ethics, the UN Security Council, it was illegitimate. Even member states are saying it was not legitimate. The purpose of the war was weapons of mass destruction. Where are the weapons of mass destruction?'

'Didn't you realise you were working for a brutal regime?' I asked.

'Every system has its own negative aspects,' he said. 'Nobody can deny that, even in Britain. Nobody is perfect. I feel sorry to see all those graveyards. Don't think that every official in the government knew all the details of what happened. We heard so many rumours but who could prove it? Some of it happened in the 1980s . . . At the time I didn't know that hundreds were killed in Hilla and Diwaniyah or Basra. Even the officials of the government didn't know. The security . . . only limited people knew about it.'

'But you stood up for the regime. You defended it against the allegations of human rights abuses,' I said.

'How can the director general of a ministry say the contrary?

There was no choice. Nobody was satisfied, even the ministers were not satisfied. All those negative aspects . . .' His voice tailed off.

He broke off to greet someone in the crowd, and again a few minutes later to look at a file or a paper that had been handed to him by one of his former staff. There was no ministry any more but Taie was clearly still in charge as he walked through the courtyard, the blackened, empty rooms of the building rising up behind him.

I asked if he knew where I could find his former minister, Mohammad Saeed al-Sahaf, who had made himself a figure of fun in the Western press during the invasion by insisting the Americans were nowhere near Baghdad even as their tanks trundled into the centre of the city. Taie said he didn't know. Some weeks later Sahaf surfaced in the Emirates where he gave his account of his Ba'athist career in a series of talk shows on an Arabic television channel. The first show began with footage that showed an exhausted and ragged, silver-haired Sahaf flying from Iraq into the Emirates with his family. Then the camera turned to the stage and there sat a rejuvenated, smiling Sahaf, his hair dyed almost jet black. He was dressed in a smart new suit, with a large watch shining indiscreetly on his wrist. Sahaf was one of the few in Saddam's cabinet who was not wanted by the Americans and he had the contacts and the negotiating power to secure himself a safe, and apparently remunerative, exile abroad. Taie, on the other hand, was left behind in Baghdad to watch his career crumble into a liability.

At times Taie seemed to admit he was under surveillance as he worked. He talked about having to be aware of his 'security' under the regime. 'How could we say this was a bad system?' Then in the space of the same breath he would return to his defiance.

'I am an Iraqi and I love my country. I believe that what I have

45

done in my domain was good for serving my country. Not the regime, but my country.'

I asked what his rank had been in the party.[8] As director general of the ministry he would almost certainly have held one of the top ranks, but Taie insisted he had been only a simple 'Udw, a member or comrade. 'I was a member of the lowest level. Being a director general I was exempted from duty in that area. They knew I was a very busy man and they said they didn't need me,' he said. As he talked he gradually began to portray himself as a man of lesser importance, not a leading light of the party.

'Even in the last three days I didn't think of going to the ministry. I was sitting at home. There was no electricity and I stayed at home. Civilians like me have nothing to do with the party. When I came back home people were kissing me on the cheek, people I didn't know, people I hadn't met before.'

It was a protestation of innocence. My own people, he seemed to say, don't hold me as a criminal so you shouldn't either. I worked for the government but I am a civilian, an innocent too. I am of the system, yet not with the system.

'I defended my country. I defended the government for the achievements that had been realised for the people. We endured three wars, martial law was implemented, we fought against Iran, we fought against the Americans and all the intruders. Orders came from the presidency to the minister and the minister gave them to us. Sometimes we agreed and sometimes we said: "This is not right."'

Then I asked him about the role of the Mukhabarat, the powerful Iraqi intelligence agency, in the running of the Iraqi state and the fact that in the final months before the war a flood of Mukhabarat agents had joined the ministry staff. His tone changed dramatically. 'Don't ask me direct questions. I am not authorised to answer.' Who did not authorise him to answer

46

now the regime was gone? Did that mean the party still operated in hiding? He wouldn't say. A moment before Taie had been only a civilian who bore no responsibility, now it seemed he was in some chain of command.

I asked what he would do now.

'Where is the new government?' said Taie. 'I am ready. I should serve my country or I could be a cigarette seller, a humble way to protect my dignity. I had a thirty-three-year career in the Ministry of Planning and the Ministry of Information. This is my reputation. I am proud of myself,' he said and walked off into the waiting crowd of his former staff.

If others were like Taie and denied first-hand knowledge of the extent of the regime's crimes it was a sign of how hard it would be for the country to reckon with the sins of the past: 290,000 people 'disappeared' in two decades of Saddam's government, according to one conservative estimate.[9] How could he not have known? How much had he helped to cover up? But did being the director general of a government ministry automatically make him complicit? I wondered about his pragmatism. Had he ever been inspired by the original ideas of the Ba'ath and its pioneering revolution or had he simply been a bright young student intent on a safe career as a civil servant? In effect he was pleading with me for absolution. He wanted the Ba'athists to be forgiven, their past forgotten and put behind them. There was too much else to get on with now. He was certainly right when he said so many functionaries had been in the party that if they were all banned from work then Iraq would be difficult to run. It wasn't just the ministries. Iraq had been a socialist command economy and the state controlled most aspects of life: schools, universities, banks, factories, businesses, newspapers. To get to the top in any of these professions had usually required overt loyalty to the party for idealists and pragmatists alike. Iraq would cease to function as a state if all these people were purged from public life.

The Ba'ath had begun in the early 1940s in Syria in revolt against French occupation and as a peasant movement fighting a feudal elite. Its intellectual father was Michel Aflaq, a young history teacher. He was an Orthodox Christian, like several of the young Arab nationalists who were searching for inclusion in the Muslim-dominated Arab world through this secular movement. He had studied at the Sorbonne in Paris from 1929 where he drank freely in the fashionable currents of socialist theory and then returned to Damascus, where his father was a grain merchant, to agitate against French colonial rule. Aflaq and his supporters produced a newspaper, *al-Ba'ath*, 'The Renaissance', and in April 1947, a year after Syria won its independence, the group held its first party congress. The ideology that was the founding stone of what eventually became the Arab Ba'ath Socialist Party was pan-Arab nationalism, and the principles of 'Unity, Freedom and Socialism'. The Ba'ath revolution was to be an 'eternal mission', according to one of its founding principles. Aflaq spoke of it in terms that were at times almost spiritual and at other times democratic and then quite authoritarian. It was to be an 'awakening', a 'rebirth of the Arab spirit'. 'Our movement is the destiny of the Arabs in this age,' Aflaq said.[10]

The party rode a wave of popular Arab nationalism in the 1950s, and grew rapidly in Syria as well as Jordan and Lebanon, finding support among middle- and lower-middle-class professionals. In Iraq, the Arab nationalist tide swept the country into a decade of chaos and violent upheaval. On 14 July 1958, a group of army officers – the Free Officers – overthrew the British-backed monarch, King Faisal II, and killed him, his uncle Crown Prince Abdullah, several royalist army officers and the powerful politician Nuri Said. Their bodies were sliced into pieces in a final act of desecration. Statues of Faisal and General Maude, the British officer who captured Baghdad in 1917, were pulled to the ground by large crowds. It was a sweeping revolution and celebrated for its reforms, but the new republic brought precious little stability. In the next decade four more coups followed, each time accompanied by a 'Communiqué no. 1' denouncing the former government and promising the rule of law. Only on 30 July 1968 did the Ba'ath finally consolidate their hold on power. Saddam waited in the wings of the upper party echelons until finally, eleven years later, he manoeuvred himself into the top spot and began to exercise his total domination of Iraq.

I tried for many months to track down someone who openly espoused the ideals of the Ba'ath but they were hard to find. Usually these people had disappeared into hiding, had fled the country or they had been arrested by the Americans. I met a couple of times with a former officer in the Mukhabarat, the intelligence service. We sat in the coffee shop of a hotel and he told me that the party was secretly re-forming, readying itself to seize power again. He wasn't happy talking about the past though, and after a while he disappeared. Eventually Qais said we might try a former drinking friend from the time he worked in the Sheraton Hotel. Fariz al-Khattab had at one time been the hotel's executive manager before he left to run a magazine called *Wadi al-Rafidain*, the 'Valley of the Two Rivers' (named of course after the Tigris and the Euphrates, which flow down the length of Iraq until they join just north of Basra at the point that legend says was the Garden of Eden). Khattab insisted the magazine had been independent of both the government and of Saddam's eldest son Uday, who was in charge of controlling Iraq's press. But it still followed a staunchly party line and two of his uncles were very senior in the party. Khattab himself spoke with a rare self-confidence about his lifetime loyalty to the Ba'ath.

He wasn't in the country very often, and he wasn't eager to meet strangers. But Qais talked him into seeing us and we made an appointment to meet at his new office on Saddoun Street, a broad, busy avenue that runs through the heart of commercial Baghdad on the eastern bank of the Tigris. It was just a stone's throw from Paradise Square, where Saddam's statue had been toppled. Opposite his office was a petrol station and a long queue of irate drivers waiting in line. A board downstairs in the hallway of Khattab's building showed most of the other small offices in this block were old travel agents or industrial-equipment companies. Qais and I walked up flights of dingy stone stairs to the fifth floor, where we were led into a freshly painted but almost completely unfurnished office. It was blank and anonymous. The little furniture to be seen was new and gave you the immediate sense that this was an office more often empty than occupied. Khattab divided his time between Baghdad, where he was now scared to show his face, and Abu Dhabi, where he ran a commercial media business and occasionally appeared on political talk shows on Arab satellite channels. He led us into his room, which had slightly more furniture than the others. We sat on a grey imitation leather sofa before his desk. On the wall were two large, ornate Qur'anic quotations in gilt frames. Khattab, who was fifty, wore a dark suit and a smart white scarf around his neck against the spring chill. A cheap kerosene heater roared in the corner and a telephone in the next room rang every few minutes for the next couple of hours.

Khattab had joined the party in his first year of secondary school, at the age of twelve. It was a few months before the July 1968 revolution. Some in his group of friends were already Ba'athists and encouraged him to take part in demonstrations against the regime, which was already beginning to disintegrate after the latest dictator, Abd-us-Salam Aref, a Nasserite army officer originally backed by the Ba'ath, was killed in an accidental plane crash in 1966. 'I was a child so I didn't attract the attention of the police or security forces and they gave me slogans to repeat during the demonstrations,' he said. He never left the party and after school he went to Mosul in the north to study engineering, and then returned to Baghdad to take a degree in what was called 'information' – a mixture of cultural studies, journalism and editing.

'The truth is that the Ba'ath Party is a political ideology,' he said. 'It is not a labour union that can be closed down when the interests it stood for are gone. It is the only Arab party that for more than fifty years stood against the international and regional changes. It is the only party that stands against the ambition of the Zionist regime. The Ba'ath Party wants to change the dark times of the Arab nation.' He was a much stauncher defender of the party than Taie the civil servant had been. While Taie sought to diminish the party's importance, Khattab was still happy to boast of it.

'What were the dark times?' I asked. I thought he meant 1967 when the Israelis defeated and humiliated the Arab armies.

No, he said, not that recently. He had a far longer sense of a people slighted. 'Since the Ottoman period. The Arab character melted in the Ottoman era and then the French and British colonialists put their fingers on the region and drew borders between the Arab countries and the Ba'ath Party tried its best to remove these borders.'

They were grand ideals but the practice was flawed. I asked about the reach of the party. I had been told that every residential district was divided into sections and that a Ba'athist who lived there was responsible for each section. It essentially meant you were being watched by some of your

51

neighbours. Depending on who these Ba'athists were it could mean nothing, or it could mean everything. Qais told me he had frequently been accosted by the Ba'athist in charge of his district who wanted to know why he wasn't attending the regular party meetings as expected. Qais charmed him and put him off and in the end resisted the pressure to attend. After the war this Ba'athist, like many others, simply disappeared. Khattab was quite frank about the system.

'The majority of commitments of the Ba'ath were concentrated on the districts and for that there was a complete coverage of all Iraq. It was a shield on the security side and stopped hostile elements from making espionage networks. The Ba'ath knew all the details of each Iraqi house, the Iraqi streets, the Iraqi universities, the Iraqi mosques, the Iraqi churches. We were in every house. The father or the brother or the mother, one of them if not all, were members of the party. There was an eye on everyone and an eye for everyone.'

I asked Khattab if he had had anyone from his home district arrested for spying or conspiring against the government. He looked uncomfortable and paused. Then he said he had suspected only one person but that they had died in a car accident before they could be arrested.

So while the grand ideal had been to restore pride in the Arab character after centuries of oppression, in fact the party concentrated most on spying on its own people. It was a quite astonishing system of collective paranoia and surveillance that Khattab was describing and defending. The UN weapons inspectors who worked in Iraq in the 1990s had uncovered traces of the spying used to track their movements but there had been little sense then of how much such surveillance had been focused on the ordinary Iraqi population. Saddam had created a web of nearly a dozen rival security agencies which spied on the entire population and then on each other. Conversations on the telephone, in coffee shops, in the school playground were overheard. Suspicions were freely and quickly reported. It was little wonder that every single genuine coup attempt, even in the fragile final years, was uncovered and the plotters executed. One morning after the war I had been talking to teenage children at a school in Karrada, a middle-class commercial district of Baghdad. They had described how much the party filled the public space at school – Saddam's portrait in their textbooks, posters of him on the walls, enforced exhortations to the leader before class and lessons in patriotism to instil Ba'athist ideology. Party recruiters would come to the school asking children aged twelve and above to sign up to join the party. Most would sign, and those who did not might be expelled, sent to another school and pressed again to sign up. One girl, aged fourteen, said even as children they were marked out by their allegiance to the party. 'There was a difference in the classes between the girls,' she said. 'We knew who was really with the Ba'ath, even in the school. We were scared to talk in front of them.'

Once the war with Iran began in 1980, the pervasive atmosphere of mistrust intensified. Shia political groups, particularly Dawa, an opposition party that was strong in Baghdad and the south, were presumed to have links with Shia Iran and were immediately regarded as agents of the enemy. Thousands of their supporters were arrested and executed. Khattab said there had been an official communiqué from the Revolutionary Command Council, the highest authority in the land, declaring Dawa to be what he called an 'agent party'. He said he remembered as a young boy – he thought it was 1970 – watching the public execution of men he thought were conspirators in an elaborate Israeli and Iranian spy plot. The victims were hanged in Liberation Square, under the gaze of the vast Freedom Monument, Nasb al-Hurriyya. The monument, a fine, Picasso-influenced sculpture which still stands in Baghdad today, captures the moment of the fall of the monarchy in 1958: a political prisoner caught in jail, a soldier wrenching open the bars of the cell, a woman holding a torch leaping free into the air.[11]

I wondered how much Khattab had been affected by the ruthless persecutions that took place after the Ba'ath took power. In 1969, when he was a young boy, a spy hunt led to the execution of fifty-three Iraqis and the following year another forty-two people were hanged or shot after a failed coup. Perhaps those were the executions he remembered. Did he find it crudely exciting or deeply traumatising? At the very least it was an early and unforgettable lesson in how politically violent Iraq had become. Power and control were associated with vengeance and death. It worsened under Saddam. In 1979, once he took over the party, he had dozens of Ba'athists jailed and twenty-two others executed for an apparently fictitious coup plot.[12] There is video footage of Saddam addressing hundreds of senior Ba'athists in a large hall. The accused, some of them once Saddam's close friends, were led out to their deaths one at a time as their names were mentioned by a witness who had apparently confessed to a plot under torture. Several accounts say Saddam led the killings but also made his cabinet and several members of his Revolutionary Command Council each take the handgun and kill. All were implicated from the start, including many of the men who stayed by his side until the regime collapsed.

Khattab did have his criticisms of the Ba'ath, but they were not of the paranoia or the ruthless violence that he had just described. That had been acceptable, even necessary, he implied. No, he believed that the problems in the party only started in 1990 when Saddam invaded Kuwait. He called it a 'big crack'. 'It put Iraq in the barrel of a cannon and gave the

54

keys of the game completely to our enemies,' he said. It had also been a mistake to militarise the party, put Saddam in charge of the army and have him appear so often in military dress. The army should have been neutral, Khattab said. Not only did Saddam destroy the army and billions of dollars of Iraqi infrastructure by bringing upon his nation the first Gulf War, but 'most importantly he destroyed the spirit of the victory among all the Arabs, which was formed when Iraq came out victorious from war with Iran.' Here again was the sense of Arab pride slighted once more. After 1991 the party changed. Weekly meetings were pushed back to monthly meetings and several party militias were created. A divide grew between the highest echelons of the party and the ordinary members, who were no longer so quickly trusted. The sense of the party's self-criticism, such as it was, had gone, he said. He said nothing about the arrests, executions or mass graves, which didn't seem to figure in his analysis.

I asked him if in that climate he had been able to speak freely in private with his family or his friends about his criticisms of the party.

'After 1991 I remained silent. The mistake had already been committed and we were not able to change the leader. He had become a military leader, he was like Stalin. He was scared of senior Ba'athists turning against him.'

Khattab said that inside part of the insurgency that was now fighting the American occupation was a Ba'athist element which wanted to return to power but to rule in a different way from Saddam. They would nationalise the oil companies and give autonomy to the Kurds in the north, he said. They had already talked about making a comeback in the future as a political party, even taking part in elections: a moderate, acceptable Ba'ath.

'Do you really think the Ba'ath still has credibility with the Iraqis?' I asked.

'After the shock, the majority of the Iraqis hope that the Ba'ath will return and, because of the horror they have seen, some of them even want Saddam back in power. The day is very near.' Khattab said. 'Saddam Hussein is not the Ba'ath. Though he committed mistakes, those are not the mistakes of the Ba'ath.' I left his office and the next day he flew back to the comforts of Abu Dhabi.

4

Order Number One

I could see that I had to leave the hotel. Over the summer I had sat with the other journalists by the pool at night, drinking and laughing at the strangeness of the country around us, but it was too transient a place to stay. I didn't know how long I was going to be in Baghdad, but it was going to be several months at least. So in the autumn after the war I moved into a house in a wealthy and quiet district not too far from the hotel. There wasn't a wide choice of houses on offer. I spent weeks looking at large, often gloomy villas whose owners were asking up to £50,000 for a year's rent. Many of them were ugly cement monoliths, built in the 1960s or 1970s, with large overhangs at the front propped up by faux classical columns. These were designed to give weight and prestige to the building, but they cast every room inside into dark shadow. It might have been a wise precaution against the relentless summer sun but it left the homes soulless and deeply depressing. If you glanced across at the Baghdad cityscape from almost any view it was grey and forbidding. The beautiful architecture of the past was now difficult to find: the narrow, shaded alleyways of the old city in Adhamiya, or the stone arches and metal balustrades of the side streets of Abu Nawas on the riverfront, or the dark, spice-clouded souk around the Shia shrine of Kadhamiya.

One of the best houses I found was an oddly designed building close to the old Australian embassy and just a stone's throw from the hotel. It had a vast salon downstairs and only a couple of small bedrooms tacked onto the back, as if this was a home for showing off not for living in. The salon was divided into six or seven separate seating areas. In the centre a tiny bar was squeezed into its own small wooden room, marked off with stained-glass windows. The house was crowded with paintings and sculptures by Iraqi artists that gave it rare warmth and the owner, Faisal Jaboori, said artists and poets had been frequent visitors in the past when they gave regular readings and had smoke-filled, late-night debates. I asked if they still came, but he said no. Since the war his artist friends had left the country or they stayed in their homes. None of them were painting any more. One of his friends who had now left Baghdad was Mohammad Ghani, a sculptor I had met before the war. He was clearly in favour with the Ba'ath, because his largest pieces were spread across the capital, though he had insisted to me he never slavishly produced propaganda for Saddam (and that was a time when some artists would paint you a portrait of Saddam in their own blood). He showed me round his studio, which was small and crowded but with a large skylight in the roof. I found on one shelf little clay figures of seven women, each bent double under the crushing weight of a large stone block. Etched on to the blocks in English were the days of the week. The point was to highlight the suffocating weight of the UN sanctions which were imposed on Iraq after the invasion of Kuwait. Another series of small sculptures in bronze depicted a line of women, again bent double, their faces empty hollow spaces, queuing before a closed wooden door. They were families under embargo again, he said. The men were missing and the women were waiting for food and medicine. Spread on shelves around his studio were dozens more hunched women, all without faces and some with babies reaching up to feed from dry breasts. These pieces had never been shown outside his studio

58

and they were very different from his public sculptures, which were colossal works glorying in the fables of ancient Mesopotamia: the slave girl Morgiana from 'Ali Baba and the Forty Thieves' pouring boiling oil into piles of tall vases, or, near the Sheraton where Qais had worked, a large flying carpet from the *Thousand and One Nights*. Ghani had been working in his studio during the first Gulf War and described how the windows had shaken and then shattered as bombs exploded nearby. He was extremely angry when I saw him, for he had realised that war was again imminent. 'The Americans think that the Iraqis are like the Red Indians and that it is very easy to kill us off,' he said. 'But Iraq is difficult to destroy. Iraqis are like palm trees that bend in the wind but never break. Now the wind is blowing stronger than ever but it will pass.'

In the end I decided to take a house that was smaller and more suitable for what I and the journalists I was to share with needed. It was in a quiet cul-de-sac blocked off with a fallen tree trunk and all the houses in the street were owned by the same family – the Khudairis, a family firmly embedded in Iraq's small but extremely wealthy elite. Next door was a vast Khudairi house that had been appropriated by Saddam's regime and used as a guest house for important visiting diplomats. After the war it was appropriated a second time by Sharif Ali bin al-Hussein, a cousin of Iraq's last king, Faisal II. He had fled Baghdad aged two when the monarchy was toppled and grew up in Lebanon and Britain, becoming an investment banker. He returned a couple of months after the war, arriving in sweltering heat dressed in a pristine, dark pin-stripe suit and wearing a close-fitting bullet-proof jacket hidden under his starched white shirt. He spoke grandly of restoring the monarchy and insisted it had been a golden age of tolerance and progress, though in reality there was to be no going back to the days of royalty. A small flock of fat-tailed sheep was always grazing in the corner of his sprawling front garden, gifts from the many tribal leaders who would visit.

The Khudairi couple who owned my house had left for New Zealand with a flood of Iraqi emigrants in 1991 and the building hadn't been lived in since then. As Baghdad houses went it was small and modest and mercifully free of the usual clutter of heavy columns, ornate marble hallways and gilded chandeliers. The furniture was old and unremarkable except for two tall, ugly glass sculptures in the front room each in the shape of a palm tree, with heavy fronds drooping to the floor. One day an Iraqi friend came to the house and as soon as he saw the sculptures he pronounced them marvellous and extremely valuable examples of Czech glass. He said they were worth perhaps £30,000.

The property was managed by an arrogant, unscrupulous agent named Abu Mustafa, who always got the upper hand in his dealings with us. He delivered a long lecture about how reverently we should treat the glass sculptures and only with great reluctance did he agree to tidy and clean out the house before we first moved in. After we had negotiated hard to have a large petrol generator included in the rental price, he delivered instead an agricultural pump that had been adapted to run as a generator. It broke down and overheated frequently and was so noisy that the neighbours complained. At the same time, though, they quietly and without asking hooked up their own homes to run off the machine. The house trembled every time the generator was switched on.

When the exiles came back to Baghdad, following in the wake of the invading American and British armies, they brought with them a clear resolve about the fate of the Ba'ath. The party was to be deleted from the Iraqi political scene, 'de-Ba'athification' they called it. In Arabic it was even stronger: *ijtitath*, which meant 'uprooting' the party. In the early months it was an approach embraced by the Americans. On 16 May 2003, four days after he had arrived in Baghdad, Paul Bremer, the new American administrator of occupied Iraq, signed into law his first order. It became one of the ideological pillars of the occupation: Coalition Provisional Authority Order Number One: De-Ba'athification of Iraqi Society. It meant a purge of former senior Ba'athists from public office. The party had already been technically 'disestablished' but this went further. Iraqis who held one of the top four ranks in the party were to be permanently barred from public office. Any former member of the party, regardless of rank, would be prevented from taking the top three positions in any government department or state-owned industry. They were presumed guilty before being found innocent. Images of Saddam and all Ba'ath Party symbols were banned.

'By this means, the Coalition Provisional Authority will ensure that representative government in Iraq is not threatened by Ba'athist elements returning to power and that those in positions of authority in the future are acceptable to the people of Iraq,' said the law.[13]

It was a sweeping step that, with the stroke of a pen, forced 30–40,000 senior functionaries out of their jobs. A week later Bremer signed his second order, Dissolution of Entities, which took the ideological approach one step further and formally dissolved the army, navy and air force, the Special Republican Guards and the Republican Guards, the state militias, the security services, the Ministries of Defence and Information, the Revolutionary Command Council, the former National Assembly and even the Olympic Committee.[14] Although most Iraqi soldiers had given up fighting once they saw the unstoppable momentum of the invading American army, this law ensured there would be no immediate return to barracks

61

even for the junior ranks and effectively meant that an army of up to 400,000 people was now out of work.

Countries have dealt with the legacy of nasty dictatorships or vicious civil wars in many ways.[15] It is the most natural human reaction to forget. This was what happened at the end of the English Civil War in the seventeenth century; it happened in de Gaulle's post-war France, in West Germany in the 1950s and more recently in post-civil war Lebanon. The past is simply left where it stands. There is no reckoning, no accountability.

Other places have made a concerted attempt at catharsis. South Africa's Truth and Reconciliation Commission is often held up as a model for others struggling with their past, although there has been regret even there that many murderers and rights abusers who ignored the commission have gone unpunished. In Germany, the official amnesia of the 1950s was later seen to be a mistake that took many years to undo. Desperate not to repeat the error once again after the collapse of the Soviet Union in 1989, there was a rush to remember East Germany's communist past. Details were unearthed, crimes brought to the fore. But it had mixed results. Large public trials often didn't provide catharsis. Purges of former functionaries were too broadly and cumbersomely applied. The former communist states also had access to vast archives of secret police files which contained detailed reports made against citizens and the names of their informers. Many governments committed themselves to making these files open to all, and in many cases this exposure of truth seemed a decent response to a difficult past. In Iraq, however, much of the equivalent archive of files was destroyed in the weeks of looting that followed the war, sometimes on purpose. There could perhaps have been a truth commission, although it is hard to see how it might have worked in the face of the violence. But this is not what happened. The Americans and their Iraqi exile allies came with a specific agenda and that agenda was to destroy the Ba'ath and purge it from society. One official in the American administration in Baghdad said in May 2003 that they intended to 'extirpate Ba'athism from Iraqi society' and to 'put a stake in its heart'.

Perhaps it was inevitable in the shifting sands of the new Iraq that one of the men selected to oversee the de-Ba'athification policy had been a Ba'athist himself. Mithal al-Alusi joined the party as a young man because he was attracted to its Arab nationalist ideology. He was given a surprisingly influential position teaching in a school in Baghdad that trained Ba'athists in the workings and thoughts of the party. It gave him access to senior figures and he said he had even spent time with Khairullah Tulfar, a close uncle of Saddam. Just before or shortly after Saddam was born, his father died. It was Tulfar who brought Saddam up and arranged for him to marry his own daughter, Sajida.

Alusi said he began to realise in the early 1970s that the party was taking a violent and dangerous new turn away from its true path. 'It was obvious to me because of my position that the leadership was going wrong,' he said. 'The scandals were every-where and it was going to destroy the whole country.' He said he began working against the party in 1973 – although he didn't explain what exactly that had involved. Three years later, when he realised he was under suspicion, he defected during a trip arranged for him by the party to Egypt. An order for his arrest and execution was issued in Baghdad while he was abroad. After that he lived in exile, first in Britain and later in Germany. He didn't return to Iraq until some months after the fall of the regime, twenty-seven years later.

I met Alusi one spring morning in the offices of the Supreme National Commission on De-Ba'athification, of which he was the director general. The offices were in a building that once belonged to the Ministry of Military Industry and was close to the palace. As soon as I stepped from the lift I entered a long corridor, lined with harrowing photographs of Iraq's many mass graves and of the scene at Halabja, the Kurdish village where 5,000 people died after the regime attacked it with chemical weapons. Such images left no room for doubt about his sense of the Ba'ath legacy. There was no grey area, no arguing about the merits of post-colonial, pan-Arab ideologies and the complexities of a paranoid state. On another wall was a sheet of paper typed with the words 'Nazis=Ba'ath'. In a second hallway was a papier-mâché model, about the size of an adult, of a three-headed serpent in green with a long, yellow tail. On the first head was a Nazi swastika; on the second head was Saddam, painted with long fangs, dripping in blood. The third was of Michel Aflaq, the founder of the Ba'ath. At the end of the hall was a large office, and in the office, behind a large wooden desk, sat Alusi. He was dressed in a black suit and tie. He was fifty-four and seemed tired and uninterested, appearing to talk out of the side of his mouth and chain-smoking his way through several Gauloise Blondes as we spoke.

Alusi was a Sunni Muslim, the minority Muslim sect in Iraq but the sect to which Saddam belonged and which the regime had favoured early on. That marked him out as unusual among the exiles who had returned, because at that stage most of the main political figures were Shia. Alusi now worked with Ahmad Chalabi, a wealthy Shia businessman who had run one of the main opposition parties – the Iraqi National Congress – and who was heavily backed by the Pentagon in the years before the war and for some time afterwards. Chalabi, an intensely bright mathematician who had been convicted in his absence in a case of banking fraud in Jordan in 1992, was credited with driving the de-Ba'athification policy, but Alusi was a willing adherent. It was as if he had lived his adult life waiting for these days to come.

In Germany Alusi had worked in trade and commerce, but regarded that as simply a way to earn money while he worked in the opposition against Saddam. He described his occupation then as 'political refugee'. In fact he was a little more than that. One day, less than a year before the invasion, he and a group of like-minded Iraqi exiles hatched a plan. Iraq was a long way off and there was no way they could realistically confront the regime in Baghdad head on. So instead they decided to attack what was technically the closest piece of Saddam-controlled Iraqi territory: the Iraqi Embassy in Berlin.

Shortly after lunch on 20 August 2002, Alusi and a group of his friends stormed into the embassy, letting off sound blasts and squirting pepper spray or tear gas.[16] He insisted they carried no guns, although witnesses heard two shots fired inside the building. There were four Iraqi staff inside. Two were either released or slipped away in the chaos of the attack. But the group held on to the second pair and tied them up – one of them was the acting ambassador Shamil Mohammed. Then a letter was sent to news agencies in Germany announcing the demands of Alusi's hitherto unknown group, the Democratic Iraqi Opposition of Germany.

The statement said: 'In the name of the Iraqi people and their legitimate leadership, the Iraqi opposition, we declare that the liberation of Iraqi soil begins today. We are taking over the Iraqi Embassy in Berlin and with this the first step in the liberation of our beloved fatherland. This first step against the terrorist regime of Saddam Hussein and his killers, which is taking place with a peaceful purpose, is intended to make the German people, its organisations and its political powers understand that our people have a desire to be free and will act on it.' The group said the German people in particular would understand the nature of a tyrannical regime: 'The Germans . . . also suffered and bled under the dictatorship and tyranny of Hitler's National Socialists. These parallels unite democrats.'

In Baghdad, the Saddam regime denounced the attack as 'terrorist aggression' by 'mercenaries of the American and Zionist intelligence services'. The Iraqi government gave permission to the German police to storm the embassy.

Five hours later, at about 7.40 p.m., a team of German police commandos assaulted the building, freed the remaining two hostages and arrested Alusi and four others. Two of the embassy staff had been injured, though not seriously. One had been squirted in the face with an irritant spray, another suffered shock.

Looking back, Alusi was rather proud of his day of activism. 'It was the right thing to do,' he said. He insisted that inside the building he had found documents suggesting that there had been collusion between German intelligence and Saddam's regime and that Saddam's regime had influenced the outcome of recent German elections. He said it was 'proof' of co-operation between the two governments. I looked for any evidence of such co-operation but I could find none.

Eventually Alusi was convicted and jailed for three years and three months, a much lighter sentence than the fifteen years he said the prosecutor had first demanded. So while American and British soldiers invaded his country and toppled the regime that he had fled nearly three decades earlier, Alusi watched it all from a German jail cell. It was only on 3 September 2003, several months after the war, that he was released. The court ordered him to stay at his home in Germany and confiscated his passport. Alusi slipped away and somehow made the journey to Baghdad – he wouldn't say how. He and four others from the group who attacked the embassy were now working in the De-Ba'athification Commission. He rummaged through the papers on his desk until he found for me a letter in English from the

German embassy in Baghdad to the new Iraqi government that proved he had indeed skipped the country illegally and was still liable to arrest.

'The director general of the Supreme National Commission for De-Ba'athification, Mr Mithal al-Alusi, has also been convicted for the occupation of the embassy. He however left Germany in contradiction to the condition imposed by the court. In case he would travel to any European destination (Schengen states) he would risk to be arrested upon arrival,' said the letter, signed by the German chargé d'affaires in Baghdad.

This of course meant that after twenty-seven years in exile in Europe, Alusi could not now return. He would have to make Baghdad his home, a decision which at the time seemed straightforward but that later came at great cost.

Alusi's attitude to the Ba'athists was as uncompromising as the posters in his corridors suggested. He referred again and again as we spoke to the 'fascist Ba'athist Nazi experiment'. 'We want to prevent this happening again,' he said. 'We want to build a new Iraq, a transparent Iraq where there will be no place for one party and one leader. We don't want to try the Nazi Ba'athist experiment again. The Ba'ath ideology is the Nazi ideology and the Ba'ath method is the Nazi method.' On the walls of his office were garish, new oil paintings that showed skeletons in jails.

He said the commission wanted all party members from the top four proscribed ranks excluded from government jobs for life. That meant, he said, as many as 60,000 people. Some in the fourth rank, 'Udw Firqah, could apply to stay on in government jobs, though not in senior positions, he told me. They would have to prove their hands were clean, which usually meant providing a letter of support from a cleric or one of the major parties. Since the parties represented the opposition and none represented the Ba'ath, these letters were not easy to obtain. Even as we spoke there were Ba'athists queuing up in the street outside to present their case to the commission, pleading for the chance to return to work. Many of them were teachers – teachers had made up a disproportionately large part of the Ba'ath membership even from the beginning. But Alusi said he had the names of 71,000 unemployed teachers who had never been Ba'athists and who were now looking for work. They deserved precedence and, after all, he said, they would make better teachers.

I asked Alusi how he could tell the difference between an Iraqi who had joined the party just to win promotion at work, and someone who had committed serious crimes under the protection of the Ba'ath. This lay at the heart of his determinations as head of the De-Ba'athification Commission.

'If we try to bring any of them before any criminal court anywhere in the world none of them would ever be allowed out again,' he said. 'All criminal law in the world that is honest says that everyone who knows about a crime, pushes for that crime or is quiet about that crime is complicit in that crime. But we know people were obligated to be members of the party so we need to find the correct solution for every man.' He said the commission had allowed hundreds of Ba'athists to return to their work, although I had met little evidence of this over the previous several months in Iraq. He wanted Ba'athists to give up their weapons and live as ordinary citizens.

'We don't want killing of the Ba'athists. We believe that if this commission wasn't here there would be mass crimes and killings of the Ba'athists in the streets. That is for sure.' Alusi said his commission acted as a mediator to channel the anger of the victims and protect the rule of law, though again I had seen little evidence of that. Few people outside the offices of the commission seemed to know much about it. Ba'athists saw it as a place they had to visit if they were ever going to get their jobs back – a sham confessional.

I asked if his time in Germany had suggested any lessons from dealing with the legacy of the Nazis that could be applied here in Iraq. He leapt on this idea. 'We have learnt that we should not give leadership to the Ba'athists again like what is happening in Germany at the moment. Do you really think Jewish people can live freely in Germany now? There are people in Germany who are killing Jews in the name of resistance.'

There seemed little room for reconciliation in Alusi's approach and every sense that the party still remained a powerful threat. I asked if it wouldn't be easier to allow the Ba'ath to take part in the political process and then see how few people supported it when given a genuine choice. That way the party might gradually shrink into a small, unimportant minority. He thought this was most dangerous.

'No,' he said. 'We cannot live peacefully and securely with the presence of the party. Germany cannot live with all these Nazi thoughts. You have Nazis in your country too, don't you?'

'Well, we have a nationalist party,' I said, 'but it is small and not many people support it.'

'Yes, but the British have experience of democracy. The Nazis are there but they have no power. You cannot compare what we have right here and what you have in your country. The Ba'athists were here for thirty-five years, they are many in number, they have many weapons. One night they left and now they want to return.'

5

Revenge

Of course no one was at hand to explain how the Americans could remove a party like the Ba'ath that had soaked itself so deeply into the fabric of society without a vast bloodletting. It was easy enough to outlaw the party, or sack people from their jobs, or force them to sign renunciations of the Ba'ath, but that only scratched the surface. After all, what was the word they used? Extirpate. Even the sound was arresting, so surgical. They weren't talking about disbanding the party, or proscribing it, or ridiculing it, or papering over it, but tearing it out from the roots. In the end there was only the thinnest line between extirpation and revenge.

Now there were rumours from the southern city of Basra that suggested some groups already had their own very clear understanding of what it meant to extirpate and that they were going about it with bloody abandon.

The looters in Basra had been rapacious. Before the war there had been a line of enormous bronze statues of Iraqi military officers standing on plinths along the Shatt al-Arab. Basra sits on the river's west bank and on the east is the border that marks the beginning of Iranian territory. All the statues had stood facing across the river, each with his right arm thrust out from the shoulder pointing damningly across the water at Iran. It was a muscular war memorial that seemed to me quite at odds with the way the people felt. The eight-year war between Iraq and Iran in the 1980s had been a long, grinding slaughter that claimed more than a million lives on the two sides. It was something to be wept over, not celebrated. What did for the statues in the end, though, was not their zealous finger-pointing but the value of their bronze. They were sawn off, dragged away and melted down. Only the concrete plinths were left, with the occasional piece of metal wire sticking up out of the stone. Then there was the Sheraton Hotel on the waterfront nearby. It had been gutted. As Basra fell a handful of thieves pushed the grand piano out of the building and away down the high street.

What distinguished Basra, quite apart from its looting, was the water. It was a city built on the fortunes of the sea. Long straight canals, clogged with rubbish, cut through the centre of the city like a network of electronic circuits. The trade that came along these waterways brought wealth and a tradition of openness. Basra had a vitality all of its own. When the city was established in the seventh century it was filled with Bedouin Arabs from many different tribes with as many different dialects of Arabic who had come there to trade. There were also thousands of Persian-speakers who had flocked to Basra, which quickly became the greatest port of its time in the Arab world. From here sailors would set off for destinations as far as China. Out of this great mixing pot emerged a man named Abul Aswad al-Du'ali, who was so worried that the precise Arabic of the Qur'an was being lost in the collision of dialects and languages that he set about establishing for the first time an Arabic grammar, and he founded a school that produced some of the greatest poets and scholars of the Arabic language. By now this rich tradition wasn't anything more than a faded memory, but it did feel that the old energy the port brought to the city had returned. Under Saddam the years of sanctions had brought work at the docks to a halt. After the war they opened again to trade and drew in huge container ships which would dock and unload vast consignments of televisions, food, clothes, spare engine parts, second-hand cars from the Gulf and used refrigerators. It was all quite legal and nothing was subject to taxes or tariffs or more than a cursory glance from customs officials. At night, the port was a different place. Smugglers would drive out to the docks with tanker-loads of fuel they had siphoned secretly from the government stores, which would be loaded onto ships to be exported abroad. Bribes kept the policemen silent and the port gates unlocked. One of the main docks was called Abu Flus, the Father of Money.

I drove down to Basra to search out the rumours of revenge. I had the name of a resourceful local journalist and he arranged for me to meet a young man called Ala Mohammad Abdul Nabi, who was twenty-three.[17] I sat with him in the corner of the restaurant in my hotel and he told me the story of his father, Mohammad, who had been a headmaster at a secondary school in Basra. Nabi said straight out that his father had been in the Ba'ath. Not just a simple member, but one of those in the top four ranks, a Branch member. But this was how it was, he said. His father had wanted to be a headmaster and only by being a senior member of the party could he get the promotion. 'To make a living for your family you had to be a Ba'athist, otherwise what were you supposed to do? Live in the desert?'

Then came the invasion and not long afterwards Nabi's father was told he was no longer needed at the school. There was a de-Ba'athification policy under way, they said, and he had to leave. For six months he sat at home, unemployable. Two of his sons dropped out of college and found menial jobs to bring in enough money to keep the family going. But this wasn't good enough for Mohammad. He went several times to the Directorate of Education in Basra, once with a cleric friend of his who was there as a character witness to say that although he had been a Ba'athist that didn't mean he had been a criminal. The cleric wrote a letter to that effect and handed it in, but still the officials refused to let Mohammad go back to work. Several weeks passed and eventually Mohammad typed out a new letter explaining that indeed he had been a Branch member of the party and that he realised he couldn't go back to his previous job but that as he was now nearly penniless he hoped for a retirement payment or perhaps a modest desk job in the administration. He put the letter in a Manila file with other documents about his case. That day and that evening his family begged him to give up his campaign. But Mohammad insisted he would go back to the directorate to plead his case. So the next morning he dressed himself in a smart, clean robe, took the file and drove into town. He parked opposite the directorate and went in to make his petition. It was not a success. The officials didn't want to listen and eventually, dejected, he left the building. It was about 1 p.m. He walked out of the gate and started to cross the main street back to his car. At that moment a white Toyota saloon car pulled up and a gunman armed with a pistol shot him twice. One bullet hit the right side of Mohammad's neck; the second entered his chest just under his shoulder. He died in hospital later that day.

Perhaps if his death had been a one-off, you could have put it down to the lawlessness of Iraq in those days. But two days earlier one of Mohammad's friends, also a teacher, had been shot as he walked away from the same office. Their deaths were part of a much larger wave of revenge against the Ba'ath in the city. The police said around fifty former party officials had been killed in recent weeks, of whom several were teachers. A number had died in the same place: in the street outside the education directorate.

You didn't have to look far to see who might have been behind these attacks. In the past few months a multitude of small, religious and extremely conservative Shia Islamic parties had sprung up in Basra with names like the Revenge of God, and the Next Islam and the 15th of Shaba'an – the date in the Islamic calendar that marked the start of the 1991 uprising. Some of them put up posters of the leader of the Iranian revolution Ayatollah Khomeini. In one party office I saw a poster announcing: 'All Jerusalem, we are coming' and another that said: 'Palestine will come back to us, Israel will disappear'. These groups were openly armed and even conducted their own night-time patrols, ostensibly in liaison with the local police but often quite independent of them. Police officers complained the parties were also trying to infiltrate the local force. The parties were not staffed by Iranians but there was little doubt their members were sympathetic to the Shia theocracy next door and probably receiving money or weapons from them. I heard several rumours that, immediately after the collapse of the regime, these groups had swiftly obtained lists of former Ba'athists with names and addresses that they were using as a database for assassinations. They were also selling the information on to ordinary people, allowing them to track down those Ba'athists who might have been involved in the death or disappearance of family members and, if they wished, to exact their private revenge. All this was happening out of sight of the several thousand British soldiers who were deployed in and around Basra. I spoke to one of the British diplomats in charge in the south. He thought the emergence of these parties was an inevitable result of the collapse of the regime. It was haphazard and not ideal, he said, but he wasn't overly perturbed. He called it the 'political oxygen' of the new climate.

By now, after interviewing several people, I had amassed good evidence that teachers were being deliberately targeted. So I went to the education directorate to confront its chief, a cleric named Sheikh Ahmed Jassim al-Maliki. The sheikh wore a white turban, which meant that he was a learned Shia cleric and qualified to lead Friday prayers. It wasn't ever clear what qualified him to take charge of the province's education system.

Maliki had always been political with his religion and was a follower of Ayatollah Mohammad Sadeq al-Sadr, a respected Shia cleric who had been a severe critic of Saddam. In 1999, Sadr was assassinated along with two of his sons. There was a very brief uprising in the Shia areas of Baghdad and Maliki said proudly that he had been involved. After that he became a wanted man and fled across the border into Iran for shelter. He came back after the war, taking control of the provincial education department more by force of will than any process of selection. He was a man who was not ashamed of his extremely conservative opinions.

Maliki was sitting behind a desk at one end of the room. He waited in silence for a minute or two, while one of his assistants hurriedly set an old video camera onto a tripod and plugged in a trail of wires that led across the floor. The arrival of a foreigner underlined the importance of the sheikh, they said. They would order the footage broadcast on the local news that evening.

Education in Iraq, Maliki said by way of introduction, must be in accordance with Islamic rules. What did this mean in practice? Well firstly, he said, it meant that women really shouldn't be teachers. It wasn't enough that they should cover their hair. They couldn't work safely in remote areas and they took too much time off work to have children. 'The psychology of a woman is different from that of a man,' he said.

Then there was the question of the legacy of the Saddam era. It wasn't just that the education system had been allowed to sink into disarray and needed modernising. That much was true enough. But there was a problem with the teachers. Too many of them had been in the Ba'ath.

'We cannot have our children educated by teachers who were teaching classes about Saddam Hussein and had pictures of

75

Saddam hanging on their classroom walls,' he said. 'They might tell the children that Saddam will return one day. They used to go into class and say to the students: "Long live Saddam!" The existence of such teachers is very dangerous.'

He told me he had arranged for 980 teachers in the province of Basra to be dismissed from their jobs because of their party affiliation. Those who only joined the party to further their careers were a different case. His department was working to allow them to come back to their jobs. It was he who pointed out this distinction.

I asked about Mohammad Abdul Nabi and the other teachers who had been killed just a few yards from the front gate of Maliki's office. He said he knew nothing of them. 'I have no responsibility for this,' he said. 'They came to our directorate in order to get their jobs back. People outside may have been watching them and may have taken revenge on them.' But this question seemed to have provoked him. I asked what he thought about the Ba'ath and suddenly he boiled over and began shouting at me. 'They have killed about five million innocent people who are crowding the graveyards! The criminals must be killed! Saddam was a criminal and his servants are criminals!'

But, I said gently, there were courts that could deal with crimes from the past. If he had evidence against particular Ba'athists shouldn't it go before an Iraqi court? He wasn't condoning people taking revenge themselves, was he?

He drew a breath and spoke more slowly. 'Society needs revenge. It is in the nature of Iraqi society to take revenge,' he said. But, yes, he agreed there were rules. He himself, for example, didn't have the right to give the order to have someone killed. But an Islamic court could give that order. And the son or brother or father of a victim of the Ba'ath, he also had the right to kill to avenge a crime. Maliki said he didn't recognise

76

the judgement of any of Iraq's civil courts, only instructions issued by the Shia clerics. 'As Muslims we should follow the regulations made by the Islamic courts because the decision of such a court comes from God.'

'What kind of punishments should these people receive?' I asked. He said the punishment should fit the crime. 'Islam says the killer must be killed.' But I suggested that perhaps that wasn't practical – it would mean so many deaths. I asked about the towns north of Baghdad in the Sunni Muslim communities which made up the majority of Saddam's security elite, towns like Tikrit, Falluja, Ramadi, and Mosul. There were whole communities of Ba'athists there. He exploded at me again.

'They must be removed from the map! They are more dangerous than AIDS and cancer! There is no treatment for cancer except to cut it out and there is no treatment for AIDS except to burn those who suffer from it.'

A couple of weeks later Maliki was fired by the Ministry of Education in Baghdad who had taken several months to realise quite the sort of man who was controlling their offices in the south. The idea that this was mere political oxygen seemed unaccountably naive. Here was a man who had really pondered the meaning of revenge, who savoured the culling of thousands of his countrymen. His answer to thirty years of dictatorship under Saddam was to call for a sectarian war of untold vengeance. Given a choice between reconciliation and revenge, he had most firmly sided with revenge. And these were only the early days – it was still less than a year since the invasion. Many months later men like Maliki would begin to play a serious role in the Iraqi government, dominating the police and security forces and hunting down on a much larger scale Ba'athists and clerics from the Sunni community. Perhaps, we realised then, a civil war was coming.

A few streets away from the directorate, in western Basra,

there was a small police station that was responsible for this area. Inside, an officer called Major Mohamed Farhan sat behind a desk on which was a heap of files and two packets of cigarettes. Every few minutes he pulled another cigarette from a packet and smoked it hungrily down to the filter. The police station was so small that the cells were only a few yards from his office. Half a dozen men sat quietly on the floor or on benches behind bars. The teacher Mohammad Abdul Nabi was killed in this district so Major Farhan was responsible for the investigation. In fact there were also a couple of streets in this area that were known dumping grounds for gangland and tribal killings so he had his work cut out. He said quite openly that he believed religious parties to be behind the assassinations. Yet even though the parties operated openly in the city there seemed to be an unspoken political pressure inside the police force that had prevented any serious arrests. The files continued to land on his desk. Several of the killings of teachers had similarities, not least the white Toyota Cressida saloon car that witnesses had identified as the gunmen's car again and again. He opened one of the files which described the death of a shopkeeper whose corpse had been found with a bloodstained piece of paper stuck inside his shirt. The paper was there in the file and still carried a dark layer of dried blood. It said simply: 'He was a Ba'athist and a member of the Fedayeen Saddam. He took part in the executions with Ali Hassan al-Majid in the Abul Khassib district in 1991.' It read like the sentencing order of a judge. The Fedayeen Saddam had been one of the regime's more feared paramilitary groups. Ali Hassan al-Majid, better known as Chemical Ali, was the cousin of Saddam who had taken part in the campaign against the Kurds in the late 1980s, during which whole villages were gassed, and who had gone on to lead the repression of the 1991 uprising.

As we were talking, one of the major's assistants brought in another file. A hospital had just found the dead body of a man who had been missing for a week. He was a former Ba'athist and another member of the Fedayeen Saddam. He had been shot twice in the head.

'What would you say to those Ba'athists who are still alive in Basra?' I asked.

'My advice is that they leave the city and not tell anyone their new address or go to their tribes in the countryside and shelter there. There is nothing else we can do.'

About a month later I was several hundred miles north in the town of Samarra, where there had been a big ambush on an American patrol. It was only three days since Saddam himself had been captured, apparently hiding underground in a carefully dug hole not much larger than a coffin in a farmhouse on a riverbank near Tikrit. I had seen the little shack of a farmhouse and squeezed myself into the underground hole where the American military said they found Saddam. It was a pitiful place to hide for a man who had once been untouchable. I had made a list of what I found in the farmhouse: ten canisters of Pif Paf insect repellent, several bars of Palmolive soap, a tub of Saj moisturising cream, ten chicken sausages, a box of Bounty chocolate, a vial of eye-drops, a jar of mango slice pickle, a stick of Lacoste deodorant, a tub of minted toothpicks, a pair of Italian ladies' shoes in a box on the floor, a pair of unworn Lanvain socks, several smashed eggs, a packet of Turkish Delight sweets scattered on the ground, and, most oddly, a series of stylised portraits of Jesus and Mary, under the words in English: God Bless Our Home.

I went to see for myself the scene of the ambush because it suggested that the capture of Saddam wasn't going to undermine the burgeoning insurgency in the slightest. Samarra has an important Shia shrine, but it is also in the heart of the Sunni belt north of Baghdad, the tranche of land that Maliki wanted removed from the map of his Iraq. I stood on a street corner and talked to witnesses who described the attack and disputed the American military's count of eleven rebels killed. I noted down what people said, looked when they pointed out the bullet holes in the nearby buildings and tried to form a picture of what had happened. As I was talking, two men in a white BMW pulled up a little distance away and beckoned me to come closer. They didn't get out of the car and that unnerved me. But since I had attracted a crowd I thought perhaps these were locals come to see who I was. If they did want to hurt me they could have done it by now, I told myself. Better to go to them and be open and friendly. So I walked over. I stood a little distance from the passenger window and explained that I was a journalist trying to find out about the ambush. Both men wore jeans and shirts and each had a red and white keffiyeh, or headscarf, around their necks. I saw immediately that they had Kalashnikov assault rifles in their laps and on a shelf next to the gear stick sat a hand grenade. My stomach turned and I tried to look calm, as if I hadn't noticed their guns. I had been trying for months to find men from the insurgency that I could interview and now suddenly they had come to me. I thought at last I might learn what really drove their fight. Neither man seemed aggressive and they sat in the car and began to talk to me.

'The operations that have happened here against the Americans are not by people outside Samarra,' said the driver. 'We are the tribes of Samarra and we are responsible for the attacks. We are fighting a war against the Americans. We are fighting because they arrested a lot of people, because they attacked a lot of houses in the night, they humiliated our sisters.'

Four of his brothers had been arrested and one killed since the Americans came to Samarra, he said. 'How do they expect us not to take revenge for this and not to lead operations against them? Where is the democracy and freedom?' Their fight hadn't begun on the first day after Saddam's fall, he told me. Instead they had waited to see what the Americans would do. 'For the first two months after the war it was peaceful in Samarra, there were no operations, no military action against the Americans,' he said.

I said that many people thought the insurgents were Ba'athists. Was this true? What did he think of the capture of Saddam?

He said this was quite wrong. He himself had deserted from Saddam's army eleven years before and several of his brothers had also dodged their military service. 'Saddam hurt us and the Americans came after Saddam and they hurt us too. Here we don't care whether they captured Saddam or not. We want to protect our religion, our freedom. Let them deliver authority to the Iraqis and then we will have nothing against them. We have nothing against the Americans. Let them leave our city and our society. As long as they remain inside our city we will continue to seek revenge until we die. We represent Samarra now.' By now there were American Apache helicopters in the sky, not above us but close enough to disconcert these two men. I asked if we could spend more time talking with them, they apologised and drove off.

6

They Said I Would be Punished

There is only so much you can learn about a country by attending press conferences, interviewing government officials, talking to witnesses at the scene of a bombing or an ambush or a grave. It doesn't get you under the skin of a place. So in the spring of 2004 I resolved to spend some time living with an Iraqi family in the hope that it might explain the most important story of all: how Iraqis felt about what was happening to their country. I wanted to meet a woman, only because so many of our stories were about men. But that was slightly complicated by delicate issues of honour and conservative family values. In the end a friend of mine arranged for me to spend a week with a distant relative. She was a widow, with three grown-up sons, she had space in her house and was comfortable about letting a stranger stay. Her name was Najwa al-Bayati and she was a veterinarian, specialising in virology, who had worked for the UN's Food and Agriculture Organisation until her contract was terminated three months after the war because of the worsening security crisis.

Najwa lived in a northern suburb of Baghdad called Hai al-Tunis, a comfortable but not wealthy district with broad streets of large two- or three-storey houses. It was one of the many new parts of town, an area that only a few decades earlier had been open fields and orchards and forests of date palms. Now it was a place for families, with small rows of shops every few blocks and neighbours washing their cars, quietly noticing every stranger who drove past. Hai al-Tunis sits on the first of the several sharp curves that the River Tigris weaves on its way down through the heart of Baghdad. A mile or so to the south is Adhamiya, a staunchly Sunni part of the old city, with tall, narrow houses and delicate wooden balconies. On the day his regime was toppled, Saddam was thought to have been hiding in the Abu Hanifa mosque in the centre of Adhamiya and despite a heavy fire fight with American troops he managed to escape. By now Adhamiya, its buildings still blackened from the fire fight, had become a refuge for the insurgency and almost too dangerous to visit.

Two weeks before I met Najwa, her brother, an artist called Samir, had died of a heart attack. When I arrived at her house there was still a black awning tied to the gate that announced the death.

The promise of Allah is right. The artist Samir Mohammad Abdul Wahab al-Bayati, uncle of Leith Omar Azad, Mustafa Azad and Ashraf Azad, has passed to Allah. The funeral will be held in this house in the Tunis neighbourhood on Thursday February 10, 2004. We are of Allah and to Allah we will return.

The front door was closed. It was always closed, I learnt later. Najwa led me in through the kitchen, then round and under the stairs and into the lounge, where an old set of armchairs lined the walls and a large television sat in the corner covered with a white, embroidered cloth. The curtains were drawn, casting the room into smoky shadow.

She was dressed in black, but it wasn't only for her brother. Her eldest child and only daughter, Samar, had died five years earlier when she accidentally electrocuted herself on a faulty light switch. A large photograph of the girl, with long, curly

83

dark hair and a garish, bright jumper hung on the wall in the front room, dominating the space, watching over their lives. Eight months later, Najwa's husband Azad (his name meant Free), had also died. He was extremely sick after spending four years in Saddam's jails and survived only a short while after his release. Najwa now lived with her three sons: Omar, who was twenty-four and had just married his girlfriend Sour; Mustafa, nineteen; and the youngest, Ashraf, who was seventeen.

She told me all of this in a rush at the beginning of our first conversation, introducing herself through a history of mourning. But despite that, I never felt the house was a particularly sad place. There was grief, but it was for the most part kept private and it is not what I remember most. I remember the laughter, the frustrations, the stories about naughty children, plans for the future and the plentiful food.

When I met Najwa, she was concerned above all else to get her job back. As an employee of the UN she had been well off. Unlike others, she was not overly affected during the sanctions years and she had spent five years at a posting in Irbil, a Kurdish town in the northern autonomous region that had been out of Saddam's control since the 1991 Gulf War. Since the UN had now largely left Iraq she wouldn't be able to work for them again, but she hoped to return to her old job at the veterinary department of the Agriculture Ministry. She was sufficiently qualified and there was work available, plus she had the necessary recommendation from a political party to be accepted back. In these times your contacts counted above all else. Najwa had been a member of the Communist Party since her student days. She was also a religious Shia Muslim. In Iraq this wasn't as much of a contradiction as it should have been. The communists were pragmatic rather than revolutionary, more like social democrats, and most of them were practising Muslims, often Shias from southern Iraq. The party was one of the few with an organised network inside the country in opposition to the Ba'athists since the early years and it still commanded respect.

She had visited the Communist Party offices several times looking for help with her job application but, though they eventually provided a letter of recommendation after months of delay, she still wasn't having success. There was the concern that, with all the more conservative Islamic parties coming to the fore in the new Iraq, the communists were not the powerful force they once were. Nevertheless, Najwa was glad that the Americans had invaded. She had loathed Saddam's regime and had cheered and danced when she watched on her illegal satellite television his bronze statue being wrenched to the ground in Paradise Square. I could understand why when, after I had been in the house for a few days, she told me about her husband Azad. I had seen a photograph of him – an old and sick man sitting in a wheelchair – but she had barely mentioned him until one afternoon, when we sat in her front room sipping cups of strong Arabic coffee. Azad had been her teacher at veterinary college. She had fallen in love with him and the couple were wed, in defiance of the social convention of arranged marriage. They lived happily with their four children until 1991, when an informer presented a report to the security services describing Azad's private criticisms of Saddam and of the war against Iran in the 1980s. He was arrested and interrogated. The directorate of National Security, Amn al-'Am, one of the most feared intelligence agencies in Saddam's Iraq, called her in for an interview.

'They told me my husband had not been charged. They said they wanted me to help them by writing reports about colleagues in my laboratory. They said if I agreed to help them my husband would be freed the next day. I told them: "I can't do it. My husband is now with you so keep him and let me live

85

with my children." They said I would be punished for saying this.'

Azad was then tried by a court with no right of appeal and sentenced to twenty years in jail. Four years later he was freed during a rare prison amnesty but he was so sick from his time in jail that he spent several years confined to a wheelchair. In 1999, he died.

She told her story in a matter-of-fact way, as if what she described had happened to a neighbour or a friend, not her own husband. She left me feeling she was a strong-willed woman, tough enough to face down the regime in her own way despite the heavy penalty it incurred. 'I'm not afraid of anyone, only God,' she used to say. But then perhaps this was also the haphazard way lives were lived under the old regime. Some people were untouched, others were arrested, jailed and died for no particularly good reason. She was probably right that once her husband had been arrested he would not be easily freed, whatever she had agreed to do. It was just arbitrary and terribly cruel.

A couple of days after my first visit, I returned to Najwa's house, this time to stay. It was a cold day but the sun shone and the field opposite the house was being cleared by fire. The rooms downstairs had been carefully cleaned for my arrival and a computer had been put in the front room, near the curtained window. I was to sleep in what had been Samar's room. Five years after her death, it had hardly been touched. There were photographs of her on the wall, and her books and bags were still there, pushed into a corner.

I stepped into the middle of an argument between Najwa and one of her friends, a woman whose daughter was to marry a dentist. The girl had just discovered that the man she loved wasn't in fact qualified. Though he had taken a dentistry course, he hadn't completed it and had been trying to impress

86

her. This was a big deal and her family took it very badly. It looked like the girl would not easily find a new fiancé and there was some argument about whether she should stick with her dentist. 'He was a big liar,' Najwa said. 'People say she shouldn't get engaged again because people will talk. But I say people will talk anyway. If she can't trust the man on this then she can't trust him on anything.'

A few minutes later her youngest son Ashraf came home from school. It was only just after 11 a.m. School had started at 8 a.m. but both Ashraf and his older brother Mustafa had stayed up so late watching television the night before that they had overslept and missed the first class. Then the teacher for Ashraf's last lesson of the day was absent. Najwa shrugged when she heard the story. The boys only ever went to school for half a day, that way the teachers could cram twice the number of pupils into the school. In the morning it was a secondary school and after lunch it became a primary school, with a different set of much younger pupils. Every three days in the six-day school week it would switch around.

A few minutes later Mustafa came home too. He had finished school and was now taking computer studies at a private college that cost £300 a year. The boys were brimming with stories of the iniquities of the education system, some apparently justified, others perhaps less so. Ashraf said some of his friends had paid bribes to get through their exams. Mustafa said the teachers had made the exams too difficult because they wanted pupils to pay the 10,000 dinar (£4) fee to re-sit them a month later. He himself had failed four subjects, although in the private college he was top of the class.

'I was very sad when I saw my results,' Mustafa said. 'Then my friend Zaidoun came to me and asked me how I'd done. I said I failed four subjects. He said: "You are a hero." Zaidoun failed seven.'

Before the war, Ba'ath officials had come to the school to recruit from among the pupils. Ashraf said some of his friends had signed up, though he did not. Those who joined were given ten extra marks in their end of school exams. If you were a particularly loyal Ba'athist you would be given fifteen extra marks. Several other families had told me exactly the same story. The final exams were marked out of 100 and your result decided not only which university or college you would join but also which subject you could study. Only those with marks in the high 90s could study medicine at Baghdad University – it was regarded as the most prestigious course on offer. Najwa had scored 75 which meant she was sent off to a technical engineering college. With the support of her family she rebelled and did what she had always wanted to do since she was a child: study at vet school. She was one of only eight girls in the entire college.

Najwa reached for another cigarette from her packet of Pines, a cheap and harsh Iraqi brand. 'Enough, Mum,' Ashraf said as she lit up.

She talked about the sons of a woman friend of hers who had been to visit the other day. She was complaining about the boys. 'They are not interested in finishing their studies. They all want to go abroad, they just want to leave Iraq,' she said. 'They've been taking drugs like Valium to make them happy. Maybe they are helpless. Most of them have no work and no money. They want to forget.' There were no reliable unemployment statistics in the new Iraq but it was obvious that, like the trauma of war, it was a vast problem. There was a hunger to escape among so many young people, a sense that the world beyond the border must somehow be a magical, sheltered place. This hopelessness hung like a dark cloud over everything that was said and everything that happened.

However long we talked the conversation always came back

to money. Najwa wasn't embarrassed talking about the family's dire financial straits. It was almost something to be proud of, as if she was saying: here I am with no husband and no job but still the boys are being educated and still we put food on the table.

Across the road, on the pavement opposite the house was an old billiard table. I'd asked about it when I arrived. She had once owned a billiards club that was managed by a friend of her brother. Now it was closed and she was selling off the tables. She said the ragged table sitting in the sunshine across the road had originally been worth 350,000 dinars but that now she hoped to sell it for perhaps 10,000. Then there was the family's large Chevrolet van, parked next to the billiard table and immobile because the engine needed some sort of repair that would cost £400. They had only bought the van five months before the war and they still owed money to the seller. On top of this was the money she owed to her friends for the funeral two weeks before of her brother, and for the wedding a month back of Omar, her eldest boy. The UN owed her six months' salary, she said, but she was still waiting. She had been forced to sell a lot of the family furniture and now they were living off her savings.

Most of all she feared sliding into poverty. Suddenly she said: 'I used to go shopping in Mansour and I would see old women who looked like they had come from wealthy families but they had become poor and they were searching through the rubbish bins hoping to find something they could use.' She shuddered at the shame of it. It was only a passing moment, but it was the one time when I felt she was really exposed. Usually she was tough-skinned and determined, never vulnerable.

That afternoon we drove into the centre of Baghdad to the offices of a newspaper that Najwa's brother Samir had visited the day before he died. The paper was called *al-Taakhi* and belonged to the Kurdistan Democratic Party, for whom Samir

89

had painted a portrait of their long-term leader Mustafa Barzani. We walked around the deserted building until we found one of the paper's editors, Hussein Jafar, who sat alone in his office. He was shabbily dressed in a black suit spotted with dandruff on the shoulders, and he offered his consolations.

'We lost a dear brother, really one of our truest friends and one of our biggest supporters in Iraq. He was a progressive nationalist,' Jafar said. He shuffled through the papers on his desk and then handed Najwa a party calendar as an impromptu condolence gift. 'He was one of the most perfect artists in Iraq and a man of principle.'

Najwa cried. Jafar produced a photograph of the painting of Barzani. It was a peculiar work: the image had been burnt onto a large sheet of what looked like chipboard. The party leader was depicted in idealised fashion: 10 or 11 feet tall, dressed in the baggy Kurdish costume and with a dagger in his belt.

We walked through the offices. 'Let's see if they are more loyal than the Communist Party,' Najwa whispered to me. Discreetly she led Jafar away and asked if the party had any money it could donate to cover Samir's funeral expenses. They talked for a few minutes but there was no money given. Instead he gave her a copy of the obituary of Samir that ran in the paper, which was headlined: 'Goodbye Samir al-Bayati'. Najwa asked if he could find a job for Sour, her new daughter-in-law, when she graduated. Jafar said he would try.

At home that afternoon, Sour's mother came round, dressed in a tight-fitting white hijab that covered her head and part of her face. She was polite but seemed very conservative, much more so than her daughter. She brought with her a friend of Sour's called Saira, who was in her early twenties and giggled a lot. Her dark, tightly-curled hair bounced about on her shoulders and she spoke good English. She was working as an

90

interpreter for the US military. When I asked if she liked the Americans she said 'Sometimes'.

Sour's mother – I was only ever introduced to her as Um Sour, literally the mother of Sour, and I was made to feel this was the only name I should call her by – was much more angry than Najwa about the invasion and occupation. Najwa believed that the Americans and British provided a bulwark against civil strife and said if they left Iraqis would have 'blood up to our knees'. Um Sour was more damning.

'Since 1980 we have been suffering and now we are suffering again,' she said. 'The day before the wedding the Americans stopped our car. They used bad words. They wanted to take Omar and his friend to prison for nothing.'

'You know, about half of everything they say is bad words,' Saira said, she looked embarrassed, her face reddening. The bad words were what she had to listen to every day at work.

'They didn't like Saddam but now they must do better for Iraq,' said Um Sour. 'The roads are dirty, you see dirt every-where. We don't just want mobiles and satellite televisions. What we need is peace. We are rich in oil and they take our oil. The Americans are destroying our country.'

'Everyone now thinks they were coming here to take the oil,' added Saira. 'And that the people were fooled by their lies. Anything the Americans want to do, they can.'

We ate dinner that evening around the white plastic table in the kitchen. The electricity supply, as everywhere else in Iraq, was intermittent at best. In those days the house received on average four hours of electricity followed by a four-hour blackout. It meant the tall fridge and the long deep freezer in the kitchen were never used properly and now served only as cupboards. Every time the power went off, one of the boys would step out into the drive and fiddle for a few minutes with the wires at the main fuse box. A wealthy man in the street had bought a large generator and sold electricity to his neighbours. The family had hooked up a wire to the generator and bought 10 amperes of electricity, which cost them 50,000 dinars (at the time around £20) a month. It was enough to run the lights, the computer and the television, but not the fridge or freezer. They fed a line to the poorer family living next door for free. The generator only worked from 4 p.m. until around midnight, except for Fridays and holidays when it started a little earlier, at around 1 p.m. In the morning if the power went out, there was nothing they could do. Before the war there had been power cuts, what they called load-shedding, but they were shorter and they were warned in advance. 'Sometimes it would be off for two hours in the night, or two hours in the morning,' said Najwa. 'It was OK because we knew when it would cut out. We could still use the fridge and the freezer.' Gas was a problem too. Her cooker ran on gas and the price of the canisters had risen dramatically. The family went through three canisters a month and before the war paid only 500 dinars for each. During the war that rocketed to 5,000 dinars, and now it had fallen back down to 1,000, still twice what it cost before. Sometimes the canisters came only half- or three-quarters full.

Still they ate well, although maybe that was because I was staying. For breakfast there were plates of cheese, slices of cucumber and tomatoes, hard-boiled eggs, piles of flat bread and cups of sweet black tea. For lunch and dinner Najwa would cook large, rich dishes of lamb or chicken, with rice, potatoes, okra or tomatoes. She took pride in her cooking, the food was delicious. We drank mineral water or Coca-Cola; there was no alcohol in the house. Every Wednesday she served fish, the *mazgouf* that was an Iraqi speciality. The fish, often carp, would be sliced in half and opened out then either roasted in the oven or, more traditionally, propped up with a row of sharp sticks and placed around the outside of a wood fire to cook for

92

half an hour or so. The salty, orange roe, prized as the best part of the meal, would be wrapped in silver foil and roasted on its own.

After dinner I sat with the boys and watched *Star Academy*, a Lebanese television talent show which they adored and hooted and howled at. It showed young men and women, dressed in tight, fashionable clothes, singing or laughing in each others' arms – a far more permissive atmosphere than you could ever hope to find on the staid Iraqi state television channels. Ashraf sat by himself at the computer playing a game called *Desert Storm*, in which he took the role of an American soldier in the first Gulf War shooting at Iraqi troops, who would scream out in Arabic as they were hit. Later, Najwa brought out a video-CD that had been shot at Omar and Sour's wedding and as we watched we all laughed at the smart clothes and awkward dancing. Each time Samir appeared on the screen Najwa pointed him out. He was dressed smartly in a suit and waistcoat, his hair and goatee beard were silver and he carried himself with a slow dignity. It was two weeks before his death and this slowness was perhaps a sign of what was to come. Najwa cried quietly. 'We had the greatest happiness and then, two weeks later, the greatest misery,' she said.

In the days that followed I accompanied Najwa as she travelled around the city trying to win support for her return to work. After her weekly visit to the veterinary directorate, she came back to the car where I was waiting. Her hands were shaking and there were tears in her reddening eyes. Inside the building she learned that a colleague who had been a senior figure in the Ba'ath had been allowed to return to work. She was then told that the ministry's re-employment committee would not begin discussing her own case until the end of the next month. 'They make me so upset,' she said. 'When you hear bad news like this, sometimes it is too much to bear.'

We drove on towards the offices of the Communist Party. On the way we stopped in an alleyway filled with small carpenters' workshops. She asked one about the billiard table: how much would it be worth? Would he buy her old table? A little further up the street she stopped at another workshop and cancelled an order she had made the previous week for a new kitchen cabinet. I was thinking there was something erratic about the way she led her life. She wouldn't explain why she had ordered new furniture when she could barely pay the children's school fees.

After several more minutes in the heavy traffic of downtown Baghdad we parked outside the Communist Party offices, housed in a former Defence Ministry building, and we walked in. She carried in her bag the newspaper obituary of Samir, as if it was an assertion of her loss. Large portraits of Marx and Lenin hung in the main hall of the building, looking down on crowds of chattering party officials, many of whom were smoking and counting prayer beads through their fingers. There was another wood-burnt portrait by her brother, this time of an Iraqi Communist Party leader Salim Adil, who was arrested and executed in 1963 in a crackdown on the party. One party official told me that after Adil was killed his body had been chopped into pieces and dissolved in a bath of acid.

Inside, Najwa complained that the letter the Communist Party had provided hadn't worked and that she still didn't have her job back. Others who had recommendations from the big Shia religious parties were finding it much easier to go back to work, she told them and she began to argue with a party official, Subhair Jumaili, who sat behind a desk in front of us. He had spent many years in exile in Britain and his family still lived there because he considered it too dangerous for them to return.

Jumaili said the Governing Council, the would-be government appointed by the American administration, was trying to set up a system so all those who lost their jobs through political pressure under Saddam could now return to work. There had been a flood of applications, he said.

'How come my colleague who was a Ba'athist got her job back?' she asked him.

'What I am saying is that all the official offices still have some percentage of staff who were part of the former regime,' he said. 'It's a problem and it takes time. It's not an easy job. We can't just dismiss them. A lot of them were forced to join the Ba'ath Party.'

'Why didn't I join the Ba'ath Party? I'm so angry about this,' she snapped.

'Don't be angry with us,' he said gently. 'It won't bring a solution to your problem. We understand the problems. All of us have ones we lost. We lost our friends, our families, our relatives, all of us. But we have to consider now we are in a new situation and we are trying to set up something right and move forward to deal with this problem. But it needs time, and money as well.'

'And meanwhile all the Ba'athists remain in their jobs,' Najwa said.

In the end Jumaili admitted that recommendation letters from the communists did not carry the same weight as those from the religious parties. The Minister of Agriculture, who oversaw the laboratory where Najwa wanted to work, belonged to a moderate Sunni party and the communists had little influence in his domain. Since the war, politics had been consumed by nepotism. Each party was trying to look after its own. Running a party wasn't about presenting a coherent political ideology. It was more about providing jobs and support for your members, particularly those who had returned from years in exile or who had spent years in Saddam's jails. Jumaili talked about the de-Ba'athification process and said he was uncomfortable with it, that he felt it was a crude broad-brush approach that was penalising too many people. This made Najwa angry.

'We want them eliminated, every member. We want even our children to forget there was a Ba'ath Party in Iraq,' she replied.

'I fully understand these feelings. We suffered from the regime, we lost many cadres at the hands of the regime,' he said. 'But we don't want other people to suffer now. We didn't get rid of Saddam just to punish ordinary people.' Because the communists didn't agree with the de-Ba'athification policy they did not sit on the committee that oversaw how it operated. Again that lessened their influence.

'We get some obstacles from some ministers. It is not something we are happy with. We want to get rid of such ideas and for this we need a transitional authority,' Jumaili said.

The Americans had promised that, in June 2004, still four months away, they would 'hand over' Iraq to a sovereign government. Few expected much would change. Jumaili said he wanted elections to be held, that this could be the only real solution. But it was a matter of finding the right time and conditions in which to hold them, he said. The Americans had come under pressure from the biggest Shia religious parties who wanted elections soon, but the Americans were reluctant to hold a vote. They, like Jumaili, felt it was too early. It went unsaid, though, that it would be far easier for the Americans to continue their military operations with a pliant, appointed Iraqi government rather than an independent, elected body that might oppose their plans. It was clear that the party wasn't going to give her any money or do more to help, so we left. She was going to have to work on her own at getting the job back.

7

New Furniture

Two weeks before I met Najwa, in fact on the day that her brother died, the lead headline on the afternoon radio news was of a car bomb in the town of Iskandiriya, thirty miles south of Baghdad. 'Reports are coming in of another car bomb in Iraq,' the BBC said. It was no longer anything new. The bombings were frequent and often targeted Iraqi police stations or army recruitment centres. As far as the insurgency was concerned, young Iraqi men signing up to join either the police force or the new army were no more than collaborators in the occupation. Already in the past month I had been to the scene of a suicide car bomb outside the gates of the Green Zone in Baghdad, which killed twenty-five Iraqis, and then to the aftermath of a twin suicide bombing in Irbil, the northern Kurdish town, where more than sixty people had been killed. In the second attack, two bombers, with explosives strapped to their chests, had walked into two crowded parties hosted on either side of town by the big Kurdish political movements to celebrate Eid al-Adha, the festival of sacrifice. The two bombers detonated their devices almost simultaneously. The next day I stood in a ballroom, where one of the bombs and exploded, and watched a man dig out, one by one, hundreds of small ball bearings that had been blasted deep into the walls and ceiling. He held the small silver balls in his fist. A dark red stain in the carpet showed where the bomber had stood. Two other men walked through the room spraying

97

canisters of air freshener which gave off a sickly sweet fragrance.

After the news broadcast, I called my driver and packed what little equipment I needed. We shoved a couple of our bullet-proof jackets into the back seat. They were too conspicuous to wear in the car, but often I would wedge them between myself and the door. No one on the outside could see them and it provided some protection. Our drivers alternated between a couple of cars but none were armoured. Instead we used old, modest saloon cars that looked like any other on the road. I always sat in the back; Qais, or one of the other interpreters I used, took the front passenger seat. Tinted windows were illegal – the police would pull you over and at gunpoint peel the dark plastic from the windows. But we had sun-visors attached to the back windows at the side, anything to make it slightly harder for someone to realise there was a Westerner sitting in the car. I'd grown a beard and tried not to dress too conspicuously like an outsider, but I don't think it did much good. Iraqis always seemed acutely aware of strangers.

On a trip like this, I carried in my bag my small laptop and a Thuraya satellite telephone, a plastic brick a little larger than a mobile phone, which allowed me to make telephone calls wherever I went. It was nearly a year after the war before there was a mobile phone network up and running, and even then it didn't work well and covered little of the country outside Baghdad. So we still relied on the Thuraya, which I could also connect to my laptop and, albeit slowly, send a story back to London. I had other satellite phones that were heavier and more cumbersome but faster. The rapid refinement in technology made journalism in countries like this suddenly accessible to anybody who wanted to chance their luck as a stringer. Even in a place like Afghanistan or Iraq you could operate with equipment that cost only a few hundred pounds.

We drove down to Iskandiriya and arrived towards the end of the afternoon. A police station and a small courthouse nearby had been destroyed in a car bomb at precisely 8.50 a.m. that day, carving a huge crater into the road. The bomber chose his time carefully: when he struck there was a crowd of 150 young men queuing up at the police station to hear whether their job applications had been successful. At least fifty of them died. The scene was still cordoned off by American troops, heavily armed and wearing helmets and body armour as they stood by their Humvees. Behind them I could see several cars overturned and destroyed by the force of the blast. Dozens of television cameramen were already standing on the roof of a nearby house, filming the scene. Just beneath them was a large tent newly set up in the road, with rows of white plastic chairs inside.

It was a funeral tent set up by a man named Ala'a, a policeman who had been in the station at the time of the blast. He wasn't hurt but his sixteen-year-old son Ibrahim had been outside on his way to bring kerosene and a heater for his father when the bomber struck. He died instantly. A second son, Ahsan, who was twenty-three, had also been outside and was now lying injured in hospital. Friends and relatives were already coming to console Ala'a, embracing him and sitting in the tent with him.

'It is a great tragedy what is happening to us,' he said. 'They are targeting the police because they don't want people to have a sense of security. They say we are co-operating with the Americans and this is what happens to anyone who co-operates with the Americans. But these people were just looking for jobs.'

It was a guerrilla war and the crowd of young job-hunters made a much easier target than the American troops wrapped in armour and holed up in their well-protected base nearby. By

99

now more than 300 Iraqi policemen had died in bombings. That number rose and rose as the months ticked by and yet still the young recruits came in their thousands.

The Americans quickly and quietly withdrew their cordon and drove away. A large crowd gathered from nowhere and moved rapidly towards the police station. I went with them and saw several cars overturned, some with their paint melted off. The engine block from what may have been the bomber's car lay on the other side of the road. The crowd began to rush forward and to clamber over the cars and then over the walls of the police station. Some were looting the remains of the scene, dragging off pieces of the cars or furniture from the police station. Others looked as if they wanted to attack the police, as if they blamed them for the bombing. It was a collective fury and I hadn't seen anything like it at the scene of an explosion before.

I stopped to ask one man what was happening. He was a guard in the Facilities Protection Service, an American-trained security force used to guard buildings and factories. 'They are all trying to loot the police station, this is not because they love their country,' he said. Perhaps the whole population despised the police as much as the bomber had. Although it was south of Baghdad, Iskandiriya had a significant Sunni population and its back roads led to the towns of the insurgent heartland to the north-west, places like Falluja and Ramadi. About six months after this bombing, Iskandiriya became such a violent refuge for the insurgency that foreigners and many Iraqis stopped travelling there. As a result our road links to the south of Iraq were virtually cut off. The fury we saw on this day should have been a warning of what was to come.

The crowd pushed in and a group of policemen emerged angrily from the station, waving their Kalashnikovs in the air. The crowd taunted them. 'You're all pimps!' they shouted at the police. 'No, no to America!' The policemen, furious now, began firing into the air to force the crowd back. I watched one policeman. He held his rifle pointing upwards and fired a round into the air. A few seconds later he fired again and he kept on firing like this every few seconds. But the rifle was heavy and each time he fired it slipped a degree or two down towards the horizontal. Still the crowd did not move back. By now the rifle was pointing in the air only a few feet above the crowd. No one had noticed. Then he fired another shot and I saw a man in the crowd, no more than twenty yards from us, collapse to the ground. He clasped his shoulder. His friends paused for barely a moment, as if they understood precisely what had happened. Then they picked him up and lifted him into a car that was suddenly next to them. They drove off through the crowd towards the hospital, honking the horn to make a way through the mass of people. We ran to a wall by the pavement and crouched down to take cover. There was blood on the street in front of me and broken tree branches and black scraps of cloth. After some minutes the police pushed the crowd back and regained control of the street. The police station was in ruins.

It was growing dark and I was reluctant to stay longer but I had to see the hospital, just a few minutes away, to find more witnesses who could talk about what had happened. Often at these hospitals I would meet young, well-educated doctors who spoke in unemotional terms about the mass of horrific injuries they had had to deal with that day. In the hospital in Iskandiriya I found a young doctor who said he had received about a hundred patients, half of whom were dead on arrival and the rest of whom were injured, some seriously. He described in an anodyne way their injuries, mostly blast wounds or glass cuts, and said his small hospital was already short of medicine. I asked him what it felt like to see such

101

violence in his town. He stopped talking like a doctor and looked up at me with a sigh.

'It is a disastrous thing,' he said. 'What had these people done to deserve this? These were honest people, not even American soldiers, and they were just going to their jobs or looking for work.'

I walked through the ward where the injured were lying in beds. One unemployed young man hoped a job with the police would mean he could save up enough money to pay for a marriage in the future. He realised there were risks involved, but he needed the money. 'I was told a religious leader said that anyone who joins the police force is a Jew. I don't believe that and I don't have anything to do with it,' he said. 'The people who did this want us to go through a civil war. They want us to fight, Sunni against Shia.'

Another man, still dressed in his police uniform, said the bombers were people who didn't want to see reconstruction in Iraq or stability. He had been in the police for eight months, earning 360,000 dinars (£150) a month, much more than in his previous job as a daily labourer. 'If I didn't join the police and others didn't join the police our country will be like something for dogs to eat. If we don't work hand in hand to protect our mothers, sisters, wives and daughters, then who will protect them?'

I closed my notebook and walked out of the hospital in a hurry to escape the smell that clouded its corridors: part disinfectant, part clotting blood. I walked around the corner of a building and found myself in front of the morgue. It was a large, white refrigerated metal cube planted in the sand. It should have been closed, for it was supposed to seal away the dead. But so many people had been killed that morning that the morgue had filled up quickly. Nine contorted and badly burnt bodies, only partially covered in blankets, lay in the sand outside waiting to be identified by relatives. Some of the bodies were whole, some were not. Two feet, still dressed in socks and shoes, stuck out from under one green blanket. The air-conditioning fan for the morgue whirred in the background and hospital staff, wearing white gloves, moved around slowly without talking to each other. They carefully loaded each body onto a steel stretcher. I stared at the corpses, expecting them to wriggle free from their rigid positions in the sand.

After a few moments a woman dressed in black from head to toe walked round the corner, supported and followed by two or three men. She was already in tears and when she saw the bodies she began to scream and then started to stab her fingernails into her face, picking and jabbing and scratching, until there were small specks of blood on her cheeks. The men tried to wrestle her arms from her face and she became more frantic. Her scream became an ululating wail, piercing and desperate. Eventually she was led away. I stayed for some time, staring. I remember feeling enveloped in the warm air and seeing a rose sunset in the distance. A flock of birds flew high overhead.

It wasn't the worst of the bombings and certainly not the last. The next morning forty-seven people were killed when a car bomber drove into a line of recruits queuing in the rain outside an army base in Baghdad. Later that week I saw a graffito on a wall in Mansour, in western Baghdad, apparently directed at the American military. 'You have been killing our men and women for ages and now you are hiding in a hole like rats. One day we will crush you with our bodies.'

Life inside Najwa's house felt comfortably insulated from the violence of the streets outside. There were always people visiting, sometimes to stay overnight, at other times just for meals. They were friends of the boys who had become part of

103

an extended family that would gather round the white plastic table in the kitchen to eat in the evenings and then sit outside in the small front garden playing cards into the night.

One day Saira, the lively translator working for the US military came over. The boys had told me she had fallen in love with an American soldier who had proposed marriage to her. He had already left Iraq and she was trying to get a visa to travel abroad to see him. She quizzed me about visas. How could she get a visa to Germany, where her soldier was based now? Would it be difficult to get a visa for the United States? How much money would it cost? Did I know anyone at the embassy who could help? She said her soldier had promised her he could help with the visa and she seemed to trust him completely. I thought to myself: she's desperate to leave but so naïve about the huge decision she is about to make, about the leap across languages and across cultures.

The two most regular visitors at Najwa's house were Haider and Leith. Haider was the joker of the crowd. He was a taxi driver and they called him Haider Peugeot, after a car he had once owned. Now he had a red Toyota, which he looked after carefully and lovingly washed every chance he could. There were furry children's toys stuck on the inside of the car windows. For a taxi driver he seemed to take very few passengers. He was always hanging around at the house, and had a knack of arriving just a few minutes before meal-times. Haider was rarely serious and spent most of his time making fun of himself and the others. Najwa and the boys adored him and he knew it. Seven people in his family had been arrested and killed under Saddam, although he never talked about it.

I asked him once what the future would bring and he admitted he was worried. 'When the Americans leave there is going to be a civil war. Everyone has a Kalashnikov and there are a hundred different parties. Everyone is going to fight everyone else,' he said.

Haider was a Shia and followed Syed Ali al-Sistani, the most important Grand Ayatollah in Iraq and a respected moderate. Sistani, an elderly Iranian-born cleric who almost never left his small house in Najaf, had been pushing hard for elections to be held since the autumn. The Americans misjudged him and underestimated his influence. Be patient, they said to the people, the time is not yet right for elections.

Leith was quite different. He was quiet and seemed poorer than the others. Often he would run errands for Najwa. He laughed along with Haider's jokes but rarely made any of his own. Leith was a Shia from Iskandiriya. He dressed all in black and was a member of the Jaish al-Mahdi, an armed militia that followed a young rebel Shia cleric called Moqtada al-Sadr. Where Sistani wanted to negotiate and talk with the American occupation, Sadr wanted only to confront it. Leith didn't seem the type to confront anyone but he found an identity and energy in Sadr's group. He was recently married and the night before his wedding, the boys told me, Leith had had the words 'Moqtada al-Sadr' inscribed on his hand in henna. I asked him what the Jaish al-Mahdi was doing in Iskandiriya. He said he and his friends would go out on patrols. 'We are working with the police to protect Iskandiriya,' he said.

I talked to Najwa about the war and the occupation and the more she spoke the more frustrated she seemed to become with the Americans. She said that at first she had waved to the American soldiers when they came down the street, and took them out drinks, speaking to them in English, making them welcome. But in the past year, she had changed. It was partly the electricity and the rising prices and the fact that she was out of work. Then there was the violence. She took me to meet one friend, a fellow student from her college days. He had been

105

attacked a month before and badly beaten. His car was stolen but he was left alive and he was furious with the Americans. 'We lost our country, we lost our security,' he said. 'Will it be OK? We don't know. Where is Iraq going? Who is responsible? They are doing nothing.'

Najwa said the Americans were rude these days and aggressive and she found this upsetting. 'At the beginning there was no resistance, but the behaviour of the American army meant resistance grew. At the beginning when they came past the house we offered them coffee. Now they have changed, they don't talk to us at all.' I asked what would happen if the Americans simply left. 'Maybe if the American army goes the Iraqis will kill the Ba'athists themselves. It has started in the south. Now the people are trying to keep everything as it is but they will take their revenge eventually. We need patience to see what will happen to our country.'

On my last day at her home, Najwa took me to a meeting of a women's league which she had recently joined and which campaigned for women's rights. On the way in the car I talked to her about the hijab she wore. I never saw her in anything other than long, shapeless, black polyester robes with a black scarf tied tightly over her hair. She explained it was only out of mourning for the death of her daughter, until then she hadn't worn one. She said her son Omar wanted Sour to wear a hijab. Where he had got this from I had no idea. He didn't seem in the least religious and would happily sit in the evenings with his brothers and watch revealingly dressed Arab women on Lebanese television. Sour, who dressed just like any young Western woman, didn't look like she was particularly enthusiastic about the idea. But anyway Najwa had intervened and refused to let it happen and Omar was never going to win in an argument with his mother. I had seen Omar briefly at breakfast that morning. He had been to the dentist the day before to have

106

several teeth removed and his mouth was so swollen he could barely talk. He still piled teaspoon after teaspoon of sugar into his tea. His mother scolded him loudly.

When we arrived at the women's league the meeting had already begun. There were around thirty women sitting on plastic chairs in an empty shell of a building. It had once been a recruiting office for the Iraqi army and was only just around the corner from the Ministry of Information. In the past, Iraqi women had fared better than most in the Arab world. The women's league, set up in 1953, was a strong voice and a woman had been appointed to the cabinet in 1959 – the first woman to sit in government anywhere in the Arab world. However, the Ba'ath had closed down the league in 1975 and the then general secretary went missing, never to be seen again.

Since the war, the league had re-formed and had again begun agitating for women's rights. They campaigned against a proposal raised by the Governing Council to make a change to the legal system in favour of Islamic clerics which would have curtailed women's rights, and the proposal was hurriedly withdrawn. Then they demanded greater representation for women on the Governing Council – currently only three out of the twenty-five appointed Iraqis were women. They wanted a minister for women and they wanted the new Iraqi government to endorse and apply conventions on women's rights. In particular they were anxious that the rise of the Islamic parties would mean restrictions on women.

When we arrived several of the women were complaining about Dr Raja al-Khuzai, one of the three on the Governing Council, saying that she was inaccessible and had done little to help their cause. One said she was too religiously conservative.

'We are not against Islamic parties but we are democratic Muslims,' one woman said.

107

'We should prove we are the leaders of our cause through our actions,' said another.

'The Governing Council is worse than Saddam's method of dealing with the Iraqis,' said a third.

They suggested making a representation to the Governing Council to put forward their complaints and highlight their demands for women. They took a show of hands and the vote was carried.

Then as the group began to chatter noisily amongst itself, a quiet woman called Betool who had travelled up from the holy Shia city of Kerbala, in the south, began to speak. The leader of the meeting slapped her folder on her lap several times until there was silence and Betool started again. She said a rival women's league had been set up in Kerbala with much more conservative opinions.

'They are telling women to stay in their houses and that girls should finish their education at primary school,' Betool said. 'They are calling for a new kind of hijab which should cover a woman's face. They said we should wear a hijab like the women of Afghanistan and that we are forbidden from looking at men in the street. Everything is *haram*, forbidden.'

She said the clerics were also trying to re-introduce temporary marriages, in which a cleric would give a blessing to a marriage that lasted only a few hours. It was a way to allow couples to have sex even if they were not properly married and it had been used in the past elsewhere to permit prostitution. She had spoken out against this and had been publicly rebuked. 'They view us as infidels,' said the woman. 'We suffered under Saddam and now we are suffering under these clerics.'

Najwa said Betool had been a strong advocate for women's rights in the students' union in Kerbala before the fall of the regime and was regarded as a liberal activist. She was jailed under Saddam and three of her brothers were killed.

'They say we are communist infidels and at the same time they are trying to introduce temporary marriages,' Betool said to the group. 'Who are the infidels, us or them?'

Her story caused much consternation and the women began talking loudly to each other. Several minutes later the meeting broke up. There wasn't a vote or a resolution about what was happening in Kerbala. It was just listened to and noted down and understood. There wasn't anything else they could do about it for now. As we walked out Najwa turned to me and said: 'Even Saddam gave rights to women and he was a dictator. But look what they are doing now. They want to remove all rights. How can women walk in the streets with these kinds of clothes? They just want women to stay at home and wait for their husbands. That's not right.'

Back at the house I said goodbye to Najwa and quietly handed her an envelope. I had written a letter thanking her for having me to stay and folded inside five $100 bills. I thought the money would help with the boys' education or with the gas or electricity costs or would go towards the costs of her brother's funeral. A few weeks later I went back for lunch. She thanked me for the money and said she was still waiting to hear about her job. As the fish cooked in the oven, she led me inside and I saw all the old furniture from last time piled in a heap in the hallway. In the front room in all its varnished splendour was a brand-new set of sofas and armchairs. I laughed to myself: who was I to tell her how to spend her money?

8

I've Changed My Mind

Some weeks before I met Najwa, on a day when the heat sat heavily on the city, I went again to see Barrak, the lawyer from Hilla. This time we were to meet at the American headquarters in the centre of Baghdad, now known as the Green Zone. The name was supposed to mean that these few square miles were safe; of course it also meant that the rest of the country (codename: Red Zone) was not. My shirt stuck to my skin and the sweat from my fingers soaked through the pages of my notebook as I queued at the razor wire to be searched. Barrak had been in the Governing Council now for two months and, though he was in Baghdad, he was cocooned from his country.

The council worked from a neat single-storey building in the palace complex. To reach it, I had to pass a Nepalese guard post and cross an immaculately clipped, square-edged lawn that glowed a defiant green against the sun-washed landscape. Inside was a stone floor lined with tall air conditioners that cooled the rooms to an uncomfortable chill. Outside, an array of walls, guards, checkpoints, fences, Humvees and Abrams tanks divided us from the rest of the country. At night, insurgents would fire mortars into the zone and, even from several miles away, you could hear the thud of the explosions and then a whining siren and the loudspeakers barking: 'Attack. Take cover. This is not a test.'

Barrak and I sat next to each other on upholstered armchairs and discussed Aqila al-Hashmi, one of three women on the council. She had been shot the day before, just a few yards from her home, and now lay in hospital, slowly dying. Barrak had visited her in the ward and wished me to have a precise account of her injury: how one 'devilish bullet', as he described it, had pierced her arm and her leg and her abdomen, drilling through her stomach, her liver and her pancreas.

Hashmi was an unexpected presence in the Governing Council. A former Ba'athist, she had been a senior official in the Iraqi Foreign Ministry until the war. A few months after the regime fell, the Americans invited her to take a seat on the council in a gesture of inclusiveness. She renounced the Ba'ath and became an ally of the occupation and, by default, a target of the insurgency. The Americans had suggested she should recruit a team of bodyguards, but on the day she was shot, as she was on her way to the airport to fly to a United Nations meeting in New York, most of her guards were either still on training courses or were working in her office as secretaries. Five days later she would be dead.

She and Barrak had been at opposite political poles in society until they were brought together by the occupation but still it was obvious he was deeply disturbed by the attack. He was worried about his own security and that of the others on the council and that led to wider questions about the steady collapse in security across Iraq. Every day we learned of assassinations of government officials, politicians and clerics, bomb attacks on Iraqi police and army units, attacks on the US and British military and a whole world of rampant underground street crime. There had been sharp disagreements within the Governing Council about how to tackle this burgeoning crisis. The only consensus was that more power should be given to Iraqis and less to the American military. Those with the biggest parties, which had armed militias, insisted their fighters be given a frontline role. Barrak and some of the others disagreed,

111

saying it would only create a climate of warlordism. Instead they suggested the police force should be expanded, properly armed and trained. He said it was becoming embarrassingly clear that the Americans simply couldn't confront the insurgency on their own. They had no local knowledge and they couldn't speak Arabic, let alone dissect different regional or national accents or tell an Arab from a Kurd, an Iraqi from an Iranian. They couldn't decipher tribal loyalties and they couldn't even read the identity card that every adult carried. They had to resort to hand signals to control the traffic but even those were foreign: it took months before people understood that a closed fist pointed at a car meant the driver was to stop. 'The best solution I see,' said Barrak, 'is not to increase the number of American soldiers or to create an international force under the UN but to increase the role of the Iraqis, the police and security forces.'

I asked about the political process. As well as appointing ministers, the council was supposed to be writing a new constitution and preparing the ground for elections some time in the future. But it moved inexorably slowly. In principle they met three days a week but sometimes so many of the twenty-five council members were away from Baghdad or abroad (most had foreign passports) that only four or five of the original members sat round the table. Decisions were routinely postponed. But Barrak insisted the fault lay with the Americans, who virtually ignored the council. There had been no consultation, for example, about the American decision to send the Iraqi police for training in Jordan, a country which many on the council regarded as an ally of Saddam, and little notice taken of the council's objections. There was the occasional successful protest, like the time when the council discovered that the US had quietly invited Turkish troops into Iraq, sparking concern about Turkish territorial ambition as well as unwelcome memories of the Ottoman Empire. Eventually the US had to scrap the idea. Barrak said that whenever the council asked the Americans about the political process, they would be told: 'Not for eighteen months.' He called it their 'magic number'. 'We ask about having a census, they say: "In eighteen months." We ask when the Iraqis will rule themselves, they say: "In eighteen months."' In fact, he said, most of what the council wanted to talk about was outside their control, particularly the most pressing issues of security and a political handover of power. They all wanted an Iraqi government established far earlier than the Americans were proposing.

I asked him about the cases against the Ba'athists, which when I first met him had been his prime concern. He said little had been done yet, but that a special court was planned which would try the main suspects in future. In fact some people on the council were by now arguing that the de-Ba'athification policy introduced by the Americans was far too tough and needed to be loosened to allow some Ba'athists back to work. They wanted committees established to provide broad exemptions for more junior party members.

Although he was surrounded by the symbols of power, escorted by aides, protected by bodyguards and working to a punishing late-night schedule, Barrak seemed strangely emasculated by his new position. He was one of the few Iraqis to have daily contact with the most senior Americans running his country but in fact he had hardly any influence. He could debate and argue late into the night, but he couldn't get things done. He had taken a great risk in joining the council, in allying himself to the occupation in the eyes of most Iraqis, and Hashmi's death showed just how much danger he faced. Yet it brought him little reward. The powerful politicians back from exile used the council to strengthen the foundations of their political futures. But for the more minor players like Barrak it became a game they were obliged to play knowing they could never win. Nevertheless, despite his increasing resentment, Barrak stood by his choice: he had decided not to oppose the Americans or to ignore them, but to work with them. It was a time when Iraqis across the country were facing the same choice: they were weighing up their loyalties, assessing when co-operation became collaboration, deciding whether to work in the post-war government, whether to join municipal councils, whether to help American or British officers, or whether to kill them.

In January 2004 I met Siham Hattab Hamdan in a council building at the eastern entrance to Sadr City, the vast, impoverished Shia slum area of eastern Baghdad. Standing in the middle of a mostly male crowd, she was dressed in heavy high-heels and a purple jubba, a cloak that covered her from shoulder to toe. Her hair was hidden beneath a carefully-arranged, matching purple headscarf. She was outgoing but conservative enough never to shake my hand or the hand of any man she met. Many women used such defined physical barriers to shield themselves and the practice became more widespread as the violence worsened, as if an extra few yards of cloth might deflect a shower of shrapnel or a Kalashnikov bullet. If you looked past Siham's barrier, though, you found an extraordinary woman. She was thirty-three and unmarried and for an Iraqi woman of her age that was unusual, suggesting independence and resistance to tradition. She was articulate in both Arabic and English and thoughtful about the moral dilemmas the invasion presented her. She lectured in English literature at Mustansiriya University where she had written an MA thesis on 'The Significance of Travel in the Novels of E. M. Forster'.

It was the day for elections to Baghdad's provincial council, the highest of the four tiers of local government created by the Americans after the war. Siham was already on her local neighbourhood and district councils and the more important Baghdad city council. She was evidently a rising star, courted by American military officers and state department officials, respected by her colleagues and tipped for a seat in Iraq's first post-war parliament. A few weeks earlier she had left Iraq for the first time in her life when she was invited with four other Iraqi women to Washington for a brief audience at the White House with George Bush. Few in the room doubted she would be voted onto the provincial council that day.

They were called elections but in truth there was little participation for the ordinary public. A month after the war someone had recommended Siham's name to the Americans and an American officer had asked her to join the neighbourhood council. Residents in the area were entitled to vote people onto that council, though in reality few knew anything about it. From then on councillors elected representatives from among themselves up to a district council and from there again up to a city council. Today the city councillors were choosing some of their own for the provincial council. It wasn't a widely appreciated system and clearly the powerful Shia religious authorities who carried considerable influence in the area felt threatened. In early October 2003, a group of protestors loyal to the cleric Moqtada al-Sadr had seized control of the building where Siham and her colleagues had been meeting and established their own, rival authority.[18] They complained about undue American influence and said they hadn't been told about the election process. Siham and the others had to meet in private in their homes for two weeks until the US military brought in a couple of tanks and regained control of the council building.

Over the previous few days, Siham had talked to me about how important these elections were for her so I was surprised

115

by what happened that morning. The councillors, Siham among them, were sitting on rows of plastic chairs waiting for the election. They had already spent an hour listening to a lecture about the purpose and structure of the whole project. Now an American woman from the State Department turned to the crowd and asked candidates for the vote to step forward.

'I don't care what anyone else has told you about whether you should run or not. If you would like to run I invite you to come forward,' she told them. 'If you meet the qualifications and you would like to be a candidate, you should come forward. Anyone found to have intimidated anyone not to run will be off the council.'

As a handful of people shuffled forward, Siham stepped smartly back. She had been plagued by last-minute doubts and decided not to stand.

'No, no. I've changed my mind,' she told the others. They were taken aback. 'I'm sorry. I just changed my mind.'

Siham was deliberately vague about the reasons for her decision, saying only that they were 'strategic'. 'I know, everyone is surprised,' she said. 'I just thought it's better to keep my seat on the city council for the time being. I have never thought of myself as a political leader.'

But everyone else had. She was well-educated, confident and eloquent, more than able to stand up to the often patriarchal men around her. After decades of dictatorial repression it was rare to find anyone who nurtured decent political aspirations, let alone an educated woman from a poor area. If she wouldn't take part, who would?

I asked Siham if she was scared. She had every right to be. Several members of councils like this across Iraq had already been killed; many more would die in the months ahead. Siham had taken a year's leave from her university teaching job because of the danger.

116

'I am a little bit frightened, I cannot deny the truth. But I have to do what I have to do. It is God's will. We all believe that when our time comes, it comes.' I asked if she was frustrated with the Americans and this seemed closer to the truth. 'It is very difficult that the Iraqis have had to suffer all these years and now they have to suffer more,' she said. 'People really feel upset because they don't see any change in their lives.'

The Americans talked proudly in public about how they were working alongside and supporting the councils they had created and yet in practice it was a much troubled relationship. Siham had experienced this first hand. One Sunday, just after the US military regained control of the city council building being occupied by Moqtada al-Sadr's loyalists, there was a fight between one of Siham's colleagues and the American guards at the gate. Muhanad Ghazi al-Kaabi, the English-speaking chairman of the council, had parked his car near the building in an area where the Americans had decided there should be no parking. Kaabi and one of the American soldiers began shouting at each other. Some suggested Kaabi refused to have his car searched, others said the soldier didn't recognise him and wouldn't let him into the council building. There was some pushing and shoving and a few witnesses said Kaabi even slapped the American and tried to reach for his gun. Another soldier raised his rifle and shot Kaabi in the thigh. It was a very serious wound and it bled heavily. The soldiers put the injured councillor on a stretcher and took him to one of their nearby field hospitals, but later that day he died. The military said there had been an 'altercation' and promised to investigate why one of their soldiers had killed one of the new class of politicians they were supposed to be protecting. There were street protests for a few days and the council had to find a new chairman but no more was heard of the military's investigation.

Before the war, Siham had hoped to be a Professor of English Literature. However, her family were marked out as suspect. Not only were they Shia who refused to join the Ba'ath, but in 1983 her nineteen-year-old brother, Karim, had been arrested. He was a first-year veterinary student at Mustansiriya University when he was accused of being a member of Dawa, the Shia opposition party. He was detained and taken away. For months the family were told nothing about what had happened to him and only later did they learn he had been executed. From then on Siham, her four other brothers and her two sisters were under surveillance, their lives in jeopardy. In 1998 another of her brothers fled Iraq. He was a poet who had refused repeated official demands to write eulogies to Saddam and so he escaped to Phoenix, Arizona, where he still lived with his wife and three children. He had never returned to Baghdad.

'It seems in our family we had a reaction, which was to go forward and to gain what we could in the future, to gain personal glories not public ones,' Siham said. She struggled to join the teaching staff at several colleges and universities, but she could get no higher than a simple lectureship at Mustansiriya. 'This was my vocation. I wanted to teach.'

I had first met Siham in a narrow office of the council building. It was cold and the electricity would come and go. The furniture was new, some of it still wrapped in clear plastic. On the opposite side of the street was a mosque loyal to the young cleric Sadr, whose followers had briefly set up the rival council. Though it was reasonably quiet at the moment, the council building was still protected by coils of razor wire and blast walls. A squad of American soldiers used it as a base and had set up an observation post on the roof, under camouflage netting. There was a Bradley Fighting Vehicle, an imposing tracked armoured personnel carrier, parked in the courtyard. You could see the soldiers wanted to protect the politicians, but

118

at the same time the effect was to give a distinctly American signature to the council.

There were thirty-seven people sitting on the Baghdad City Council and Siham, one of just six women, was the deputy chair. She was excited by the concept, which she said was a 'link' between the Iraqis and the Americans. 'It is a new experience, the first time that Iraqis have had such a council,' she said. 'Before, everything came from above. Nothing came from the grassroots.'

'What do people living here tell you they want?' I asked.

'This part of the city was almost completely neglected under Saddam. You can see there are hardly any road surfaces. We went through a very difficult time,' she said. 'The biggest problem is the sewage. You ask anyone here and the first thing they will say is: Repair the sewage system.'

In the years after the Free Officers coup in 1958 there had been a programme of ostensibly radical land reform that had included the construction of this suburb of Baghdad. They hailed it as Madinat al-Thawra, City of the Revolution: thousands of homes with electricity and water in eastern Baghdad were provided to alleviate dire slum conditions. In later years the Ba'ath claimed it as its own, renaming it Saddam City. However, though it had first been built out of aspirations for change, it rapidly became a symbol of persecution. It was a predominantly Shia neighbourhood and, deprived of government investment, it remained remorselessly poor. While Ba'athists built themselves sprawling villas under the shade of date palms in the broad avenues of districts like Mansour and Yarmuk, the narrow streets of Saddam City slid quickly back into the slums they were intended to replace. Richer Iraqis saw it as wild and restive, a den of thieves. Saddam sent tanks into the area in spring 1999 to crush street protests after his regime assassinated Ayatollah Mohammad Sadeq al-Sadr, the father of young Moqtada. Immediately after the war, the clerics renamed the suburb once again in the dead ayatollah's honour: Sadr City. You could pick out those who felt uncomfortable with the rise of the Shia clerics, or still clung to the ways of the old regime, because they would call it al-Thawra. Vast hagiographic portraits of the leading Shia clerics, particularly from the respected Sadr family, quickly appeared on billboards but they looked down on roads still scarred with potholes and gushing with effluent. The water pipes were not just broken, they were rusted and decayed beyond repair. The electricity supply was intermittent at best. It was no surprise that these were the first complaints of the people Siham represented.

The council had tried to help. There had been a crisis over the supply of propane and kerosene for heating and cooking and they had spent several days trying to curtail the black market. They introduced rationing and it went some way to solving the problem, although it was only a temporary fix. But the council had no budget and no power to authorise repairs to the roads or the sewage pipes.[19] They could recommend and complain but no more. It was a distinctly curtailed exercise in democracy: Siham could only plead with the Americans to do the job.

'We were told the sewage system couldn't just be fixed because it was so out of date. It had to be completely rebuilt. That requires money and a lot of time,' she said. 'Though we try hard, it is very difficult to get what we really want.' Her neighbours were unimpressed and she admitted it. 'We can't fulfil the ambitions of our people. Because of the injustice and the tense atmosphere we lived in we imagined that with the fall of the regime we could have a very different life. But things haven't turned out like this. No one has a magic wand to turn things over. It will take a long time and this will make people even more frustrated.'

In the end, every conversation always found its way back to the same question. 'What did you think of the war?' I asked.

'It's a kind of controversial issue. It is two-sided,' Siham said. 'It is very difficult for us. We had run out of patience with the last regime so we felt that it had to end. Iraqis were so tired, economically and psychologically, that they didn't have the capacity to face the regime. He was so powerful, so, so powerful and the Iraqis were weakened by years of sanctions and wars.'

She rarely used his name, Saddam. 'He' was all she would say.

'But then the occupation of this country is so difficult,' she said. 'These are two evils and we have to choose one of them. But occupation is so hard for us.'

'If you feel so torn, then why are you sitting on the council?' I asked. 'Why are you co-operating with the Americans?'

'I don't work for the coalition forces, I work for my people. I have to,' she said. 'I can't just hide myself and say I will not deal with the Americans because if we all refrain from co-operating with them then nobody will care about our society. The coalition forces will not know what the people need.'

Not long before I met Siham, the American administration had drastically revised yet again its political plans for Iraq. Originally, as Barrak the lawyer said, the Americans were hoping to wait at least eighteen months before holding elections for a new government. It was too violent to hold a vote sooner they said, and besides they wanted a new constitution written first under the occupation which they said would be a foundation for the future. But shortly after the war it became clear that this was deeply unpopular. Even the leading Shia religious authority, Grand Ayatollah Sistani, who outwardly insisted he had little interest in politics, had been demanding an elected Iraqi government. He called the American plan 'fundamentally unacceptable', particularly that a constitution

121

should be written under occupation. Why should the invaders write the future?

In a rush the Americans put together a plan for a series of complex, indirect elections which they called 'caucuses' to allow the Iraqis to choose a government that would take over in the summer of 2004, a little over a year after the war but much earlier than their original plans. Sistani had just lambasted this idea too and wrong-footed the Americans by demanding full, democratic elections. Although one of Washington's intentions in invading Iraq had been to spread democracy throughout the Arab world, now came the supreme irony: a conservative Iranian-born cleric was complaining that their plans were not nearly democratic enough.

Before Siham had dropped out of that day's provincial council election, I asked her what she thought about the row and whether she would consider taking part in the new government. The deadline for candidates to apply was only a few weeks away.

'I agree with the principle that we need some kind of election,' she said. 'It may not be a real one but we have to make the public participate. They have a right after all these long years.' But she well understood what was later to become the heart of the crisis when she confessed she was worried the new government might not have enough legitimacy without full elections. 'If it doesn't have this legitimacy there will be a gap between the population and the government. This is one of my greatest apprehensions. We don't want to separate people from their government.'

9

Serving Falluja

Mohammad Hassan al-Balwa took me to see the house he was having built in Falluja. He was sitting at the wheel of his new, olive-green Hyundai four-wheel drive and one of his two bodyguards sat up front with him, his black submachine gun wedged awkwardly between his knees. As we drove, Balwa pointed out the several properties he already owned across the town. We had set out from his home: a squat two-storey family house almost completely hidden behind a black metal fence. A few minutes' drive away were a row of shops and a car park belonging to him, then the house behind them and another house over on the high street. Not long afterwards we came to the large area of barren ground in a comparatively undeveloped suburb where the new house was being built. There were workmen busy on the site but not much else. Balwa had bought the land ten years ago but building work had only started in the last six months, since the war. The land alone had cost him 500 million dinars (£200,000), but then this was the most expensive suburb in Falluja. It was where a wealthy businessman like Balwa felt he ought to be living. So far, all he had to show us was an underground garage, wrought, rather unattractively, entirely from concrete. Across the rest of the site were piles of bricks and thick metal wires rising out of the ground from which he hoped would eventually emerge a large, sweeping seven-bedroom house enclosing in its heart a small ornamental garden. He showed me an architect's sketch. Our tour that morning was not intended to be ostentatious, for wealth here was something to be proud of, a sign of success and status and Balwa was one of the richest men in the province.

The Falluja I saw that day was a quiet town of perhaps 350,000 people, lying forty-five minutes west of Baghdad between the highway and the Euphrates River. It could hardly be called affluent. It had a bleak industrial area, filled with mechanics workshops and small family businesses, a meat and vegetable market stretching through a warren of narrow streets, and a small, poorly equipped hospital across the river. Fallujans liked to boast of Haji Hussain's, a fine kebab restaurant on the main street, but there was little else that stood out in the town apart from its deep religious convictions: they called it the City of the Mosques. Many of the young men born here became either truck drivers on the highway to Jordan or else were recruited into the most feared security forces of the Saddam regime, for Falluja was deep in the dictator's loyal Sunni heartland. Being from a wealthy family, Balwa had escaped both careers. Instead he had received a good education, spent many of his adult years abroad and prospered in business. He was more fortunate than most Fallujans and didn't have to live here still. I took Balwa's properties as a sign of attachment to this small, fiercely proud place. He liked to describe himself as 'a son of this city'. He could easily have bought a comfortable villa in a respectable suburb of Baghdad, where his import-export company already had an office and where he would have been close to those in power, but he chose instead to stay where he had always been.

Balwa was forty-eight and perhaps 5 foot 8 inches tall. He wore large, rectangular glasses with tinted lenses and carried a set of prayer beads, which he would worry at through the day. He dressed always in a neatly pressed suit a little long in the arms (except at home when he wore a cheap cotton tracksuit and sandals) and took an obvious care with his appearance, always smelling faintly of cologne. He took a similar care with his choice of words, speaking slowly and quietly and never shouting or braying as others around him did. It meant that you might not notice him at first, particularly when he was in a crowd of tall, plump tribal leaders dressed in their long dish-dashas. But when you did find him you would approach him as an equal.

I stayed at his house and he laid mattresses on the floor for me, my photographer and our driver and guide in his long front room, a place for meeting guests and for late-night discussions. Every home had a guest room like this; it marked the clearly drawn line between public and private affairs. You are welcome this far into my house, it said, but no further. A row of gilded armchairs and sofas stretched round three of the room's walls and a long table in the centre was laid with dozens of pieces of Czech crystal, a leather-bound Qur'an and a small photograph of Balwa framed in silver. That morning for our benefit he produced a breakfast of omelettes and *gaymr*, a thick cream of buffalo milk, served with flat bread and bowls of strawberry jam. The cream was special to Falluja, rich and luxurious and often served on the morning of Eid, the festival at the end of the month of fasting. Balwa didn't touch it. Since the war he'd been diagnosed with diabetes and it was affecting him badly; he felt continually worn down and was losing weight.

As you drive into Falluja from the east there is one straight, broad high street that cuts through the centre of town, crosses the Euphrates River and then stretches on towards the western deserts. Balwa's office was on this high street, set back a little from the road. Here he worked as chairman of the city council. It was mid-morning when we parked a little way short of the building. We walked the last few hundred yards and saw work-men using a small crane to lift huge concrete blast defences from the back of a truck to form a wall around the compound of his office. Balwa had been arguing against the wall for days. It was a public admission that the council members didn't feel safe in their own town. Balwa thought it was inviting trouble and wanted to move to a private office nearby in one of the buildings he had shown me that morning.

There was already a crowd waiting for him. The four sofas in front of his desk were full of petitioners and there were others standing in the corridor outside. No sooner had Balwa sat down than the first man nearest to the desk began to speak. He and several others in the room had come to complain about the local bus station, which was next to the police headquarters a few hundred yards down the road. Falluja was already perhaps the most dangerous town in Iraq and the police building in particular had become a principal target of the insurgents: two weeks back more than twenty policemen were killed when gunmen stormed the building and freed dozens of prisoners. It was now barricaded by a concrete blast wall, of the sort being put up around Balwa's office, and that morning the police chief had closed the bus station next door in a further attempt to protect himself and his men.

'The police fired over my head when I tried to get on a bus this morning,' said the first petitioner.

'Is the police chief going to close everything?' asked a second.

Balwa turned to his staff. 'I want to talk to the police chief on the phone now,' he said. 'If he can't protect himself, how is he going to protect us? Is he going to shut down every building around him?'

The staff tried to reach the police chief, but he was out.

'If he doesn't deal with it then the council will take a decision,' Balwa reassured the petitioners. He wrote them out letters, promising his support.

His next task was to sign a paper on his desk listing some of the latest decisions by the council. It announced that from now on the new internet cafés that had sprung up since the war would be carefully monitored and any caught showing 'disrespectful' or 'immoral' websites would be closed down. This, it said, was to 'prevent the spreading of bad morals through the pure atmosphere of Falluja, which is full of the houses of Allah'. A second decree banned the sale of alcohol or illegal drugs. At the foot of the document announcing the new orders was a stamp which read in Arabic: 'Satisfying Allah is our aim and serving Falluja is our plan'.

We never talked about how he inherited his family name, Balwa, but it meant 'disaster' in Arabic. His life so far had been anything but. Having been sent by his well-connected family to Romania to take a degree in civil engineering, he moved to the Emirates and worked as an engineer, saving enough money to return to Romania to complete a PhD. The certificate from the university hung on the wall in a back room at his home. He returned to Iraq and to Falluja in 1986, shortly before the end of the war with Iran. Balwa avoided military service and instead worked as a teacher, then taught civil engineering in a local college and finally set up several small trading companies, which eventually managed to produce handsome profits despite the years of war and sanctions that followed. He insisted he was never a member of the party and I had no evidence to challenge him. Perhaps if you were well-connected, agile and uninterested in politics it was possible to be wealthy and independent of the Ba'ath.

Balwa was in Falluja when America invaded his country, though the war barely touched his town. Since Turkey refused permission for the US military to cross its territory there was no invasion from the north and so troops did not reach Falluja until after Baghdad had fallen. By then the Ba'athists and security elite were wise enough to lie low and there was no fight for the city, simply an acknowledgement of the new reality of power. Within days, and without prompting from the Americans, the Fallujans formed their own ruling council and the tribes organised armed men to protect the hospital, banks and local administration offices to prevent any looting. A few months later Balwa was invited to join the council and towards the end of 2003 he was elected their leader. Yet unbeknown to the Americans, Falluja was quietly becoming a rallying point for the Sunni insurgency and American commanders in Baghdad were caught in a fatal misconception of the town's mood. One day I listened to an American military spokesman in Baghdad insist that 95 per cent of the people of Falluja 'are fully supportive of the coalition'.[20]

Unlike many around him, Balwa wasn't fiercely opposed to the Americans. He believed that, with its high standard of education and oil wealth, Iraq deserved to be a great power and America could help make it so. 'America is a great state and has a huge military force and the greatest technology in the world,' he said. 'We should deal with this power and use them to transfer this technology to our country. We could benefit from building and developing Iraq through them and then we could have America as an ally and friend of Iraq, not a country of occupation.'

However, when I met him he seemed deeply disappointed in the Americans, as if they had behaved with unaccountable disrespect in his country. He was offended and he, like many others in Falluja, could trace the day it had begun. It was late in April 2003, just a few days after the war, and soldiers from the US 82nd Airborne Division had taken over the al-Qa'id primary school in Falluja as one of their bases in the town. It was an unpopular move, because the school was in the centre of town and because Fallujans felt they were being spied on in their homes. Some thought the troops could use their night-vision goggles to see through women's clothing. The soldiers decided to leave the school, but on 28 April, Saddam's birthday and the day before they were due to withdraw, a large crowd gathered outside for a protest. There had been gunfire across the town that day and as the protest grew more raucous the troops, thinking they saw guns in this crowd, opened fire. Seventeen protestors were killed. A second demonstration was held two days later, again the soldiers opened fire. Three more protestors died.[21]

'This incident was the starting point of the resistance against the occupation. It was the beginning, the spark,' said Balwa. 'We asked the Americans to apologise to control the situation. We explained the tribal nature of this town. It is a society that doesn't forget revenge. But they were so late in their apology.'

In the months that followed several different units of American troops passed through Falluja, each equally confident of calming the brewing anger. None succeeded. Balwa said the American commanders were making contacts with people who had little real influence, and were awarding contracts ineptly.

'They are opening channels with the wrong people. Falluja is a mix of traditions. It is run by tribal law and religious law, by nationalism and by a group of well-educated people. Whoever wants to control Falluja should open channels with these people.' He was no Saddamist and like others in the Sunni elite he resented the idea that his community was being branded with the same brush as the dictator and passed over as possible rulers for the first time in their history.

He said if the Americans withdrew from the town and left Falluja to run itself, there would be less hostility on the streets. 'If we had independence, a central government, a constitution and a legal system then we would see some peace and order. In the space of a few months there would be security. That is all we need.'

Balwa was married and had five children. I never saw his wife or his three school-age daughters. They were kept behind closed doors, in the back of the house, unseen in this intensely male world. His two boys, Hassan, the eldest, and Mohammad Yahir, the youngest, I was allowed to meet. They wandered freely through the circle of adults, unafraid of the armed bodyguards who lived in the house or the conservative clerics and tribal leaders who came to visit and discuss politics late into the night. They sat at their father's feet, listening intently. Hassan, a baby-faced boy of twelve, was particularly bright. He spoke good English and his father had just bought him a new, expensive desktop computer, which absorbed him for hours at a time. One evening when we stayed over, he casually took it apart, added in new electronics boards and put it back together again. Some months later Balwa proudly told me how young Hassan had answered a ring at the door on a night when his father was out only to find himself facing a wanted man from one of the fiercest Islamic insurgent movements, which was responsible for the gruesome murders of dozens of hostages. It turned out to be a courtesy visit – the fighter wanted to talk politics with his father – and Hassan, unafraid, shook his hand, talked with him and took a message for his dad. This was the world of men.

I was surprised at the boy's education and I asked Balwa about the schools in Falluja. Were they unusually good, or was Hassan just unusually bright? 'Compared to the rest of the world our schools are so old. It's not what we want or wish for,' he said. 'If there were good schools, our kids would be brilliant.'

Thousands of American reconstruction dollars had been spent repairing schools in Falluja and elsewhere across Iraq to little effect. Balwa had papers that showed that at least a third of the $3 million-plus the Americans had spent in Falluja and the surrounding area had gone on schools and yet there was virtually nothing to show for it. The problem was that sub-contracts to rebuild schools had been shared out between several tribal sheikhs to keep them acquiescent. The money was given out quickly and with little oversight. The sheikhs kept most of it for themselves and spent only a fraction on the schools – a quick repaint, a couple of ceiling fans, a new blackboard and little else. The head of the city's education committee had come to the office that morning to complain that a man posing as a contractor had visited a school in the village of Garma, just east of the city, saying Balwa had sent him and demanding payment. The contractor was lying, a small swindle at a time when Iraq was swimming in an ocean of corruption.

Balwa led us out of his office and we walked a few hundred yards around the corner to see his old secondary school, the Falluja Preparatory School for Boys. It had been new when he attended and was still the best school in the town. Since the war, several thousand American dollars had been spent rebuilding it, although you wouldn't have known. The head-master, Taiseer Omar, led us from one shabby classroom to the next. Windows once repaired had been smashed. The chemistry lab had only a few dusty bottles of expired chemicals on its shelves; the physics lab had not a single piece of equipment.

'You can see we have nothing,' Omar said. 'We have no equipment and we haven't had new instruments for a decade. We don't have enough text books. It's a real crisis.'

There was no air conditioning, only ceiling fans, though the summer heat here was almost insupportable, and there was no generator to cover the frequent and lengthy power blackouts.

'This is no reconstruction. The Americans came last year and checked the school and promised they would support us but there was nothing after that,' the headmaster said.

Across the courtyard he took us into an English class where

131

the boys were sharing between two or three their copies of *The Merchant of Venice*. There was no sports ground, just a concreted yard at the back for football, and there were no arts or music classes.

In some ways Falluja had benefited under Saddam: many of the town's young men were employed and powerful with well-connected military or security jobs and there wasn't the systemic poverty that racked the persecuted Shia towns of the south. That's what American officials in Baghdad liked to say: Falluja had prospered under Saddam. But it can't have been much of a golden age either. Most houses needed a generator even then to take over during the frequent power cuts, the schools were worse than Baghdad's, the hospital too. It would be a mistake too to think the tribes had always shown the dictator loyalty. In 1995 an army general from the Dulaim tribe, which is settled in Falluja and the town of Ramadi just to the west, was arrested, tortured and executed for his part in an apparent coup attempt against Saddam. When his battered body was sent home it triggered riots that were only quelled after the army was sent in and hundreds of Dulaim tribesmen were killed or injured. Balwa had been lucky to spend most of his early adult life abroad.

He took us across town to show us what he regarded as the worst school in Falluja, the other end of the scale from his own: the Osama bin Zayed primary school. I thought at first the building had been abandoned: the outside wall was crumbling, rubbish was piled high in the playground and the concrete ceiling on the second floor looked precariously buckled. But no, it was just an ordinary school day with hundreds of young children sitting in lessons. Again there were no air conditioners and no generator. But then few of the rooms even had light bulbs or switches. Bare wires dangled from cracks in the plaster and a pile of broken desks and chairs blocked one corridor.

American troops had been here too and had spent thousands of dollars trying to effect repairs: you could see the same new blackboards and again some repainting on the walls.

'Is this a school in the twenty-first century?' Balwa said. 'It's unbelievable.'

I looked through one broken window into a class and a boy looked back at me, picked up the text book in front of him, opened it to its first page – the old obligatory photograph of Saddam – and tore it out, screwing the paper up into a ball with a squeal of delight.

The education committee head, who had come with us, wasn't embarrassed at the miserable state of this school, just helpless. All reconstruction money came from the Americans and was distributed by them. The council, of course, claimed they would have done a better job if they had the money, though that wasn't at all assured.

'They told us to be patient. But is it possible to be patient?' he said. 'It is not fit for animals, let alone humans.'

Walking with us was a man called Hekmat Jabbar, head of the town's teachers' union and a man dressed in a Ba'athist style olive-green safari suit. He was silent throughout our visit and then he turned to me as we left. 'If you wonder why there are demonstrations in Falluja,' he said, 'then you should know it is because of this.'

Later that afternoon I sat in as Balwa led a meeting of the city council: four dozen of Falluja's most powerful men – clerics, tribal sheikhs, former party officials – and Balwa, smart and somehow different, at the head of the room. Balwa wore a suit, but most of the others were dressed in fine dishdashas and keffiyeh delicately held in place with an agal, a black length of rope balancing on the crown of their heads. One of the men nearest me had the name of his weave printed along the seam of his cloak: 'Top Harry As In England'. The education committee

133

head, who had been so helpless at the sight of the schools, stood up and warned the council to be wary of outside companies wanting to rebuild schools in Falluja. They were all really spies working for Mossad, the Israeli intelligence service, and sent to disrupt life in Falluja, he said. Most people in the room nodded silently in assent. This town was so deeply smothered in suspicion and hostility that there was barely room to breathe.

Balwa seemed an outsider in his own polarised town. He was neither with the rebels nor against them, neither with the Americans nor against them and Falluja allowed little room for the comfortable middle ground, for those caught between the past and the coming changes. He was well-educated and apparently uncluttered by too much of the tribal code that shaped so many people's lives in these areas. After the war the tribes had become strong once again, for the first time in several decades. When the British were in Iraq, at the beginning of the twentieth century, they thought the tribes were an important instrument of control and so they appeased them. They even gave them their own separate civil code, just as they did in the North-West Frontier on the troublesome western edges of colonial India. But after the fall of Iraq's monarchy in 1958 there came a wave of land reform and urbanisation that undermined the influence of the tribes. The number of people employed by the government rose dramatically and the state, not the tribe, had the balance of authority. When Saddam took power he, like the British before him, saw that the tribes still had a strength he could harness. This time it was less appeasement than naked self-interest. For some years the men from his tribes in Tikrit, the large town closest to the village where he was born, had traditionally joined the military. Saddam accelerated this process until the upper levels of the military, security and intelligence services were stuffed with Tikritis who bore him a deep allegiance. Then, after the first Gulf War and the crisis of

134

the 1991 uprising, he turned to the sheikhs of Iraq's other tribes. Those who bowed to him were rewarded with his recognition and the right to arm their tribesmen. Those who refused to submit to his will were disposed of with his signature brutality. In spring 2003, the American invasion suddenly left a vacuum of power in the state and it was the tribes and the clerics who now stepped forward to command influence once again.

Balwa was obsessively concerned that the council had little authority and little respect amid these competing powers. A week before I went to see him, the Americans had raided one of the main mosques in the town, looking for the imam, Abdullah al-Janabi. They believed Janabi, who was a member of Balwa's council, was working secretly with the insurgency and was hiding Arab fighters and weapons in the mosque. They were right that Janabi was linked to the insurgency; in the months to come it became clear he was virtually the spiritual leader of the militants in Falluja, an influential firebrand cleric who always seemed to evade capture. But the troops were wrong about the Arab fighters and the weapons. They found the mosque empty. The raid triggered a huge street protest in Falluja the next day. Balwa went to the mosque himself and addressed the crowd, trying to calm them. It worked, at least for the moment, and Balwa was greatly relieved.

'It was the first time the local people have obeyed the instructions of our council,' Balwa said. 'Our statement swallowed the people's anger.'

He told me how he had encouraged the imams to call off another demonstration planned to take place after Friday prayers, and how, at his weekly meeting with the American commanders, he had reprimanded them for the violation of the mosque.

'I told them they were making a mistake by raiding the mosques,' he said. 'I told them they always did what they

135

wanted to do, but that it was not always the right thing.' He asked for a promise that American troops wouldn't enter a mosque again. The Americans, of course, refused, but Balwa at least thought he was having some influence in Falluja.

One afternoon he took me into the butchers' market. It was a rough area of town and we walked with Balwa's two armed bodyguards by our sides. One was a nephew, the second, a much tougher man, had been the bodyguard of Jamal Kamel, a cousin of Saddam whose two brothers had been married to Saddam's daughters. The two brothers defected in the mid-1990s and fled to Jordan calling for an uprising against the Ba'ath. Saddam enticed them back home, promising an amnesty, and then a few days later had the two brothers killed, along with their father, their sister, her four children, a second sister and her son. Their mother was stabbed to death later. Jamal Kamel was the only member of the family to survive. When I first met the bodyguard he rolled back the sleeve of his shirt and showed me a deep, horrific scar that curved like a steep valley through the thick flesh of his forearm. Saddam's eldest and hot-headed son Uday had walked past him once and the bodyguard hadn't stood to attention or hadn't got out of the way quickly enough. Uday pulled out a sword and swung it down with tremendous force, slicing into his arm up to the bone. He had been lucky to survive.

The point about the butchers' market, Balwa said, was that I should understand that the ordinary people of Falluja were perfectly decent and wanted only what everyone else in Iraq wanted: jobs and enough food on the table. One man complained about the price of tomatoes, another about the shortage of work. Nearly everyone we spoke to was violently anti-American, pledging to fight or describing how American troops had violated their traditions.

At one point Balwa quietly asked one of his aides about the

136

posters the council had been putting up asking people to keep Falluja clean and to obey the city's rules.

'Where are they?' Balwa asked him.

'At night they keep taking them down,' the aide said.

'Oh,' Balwa sighed.

I never saw his posters. I only saw posters put up by the insurgents. Once I saw several identical sheets of paper pasted to traffic bollards in the high street. They offered a carefully worded warning to motorists.

To all drivers: We have already told you not to stay close to American vehicles or American convoys and now we are warning you for the last time and telling you that keeping close to these vehicles will put you in danger of being shot so keep away from them because they are subject to attack and destruction by the mujahideen at any time. Signed, The Iraqis.

Later that evening Balwa asked me what I'd thought of the butchers' market.

'Were you scared?' he said.

'To be honest, yes I was. Of course,' I said. 'I was glad we had your guards with us. But you knew we'd be safe, didn't you?'

'I wasn't sure,' he said. 'I didn't know we would be OK until we left. I wanted to see what people think of me. It was a test. They respect me, don't you think?' He laughed.

I was staying at his house which meant it was his duty to protect me. 'Ayni,' he said. 'You are my eye.' I was his guest and because of that no one we met in Falluja when we were together would harm me. It was the tribal code and I was grateful for it. But still that afternoon left me with the uncomfortable feeling that even Balwa knew he wasn't quite accepted in a town that was so quickly becoming a redoubt for the most extreme among the insurgents.

There were others in Falluja who also found themselves trapped between their own people and the Americans. That evening Balwa took me to see a Sunni cleric, Sheikh Hosham al-Alousi, who had been shot outside his home by insurgents at dusk one evening. Was Balwa quietly trying to show me the danger he faced or perhaps the divisions tearing Falluja apart? I don't know.

The sheikh's brother said he thought twenty shots had been fired into the car, but only one hit its target. The sheikh was hit in the abdomen and after several days in hospital he was now recovering in a front room on the ground floor of his house. He was a recognised figure in Falluja. For the past decade or so he had run the Islamic Benevolence Union, a religious charity that took donations and distributed them to health clinics and to feed hundreds of poor families. He ran a religious school and sat on the local clerics' *shura*, or council, as well as Balwa's city council. No one would tell me precisely his crime in the eyes of the insurgents. Some said he was not sufficiently anti-American in his views, others said he had been seen going into secret talks with American officers. Whatever he had done had almost cost him his life. I was given tea and sweets as I waited in the hallway while Balwa went to talk to him. Eventually I was led in and saw the sheikh lying in a large and expensive hospital bed that almost swallowed up the entire room. He was a ghastly grey colour and too weak to sit up, too weak I thought even to talk to me. But he described in detail what had happened that night: the grey Opel Omega car that had driven towards him, how he had a sense just a few moments before the shots were fired of what was about to happen, the two gunmen and the hail of bullets, his passing out, his extensive treatment in two different hospitals.

'Why do you think you were shot?' I asked.

'We are living in a messy situation and it's still strange to us. It is not usual in our country to target clerics,' he said. 'The attack I suffered didn't come from the Americans. It is so important for you to realise the Americans didn't attack me. I am not fighting them, I am working through negotiations. It wasn't the Shia that struck me either.

'Those who issued the fatwa to attack me are from the local people of Falluja. And it was for nothing. Just because they are jealous of me because I am active in politics.'

I tried to ask more questions, but he lost interest. Instead he wanted to tell me about the visions he had had in hospital five years earlier after a car accident in Baghdad. He was convinced he had seen Jesus approaching his bed and described a man with long, blond hair down to his waist. Later he saw Fatima, the daughter of the Prophet Mohammad, and then Moses, and then his own mentor, an elderly Sunni cleric named al-Nabhan al-Halibi whose white-bearded portrait was hanging on the wall by the bedside. I stopped taking notes. He turned to me and gripped my forearm.

'Do you believe me? Say you believe I saw these people. Can you believe? That is all I want to hear,' he said.

'I believe you,' I said.

10

The Narrow Thread of Trust

Soon after moving into the house, I and a couple of other journalists took up playing squash in the evenings at Baghdad University. Like a lot of places in the city, the campus had once been modern and well-equipped. There was a separate sports block with a large grass running track, a handful of broken hurdles and the shell of what had once been a row of banked seating. Inside was an Olympic-size swimming pool, which was drained throughout the winter, and beyond the classrooms was a large weightlifting hall and a separate fencing hall, both permanently locked, and a row of half a dozen squash courts. We persuaded the dean to give us a letter that would allow us past the armed guards and in return we bought from him four over-priced Chinese squash rackets. The campus was only a few minutes from home and at the beginning we would walk or jog there. Later we only drove. The guards were bemused but would happily let us in, unlock the large chain holding shut the main doors and occasionally sit in the gallery smoking and watching us play. They had laid down mattresses on the floor of the hallway and they slept there all night, protecting the building from looters. American military helicopters flew regularly overhead and even though it was clear we were from those foreign nations which had invaded their country and brought such violence, the guards never once treated us with anything but grace. These short trips to the university were a rare effort to live normally in a city that was deteriorating around us. We would cook in the house, shopping for food in vegetable stalls or at two nearby supermarkets, both of which were run by Christians and stocked with expensive Western imports from Jordan or Lebanon. There were small off-licences, also Christian-run, selling alcohol but as the months went by they began to close down in the face of a wave of attacks from Shia and Sunni extremists. One of the supermarkets, the Honey Market, had an off-licence next door and that soon closed too, though if you asked quietly the staff would lead you around past the sandwiches and the milk, through a set of curtains and down into the back of the off-licence to shop for Lebanese wine. One day the owner of the supermarket was robbed at home. Someone knew he kept the shop's takings in his house not in the bank and he lost several thousand dollars.

There were restaurants too, though not as many as before the war. There were not so many crowds either. Before the invasion, families would fill the most expensive restaurants along Arasat Street. Young men from the party elite would race their BMWs and Mercedes down the road outside and the wealthy would fill their stomachs with rich food. One night before the war at the Black and White restaurant I saw a group of middle-aged party officials. One had a pistol in a holster on his belt and they had brought with them a set of crystal glasses and an icebox holding an expensive bottle of cognac. I had noticed on that trip the steady trade in luxury goods. The shops on Arasat were attuned to the needs of a corrupt, third-world elite. There were wide-screen televisions for sale, chrome parts for Toyota Land Cruisers, imported foreign cigarettes and genuine Cuban cigars starting at £100 a box. Of course there had been twelve years of punitive UN sanctions, but that did not seem to have constrained the tastes of the wealthy. The people who really suffered from the sanctions that followed the first Gulf War, as the UN and the West knew well enough, were not

141

the party elite, but the middle class. In less than a generation, professors, musicians, writers and artists had become taxi drivers and cigarette sellers. Even before the occupation came, the economy was so ground down that most people were already extremely vulnerable.

And so for several months my colleagues and I went out in the evenings, shopping, playing squash, meeting Iraqi friends or eating in restaurants. Gradually, though, this public space was closed to us. On New Year's Eve one of the popular restaurants in Arasat Street was bombed and eight people were killed. We stopped eating out at night. Not long after that the guerrillas began to kidnap foreigners. We stopped playing squash. Then I asked my Iraqi drivers to do our shopping. How quickly we were cut off.

I couldn't say exactly when it happened but at some point the narrow thread of trust that tied the American military to the Iraqi people snapped and the belief that the invasion and overthrow of Saddam would inevitably herald a better future collapsed into frustration and resentment. Some Iraqis, of course, were opposed from the very start. Others, among them many senior American commanders, never even realised the thread had been cut.[22] For the rest it happened in the first months after the war. It was what Siham had been talking about when she spoke of the gap between the people and the government. It was a sickening and swift disillusionment. Perhaps expectations were unrealistically high from the start, perhaps failure wasn't always certain, but there was no way to re-tie the thread.

For many living outside Iraq the moment when they realised that the trust was broken came in the spring of 2004 when the photographs of the abuse at the Abu Ghraib prison began to emerge, images of prisoners humiliated and violently abused.

142

For most Iraqis, though, it happened much earlier when they witnessed the kind of incidents that got less coverage in the press: relatives accidentally shot by belligerent soldiers, cars crushed or houses damaged by hefty military machinery, homes wrongly targeted in raids. Compensation was available and in the end millions of dollars were paid out for property that had been destroyed or for the lives of people who had been wrongly killed. Sometimes the money came with an apology, often it did not. For the family of an Iraqi accidentally killed by American soldiers, $2,500 was paid. It did not go far.

One of the most galling episodes happened in Basra. Although the Shia Muslim majority here appeared willing to co-operate with the British military as long as it suited them, the British still conducted raids looking for major thieves, or smugglers, or illegal arms stocks. On 14 September 2003, a squad of British soldiers led just such a raid on a hotel, the Ibn al-Haitham, in the centre of town.

Although the hotel was on a main street it was of only modest quality and often quiet. Guests tended to be Iraqis from upcountry who were making the pilgrimage to Mecca. They would drive down, dressed for the journey in sandals and pristine white robes wrapped over one shoulder like a Roman toga. Here they would stay the night before crossing the border into Kuwait and driving into Saudi Arabia. At dawn that morning, when the soldiers stormed the hotel, Baha Mousa, the night duty director, was behind the reception desk. He was twenty-six and tall and good-humoured. He worked a long, twelve-hour night shift for which he was paid just $100 a month, though he could double that in tips if he was lucky. A family photograph I have shows him standing plump and broad in an open-necked white shirt, smiling as he cradles his infant son Hussein in his left arm. Next to him, holding their second son Hassan, is his wife, who died of cancer six months before the raid. Almost as tall as her husband she looks into the camera lens, intent and happy.

Witnesses say the soldiers ordered Mousa to lie on the black tiled floor of the lobby with six other hotel employees, their hands on their heads. The building was searched and at around this time Mousa's father Daoud arrived to collect his son and take him home for breakfast. Daoud was a stout man, a colonel for twenty-four years in the Basra police force. He watched from outside as the soldiers poured through the hotel. At the reception desk they found three Kalashnikov rifles kept for hotel security. In a front room used as an office by a businessman named Haitham Baha Ali, one of three partners who owned the hotel, they broke into a safe. Inside the safe they found an olive-green Ba'ath party uniform, some party medals, two pistols and two small automatic rifles. Ali, who had been in the hotel earlier that morning, had disappeared by the time the safe was opened. He appears to have been the target of the raid and has been in hiding ever since. Some reports suggested the soldiers believed that Ali or others at the hotel were linked with the death two weeks earlier of a British army captain, who was killed in a roadside bombing. It was certainly an unusually important operation because it later emerged that standing on the roof of the hotel throughout the raid had been Brigadier William Hewitt Moore, commander of the UK 19 Mechanised Brigade and one of the most senior British army officers in the country.[23]

Daoud said he saw soldiers removing bundles of Iraqi dinars from the safe and that some of them stuffed the money into their pockets and under their shirts. He said he pointed this out to one of the soldiers, who made them return the money. The seven hotel staff were then arrested, their hands tied with plastic cuffs and they were driven off in a military vehicle. A British soldier told Daoud not to worry and said the arrest was

144

merely a formality. His son would be back within two hours, he said. But Daoud never saw his son alive again. Four days later he was called to the British military morgue to identify Baha Mousa's corpse. He found it bruised, bloodied and badly beaten.

'When they took the cover off his body I could see his nose was broken badly,' he said. 'There was blood coming from his nose and his mouth. The skin on his wrists had been torn off. The skin on his forehead was torn away and beneath his eyes there was no skin either. On the left side of his chest there were clear blue bruises and also on his abdomen. On his legs I saw bruising from kicking. I couldn't stand it.'

We were sitting cross-legged on the floor of his home in Basra and his two grandsons Hussein and Hassan fidgeted before us, too young to understand what was being described. Daoud Mousa began to sob, his broad frame shaking like a child's.

A British forensic specialist was flown out from England to conduct an autopsy on Mousa. Daoud met the man and spoke to him briefly but was not allowed to see a copy of his autopsy report. Instead he was given a death certificate, dated 21 September 2003, which recorded the cause of death simply as 'CARDIORESPIRATORY ARREST/ASPHYXIA'. All the more detailed questions on the certificate that might help explain the death were left blank. Daoud was told no more, save that the Royal Military Police were investigating his son's death. On 2 November the British gave him $3,000, which they described in a letter as 'a part payment of compensation'. It said the investigation was continuing.

There the matter would have rested, inconclusive and tragic, had it not been for the other hotel employees. Mousa had died, but the other six had lived and they had a terrible story to tell. The most articulate of them was a quiet, thoughtful, forty-four-year-old maintenance engineer, a man named Kifah Taha. I met him at the hotel one afternoon, four months after the raid, and he described slowly and in careful detail what had happened to him. He had been working on the hotel generator the previous night and was asleep in a second-floor room when the soldiers raided the hotel. He was soon woken, cuffed and arrested along with the others. The seven were then driven off and taken to a British military base. Hoods were put on their heads. 'They started beating us as soon as we arrived,' he said. 'From the first second they beat us. There were no questions, no interrogations.'

At first the men were ordered to lean with their backs flat against the wall and their arms straight in front of them, palms together with their thumbs pointing up. Taha demonstrated for me – it was what the military would call a stress position, designed to break a captive's will without causing signs of physical damage.

'They were kicking us in the abdomen, like kickboxing. They were laughing. It was a great pleasure for them. We were in so much pain. We became so tired and any one of us who fell to the ground would get beaten more than the others.' Later the soldiers forced the men to crouch on the floor, their arms still straight in front of them, palms together, thumbs up. Taha showed me again, another stress position.

'We were like that for several hours and they continued beating us,' he said. Each prisoner was given a footballer's name. 'They called us names, like Van Basten, Gullit. They said if we didn't remember our names they would increase the beating. They shouted: You must remember your name. Don't forget your name.' The soldiers poured freezing water over their heads and their bodies and delivered food: rice and beans. The Iraqis were too scared to eat. The kicking and beating continued.

Mousa appeared to suffer most from the beatings. For the first day and night the seven men were kept in the same room. On the second night he was taken away to another room but his friends could still hear him moaning through the walls.

'I heard his voice,' Taha said. 'He said: "Blood. Blood. There's blood coming from my nose. I'm going to die. I'm going to die." After that there was nothing from him.'

After that night the treatment changed. The hoods were taken off them and their cuffs cut off. The next day, the third day, the surviving six men were taken to Camp Bucca, an American-run detention camp at Umm Qasr, a small town to the south of Basra and close to the border with Kuwait. Taha was so badly injured himself that he was taken straight to a military hospital with one of the other six hotel staff who was also injured. Taha showed me a letter he had that explained his case. It was written by a Major James Ralph, a consultant in anaesthesia and intensive care. Taha, it said, had been admitted to the Shaibah military hospital at 10.40 p.m. on 16 September 2003, suffering 'acute renal failure, secondary to rhabdomyolysis.'

Acute renal failure means simply that Taha's kidneys stopped working. They stopped because of rhabdomyolysis, which is what happens when muscle fibres break down and release a protein called myoglobin into the body's circulation. Myoglobin is toxic to the kidneys and frequently causes damage that can be life-threatening – in Taha's case, kidney failure. There are several apparent causes of rhabdomyolysis, from alcoholism to marathon running to overdosing on cocaine. One of the most common causes, though, is trauma so serious that it damages the skeletal muscles. It was first used as a diagnosis in the early 1940s to describe the crush injuries suffered by victims of the German bombing raids in Britain and here it was re-appearing in Basra in 2003.

Lest there be any doubt precisely what had happened, the letter continued: 'It appears he was assaulted approximately 72 hours ago and sustained severe bruising to his upper abdomen, right side of chest, left forearm and left upper inner thigh.' He spent two months in the hospital recovering from his injuries.

Taha's account, as well as that of the other men who survived, was confirmed by these letters, letters written in English, on headed military notepaper, by British army doctors. It would seem that there could be little doubt that the men had been severely kicked and beaten, so severely that Baha Mousa suffered for many hours until he died. None of the men arrested nor any other hotel staff were ever charged with any crime. Later, Mousa's family was offered a final payment by the British Army of $5,000, but by then Daoud was so angry that he turned it down.

'That was an insult to our dignity,' said his other son, Ala'a. 'It is an ugly crime and nothing except full justice will get rid of the ugliness of this crime. It will become more ugly if there is no justice. The children will talk about it for thirty, forty or fifty years, how ugly it was, how ugly the British Army were. It will be a medal on the chest of the children.'

His father had sat listening to this and then turned to me and said: 'My son didn't die on the street, or in the hotel, or in my house. He died in custody and it wasn't a natural death. There should be a just trial and compensation for his children.'

Daoud knew there was an army investigation: he had been given letters about the case that showed that the Special Investigation Branch of the 3rd Regiment Royal Military Police were making an inquiry. The incident had a case number, 64695/03. Taha had been questioned in detail by the military investigators and was even shown video footage of some British soldiers, although, since he had worn a bag over his head for most of the beating, he was unable to identify any of those responsible. But for months the military were silent. Eventually, Daoud's complaint was taken up by a lawyer in Britain who brought a case against the British Ministry of Defence arguing its troops were bound by the new Human Rights Act and demanding the government hold an independent inquiry. Taha was flown to London to testify in the High Court and, on 14 December 2004, the judges agreed that the soldiers involved were operating under the Act from the moment Mousa was in a British prison.[24] It was an historic ruling that meant British soldiers now faced the possibility of being put on trial for human rights abuses if they mistreated their prisoners. The judges called it a 'difficult and troubling case' and noted what they termed the 'dilatoriness' of the military investigation (although the Court of Appeal later said that it was too early to determine whether a proper investigation had been carried out).[25] Despite this ruling, the investigation dragged on slowly. It was nearly two years after the raid before anyone was charged in connection with Mousa's death.

The point wasn't just the spectacular failure to prosecute the guilty in the case of the killing of Baha Mousa. It was the fact that his death was just one in a series of cases of alleged abuse, beatings or killings committed by soldiers sent to Iraq as liberators. British military investigators alone were looking at several other incidents including one in which four soldiers were eventually jailed after they took photographs of Iraqi prisoners at a camp in the south: one Iraqi was strung up in a net from a fork-lift truck; another was made to simulate sexual positions. There were other cases in my notebook that were being investigated: Ather Karim Khalaf, a driver whose family claimed he was shot dead as he queued for petrol; Abdul Jabal Moussa Ali, a primary school headmaster who, it was claimed, was arrested at his home, beaten and died in custody; Ahmad Jabbar Kareem, a sixteen-year-old boy who was supposedly thrown into a river, forced to swim and eventually drowned (four soldiers were later charged in connection with his death,

149

but eventually cleared); Hanan Saleh Matrud, an eight-year-old girl shot dead as she played outside her home; Ghanem Kadhem Kati, a young man who died after he was shot twice in the back at the door to his home.

It wasn't just happening with British soldiers. The horror of prisoner abuse at Abu Ghraib became an indelible sign for most Iraqis that the Americans could be as brutal as the regime they had overthrown. Then there were countless other incidents in which American troops had allegedly been involved in killings, beatings, abuse, and unjustifiably aggressive behaviour. In May 2004 American military helicopters attacked what they called a 'suspected foreign fighter safe house' at a village called Mukaradeeb near the Syrian border. At least forty-two people were killed. I went to their funeral in Ramadi, the nearest major town, and there it became clear that in fact the Americans had bombed a wedding party and that among the dead were musicians from a local band and perhaps two dozen women and children. I spoke to women and children in hospital and listened to dozens of survivors giving detailed, matching accounts of the party and the subsequent attack. Yet the military continued to insist it had struck the right target, even when video footage emerged showing the burials of young children killed by horrific shell injuries. 'I have not seen the pictures but bad things happen in wars,' Major-General James Mattis of the 1st Marine Division said at the time. 'I don't have to apologise for the conduct of my men.' Some months earlier I had spent a day with a woman called Siham al-Tamimi as she tried to obtain compensation from the US military because a soldier in an observation post on top of a police station had shot dead her husband Sami without any apparent reason as he drove home from work. Another day I came across the case of Mohammad Khadum al-Jurani and his wife Hamdia who were driving home with their three daughters in their Volkswagen

150

Passat when suddenly an American Abrams tank rolled directly across the highway, crushing their car. The two adults were killed and their daughters were left seriously injured. The contorted shell of their little car was still parked outside the house.

There were thousands of similar cases across the country, a vast and little-known toll of death, injury and humiliation. The occupying armies too frequently excused their mistakes by citing their broad and secret rules of engagement. Yet Iraqis knew about these stories, and this brutality and arrogance was for them precisely what a foreign military occupation meant.

11

They Just Don't Get It

The next time I went to Falluja it was on the first day of April
2004, the morning after four American security contractors had
been killed. The men, well-paid former soldiers, had been
driving their two four-wheel drives through Falluja when they
ran into an ambush on the high street. They were shot dead in
a hail of gunfire and then their cars were set alight. A crowd
appeared, tied the bodies to the back of a couple of cars and
dragged them through the streets before hanging two of the
corpses by their feet from a green metal pontoon bridge over the
Euphrates. The next day newspapers across the world carried
photographs of the two ragged black forms, barely recognisable
as human bodies.

The men worked for Blackwater Security, a private company
set up by former US Navy Special Forces commandos and one
of several such firms operating in Iraq alongside the American
military. Blackwater described itself as the 'most comprehensive private military company in the world' and offered 'the
solution to fourth-generation warfare', by which they meant a
fight not between battalions of carefully manoeuvred, opposing
armies but between an army and a group of insurgents. There
were thousands of such men operating in Iraq, a new private
army whose wages were paid by eager Western governments.
The killing of the four Blackwater employees became one of
those individual moments that changes a course of action.
Because of the nature of those deaths on that day the American

military began a much more aggressive policy towards Falluja, invading it like an army rather than merely trying to police it, destroying it to save it. In Baghdad the same American officer who had said that 95 per cent of Fallujans fully supported the Americans, now said: 'Falluja remains one of the cities in Iraq that just don't get it.'[26]

The highway to Falluja was blocked that morning by a group of American soldiers, one of them in a bomb-disposal suit, inspecting the surface of the road. My driver took one of the other roads in and we crossed easily through a cursory police checkpoint at the entrance to the town. There were no American troops to be seen. I went first to the walled compound that was the base for the Iraqi Civil Defence Corps, a para-military force established by the Americans to be halfway between the police and the new Iraqi army. They were dressed in brown camouflage uniforms and wore bright red berets. The Iraqi colonel was so scared that he would only talk to me once we were seated in his office with the thin metal door bolted. It was so small inside it felt like a garden shed and offered about as much protection. There were glasses of tea on the table, a small radio on the shelf and the men's Kalashnikovs propped up against the walls or lying on chairs. The compound was two or three minutes' drive from the scene of the previous day's killings but the colonel said he and his 900 men only heard about the incident when it was over. 'By the time we arrived there was no one there,' he said.

Despite the killings he tried to argue that security in Falluja was good, though he said there was no town that was free of insurgents these days. It would be a lot better if the Americans could step back and hand power to the Iraqis, he believed. 'If there were no Americans here then why would the insurgents attack?' he asked.

He thought the killers were not the 'restorationists' that the

Americans had described, fighting to restore Saddam to power, but instead an 'Islamic movement' fighting to force the Americans out of their country. Here was the heart of the matter. Some in Falluja had done well under Saddam's years, but the fight was not led by those wanting to restore their toppled dictator. This was a fight fuelled by a burgeoning Islamic extremism and supported by the networks of the tribes. Some fought for their God, others for their honour or national pride. They scoffed at the naivety of an occupation force that dismissed them as 'dead-enders'.[27]

I spoke to a group of Fallujans queuing at a small stationery store, one of whom said the killings were too much, they were un-Islamic. Another man, hectoring, interrupted and said resistance was a 'matter of self-defence' against the occupation. 'Anything could happen in this city from now on,' said another.

I went to Balwa's council offices. He was out but I spoke to some of the sheikhs on the council, who had been meeting that morning to discuss a response. One said he too felt the killings had gone too far but then blamed the crowd's anger on unemployment, corruption and heavy-handed American soldiering. The entire city, he said, was against the occupation.

I met a friend, Mohammad, at the council office. He was worried to see me in Falluja and drove me quickly to his office, where he worked as a freelance television cameraman with a group of four or five other young Fallujans. They would shoot footage of protests or the scenes of ambushes and then sell them to the Western news agencies in Baghdad, sometimes for hundreds of dollars. There we watched the footage he and his friends had shot the day before. The two four-wheel drives had been ambushed in the road almost directly outside their office and their shaky video showed the cars burning and a crowd dancing around them. It cut to an image of a white Toyota car trailing from its bumper a charred corpse. Dozens of young men

154

danced and chanted, many of them holding up posters of Sheikh Ahmed Yassin, the wheelchair-bound spiritual leader of the Palestinian militant group Hamas, who had been killed by an Israeli missile a week earlier.

'What was it like being in the crowd, Mohammad? Wasn't it dangerous?' I asked.

Mohammad was tall and rangy, young and excitable. Before the war he had worked in Falluja for al-Shabab television, Youth TV, run by Saddam's eldest son Uday. He smiled.

'Sure it was dangerous,' he said. 'But in those situations we chant with the crowd. We have to show we are with them. It's the only way.'

He and his friends had stories about how many times they had been arrested, about how they often took tapes from their cameras and passed them to strangers in the crowd to stop them being confiscated by the troops, about how couriers in cars or on motorcycles raced back with them to the agencies' makeshift studios in Baghdad. It was a dangerous game they played but they revelled in it.

We watched a little of the news on the television and footage came up of a burning Humvee on the outskirts of Falluja. It had been filmed early that morning by one of the group and was already on television. The Humvee had hit a roadside bomb and a couple of soldiers were thought to have been injured, perhaps killed. The cameraman, tipped off by a friend, arrived sometime after the bomb had gone off. By then the military had abandoned the vehicle and rushed the injured soldiers back to a field hospital. I was thinking there was something odd about the footage. The soldiers had gone, but the Humvee was still on fire. I couldn't understand why it was still burning so intently.

'Was the Humvee still on fire when you got there?' I asked.

'Oh no,' said the cameraman. 'The resistance set fire to it when I was there and they danced around it.'

155

'How did they set fire to it? Did they bring their own petrol?' I asked.

'No. I had some spare in the back of the car. I gave it to them,' he said. I looked a little shocked. 'This is the way these things are done,' he said and smiled back at me.

A couple of days later the US military began Operation Vigilant Resolve, a major assault on Falluja and what they promised would be an 'overwhelming' military response to the insurgent violence of the previous months. By then large numbers of young Shia men had also suddenly taken up arms against the Americans in Sadr City, in eastern Baghdad, and across the southern Shia towns. It was the first time since the war that both Sunni and Shia guerrillas were fighting against the Americans. For several days the US military lost control of the main roads leading out of Baghdad to the west as well as the road to Baghdad airport.

Falluja was now too dangerous to enter so I went instead to Garma, a small village to the east of the town. It was mid-morning on the third day of the American assault and we could hear fighter jets dropping barrages of bombs close enough that they shook the ground we stood on. A small reconnaissance drone buzzed through the air above us, unseen. At a crossroads in the village we suddenly came upon a large group of masked, heavily armed men standing around chatting. The road was too narrow to turn round quickly and, before we knew it, we were among them. So we stopped and asked one of the shopkeepers who was looking on unperturbed to introduce us to the leader of the group. Better to talk than to run away, I thought. One fighter stepped forward. He was dressed in blue jeans and a black shirt and had a red and white keffiyeh wrapped around his entire face so that I could barely see even his eyes. He was young and rested a loaded rocket-propelled grenade launcher on his right shoulder. He balanced the weapon awkwardly as he

156

put out his hand to shake mine. I said I was a journalist and carried no weapon. I came only to listen. Would he tell us why he was here?

'The Americans are accusing the people of Falluja of being terrorists while they themselves are harassing our women and girls, attacking our families and terrifying the civilians,' he said. 'We told them it was forbidden for Americans to enter Falluja but they are not respecting our words.'

'How can you fight against an army which has weapons that are so much more powerful than your own?' I asked.

'The Americans think we are afraid, while we recognise them as cowards. We have many heroes who are standing here and elsewhere. We will not be afraid of their tanks and their weapons and their other equipment. We will stay until we defeat them. We are fighting *li-wajihillah*, for the face of Allah.' It was a religious expression which meant for no other reward than the pleasure of God.

'All those who are fighting here in Falluja and across the south of Iraq are good Muslims and they know very well that America is wrong and that we are right. They will have no choice but to leave our country.'

He stopped and looked back at the other fighters. In the distance they heard the sound of a helicopter approaching and they scattered quickly, running from the open street into alleyways and houses nearby. Within a few seconds the crossroads was deserted and we turned back and drove quickly away.

Balwa had left Iraq a few days before the American attack on Falluja. He said he went for treatment for his diabetes, but there was little doubt he saw the fight coming and wanted to get himself and his family out of danger. He went to Dubai for a few weeks and I spoke to him by telephone a couple of days into the battle. He had decided to resign from the council and had sent a letter to the others explaining his protest. However, by then there wasn't even a council to resign from. The whole of the city's administration had collapsed, along with the police force and the Civil Defence Corps, most of whom either ran home or joined the insurgency. Balwa, of course, was livid about the attack on his town and the destruction and death it had caused and the infamy that now lay like a thick dust over Falluja. This time he wasn't calm or controlled. The words poured out of his mouth as if he was inciting a crowd. He barely paused to breathe.

'It is a big crime and a spot of shame on the face of humanity especially when we live in the twenty-first century in what they say is a free world. They have done nothing to rebuild Falluja. Our people in this heroic city are terrified and they are suffering from the terrorism of a state which pretends to be the godfather of democracy and the protector of human rights. Is this crime less than Saddam's crime? Falluja is a city that should be the pride of Arab nations and all the world. It is a city that became a symbol of rejection and the refusal to obey an occupying force. The behaviour of the Americans has only increased sympathy for the resistance. The Americans refused to listen to our advice and refused to understand our city.'

Balwa had fled but there were others who, despite it all, were still prepared to try to build a bridge between the Americans and the insurgents. In a Baghdad office, where the air conditioning was set to extreme cold, I met Hajim al-Hassani, a man who had found himself involved in the ceasefire negotiations to halt the battle of Falluja.

Hassani was a heavily framed man, with a trim grey beard and a faint American accent. Like Balwa he was a Sunni and he represented the Iraqi Islamic Party, a Sunni political movement that was founded in 1960 and had long been in opposition to Saddam. He was born in Kirkuk, a part-Kurdish, part-Arab city

158

north of Baghdad that sits on one of the world's largest oil reserves. He studied at the university in Mosul, another northern town. He had fled the country in 1979, the year that Saddam came to power and a time when many Iraqis realised what was coming and ran. As a student Hassani had been an Arab nationalist, not a Ba'athist, but a nationalist none the less. But it was a more ecumenical time than now. He had four close friends. Two were Shia, and were members of the outlawed Dawa party, the other two other were Sunnis. Despite their different religious backgrounds they were close. In 1979, the four were arrested: the two Shias because of their affiliation with Dawa; the two Sunnis had been working in some way against the government, although Hassani wouldn't tell me how. He feared his friends would be tortured and that they might be forced to give up his name as well. So he left the country. The two Sunnis and one of the Shia were killed. The fourth survived the purges but spent the next twenty years in prison. About a year after the war Hassani had met up with him again. He was reluctant to talk about it and said only that it had been a touching moment and that although his friend had survived prison his life was still hard.

While his friend had been in jail, Hassani had travelled to the US and had begun a new life. He finished a PhD in agricultural economics in Connecticut and then moved to Los Angeles. He ran various businesses and at one time tried to ride the dot-com bubble, investing his money in an internet firm and losing heavily when the bubble burst ('It failed miserably and we lost a lot of money. We sold it for pennies,' he said). He married an American woman and even though his life there was comfortable, he always felt torn from his country. Later the couple divorced and he said it was largely over the question of Iraq. He wanted to go back one day, she did not. In the late 1980s, just before Saddam invaded Kuwait, Hassani joined the Iraqi

Islamic Party in exile and worked with the Iraqi opposition for more than a decade. He married again, had children, and travelled from one opposition conference to the next. In the final months before the war he moved between Syria, Turkey and Jordan, meeting others from the opposition and waiting for the invasion to come. When the regime fell he crossed from Syria over a river and into the Kurdish regions of northern Iraq and from there he travelled to Mosul where the Islamic Party already had an office established. A few days later he was down in Baghdad.

Now, whenever the head of the Islamic party, Mohsin Abdul Hamid, was unable to take his seat at Governing Council meetings, Hassani would step in instead. The Islamic Party leadership counted Falluja as the sort of middling Sunni town that ought to give them backing. They had an office there and a growing membership so the task of negotiating a ceasefire was given to them.

Hassani spoke his perfect English quietly and chewed his words so that you had to lean forward from your seat to hear him. Here was a man who was open and charming, reasonable and neatly argued and yet, even though I was to see him several times over the months ahead, I could never get the measure of him. Why did he, why would anyone, return to the violence of Iraq after half a lifetime living well in exile in the United States? It is not a question an outsider can easily answer. Hassani said he was committed to helping re-build his country. Is altruism such a powerful motivation? Perhaps Hassani truly had it, I do not know. There is something almost as powerful about an exile's hunger to return one day to his or her homeland, to see what has become of it, to escape the isolation that exile can bring. And returning home can bring with it a status that for someone like Hassani would be greater than the status of an exile abroad. Later he told me he looked forward to a good position in the Iraqi government. He was well-educated and a decent man, so if he was elected or appointed fairly then why not a good position indeed? But Iraq was also dangerous and it wasn't as if he was entirely behind the American endeavour. He saw that it was wrong and yet he stuck with it. Perhaps the battle of Falluja was the first sign of that for him: there he was negotiating on behalf of the Americans yet he was set against their policies. He was angry that the US Marines had invaded the town. It was a mistake, he said, to respond to the killing of four contractors by attacking an entire town. It was, he said, collective punishment and that was immoral.

'The mistake of the coalition is that they don't understand our culture,' he said. 'These are tribal areas and you cannot deal with them in the same way as you deal with people in Britain or the US. Here the people look at the Americans as an occupying force. I think there were better ways to handle the situation.'

He was also angry, he used the word 'sickened', by the earlier decision of the Americans to dissolve the Ba'ath and the Iraqi army. These were decisions which affected how people in towns like Falluja, people who had been heavily represented in the party and the army, reacted to the occupation.

'Using force in the way they used it in Falluja made people fight,' he said. 'It isn't like these people were terrorists. They were normal people and they had children who were dying and so everybody started to fight.'

Hassani had been in Falluja at the beginning of the nego-tiations. A few days after the assault on the city began, he braved the fighting and drove into the town in a conspicuous four-wheel drive. There he spent several hours holed up in a mosque talking to the city's elders. Not everyone from Falluja wanted to begin negotiations and many were suspicious of Hassani and his delegation. They were lucky to make it back to

Baghdad unhurt. In Baghdad they conveyed to the American generals what they had heard and then began shuttling back and forth between Baghdad and Falluja. The negotiations went in fits and starts. A ceasefire would be announced and then one side would break it and fighting would continue sporadically for a few more hours or days until another ceasefire was agreed. Should there be free access to the hospital? Should all weapons be handed over? Should all foreign fighters in the city be forced to give themselves up? How was Falluja to be run after the fight? There was still much to agree.

'I would say I am an optimist and a pessimist. The road ahead still isn't clear to me,' Hassani said. 'I like some of the stuff we have done and I don't like other stuff we have done. I told the Americans they were listening to the wrong people and following the wrong policy. I think they were divided on this issue of Falluja and we are all paying the price for it.'

Four weeks later the fighting ended. The Americans had only managed to capture small areas of Falluja, while the insurgents held on to the heart of the city. The cost: dozens of dead American soldiers, several hundred dead Fallujans including many civilians, considerable damage to property, and the recognition that the world's most powerful army was not always invincible. The insurgents considered themselves the victors.

I went back to the town on the first day it opened, along with hundreds of Fallujans who had fled in the first days of the battle and now wanted to reclaim their homes. At the US Marine checkpoint on the edge of the city boyish soldiers handed a leaflet in Arabic to all the drivers, explaining how families could claim for compensation for damaged property if they provided photographs and details of when and how the damage occurred. It promised there would be 'rehabilitation' and

162

'cleaning' and 'rebuilding of schools' now that security had returned. It also offered an account of why the US military had just spent four weeks bombing Falluja, killing so many people. It implied a battle fought and won.

> The Marines [the leaflet said] came thousands of miles to help the Iraqi people to restore security and to live a good and prosperous life. Instead of greeting the Marines these terrorists and criminals inside Falluja attacked them. These criminals have chosen to hide in your city and your houses, using your women and your mosques as shelters. They brought you nothing good, only fear and war. If you have any information about these criminals please inform the coalition forces.

Beyond the checkpoint there were a handful of Iraqi police and Civil Defence Corps soldiers standing along the high street and a fire truck driving past in no particular hurry but with its lights flashing. Yet when we drove a block deeper into the city it was clear how little the battle had accomplished. Armed guerrillas, their faces wrapped in keffiyehs, manned their own checkpoints on all the major roads, checking cars and demonstrating their authority. I saw young men queuing at the Civil Defence Corps headquarters to sign up to a new Fallujan security force created under the ceasefire agreement and to be run, remarkably, by a former general from Saddam's Republican Guard. The recruits each received new boots and uniforms and I watched as they walked round the corner and began selling the kit: boots going for 15,000 dinars (£8) a pair. The recruits I spoke to believed firmly that the insurgency had won the battle; some had even been fighters themselves.

'You know this big battle in Falluja wasn't just to get the Americans out of our city, it was to get the Americans out of

Iraq. We have had a great victory in Falluja. The Americans have all these weapons and we had nothing and we fought them,' said one.

Further on, towards the Euphrates, was the city's football pitch. It was not so much a stadium as a large patch of dirt with a couple of cement benches surrounded by a tall brick wall. A pair of goalposts stood at one end of the ground. During the month-long battle it had become an impromptu cemetery and now a white cloth banner hung from the gate bearing the words: 'The Martyrs' Cemetery of Falluja'. The grave mounds stood in dozens of straight lines, most marked with a simple concrete slab for a headstone on which had been painted a name, and sometimes a short epithet. A US military drone buzzed overhead.

'THE COURAGEOUS MARTYR NASSER HUSSEIN. KILLED DOING HIS DUTY ON APRIL 15 AND BURIED THE SAME DAY.'

Others gave no name and hinted at the desperation of the gravediggers:

'HERE LIES AN UNKNOWN MARTYR, A BIG SECURITY GUARD WITH A BLUE SHIRT AND A BLACK DISHDASHA, FOUND NEAR THE INDUSTRIAL AREA WITH A CHAIN OF KEYS.'

'UNKNOWN FEMALE MARTYR FROM AL-BASRA BURNED INSIDE A MITSUBISHI CAR WITH SEVEN MEMBERS OF HER FAMILY.'

A pair of brown boots stuck out from another mound: 'AN UNKNOWN WORKER FROM THE INDUSTRIAL AREA, WEARING A BLACK SHIRT WITH YELLOW TROUSERS, FOUND INSIDE A WHITE OLDSMOBILE CAR.'

Judging by the names on the headstones some were women, and others contained more than one body. There were many Iraqis walking, like us, slowly up and down the rows, reading the stones and looking. Some were perhaps searching for relatives, but others came just to witness. I spoke to a few but they were angry and said little.

'What can I say?' said one man. 'Just look for yourself at this.'

'God is the one who will take his revenge,' said another.

On another stretch of dirt to the side of what had been the football pitch more graves were laid out row by row. One man lent over a grave marked 'AHMED ABDULLAH KHALIL FROM BAGHDAD WHO DIED ON APRIL 14TH' and gently poured water from a tin can over the mud, smoothing it into place. Two palm fronds stood at either end of the grave.

We drove through the town and saw deserted streets, shop fronts shuttered and families starting to return to their homes. On every street there were two or three homes that had been completely destroyed, sometimes more. Some sections of the city were worse hit than others: some with roads scorched black by fire, others little touched. In the market there was a truck off-loading boxes of garlic and cucumbers – the first fresh food into the city in a month. There was the litter of a foreign army: plastic mineral-water bottles and beige-coloured 'Meals Ready to Eat' wrappers. And there was Arabic graffiti from the fight still sprayed across the walls.

'You are bombing the house of the families of Falluja and it will not be forgotten. We will take revenge, I promise you,' read one. Another: 'To the American soldiers: We don't want to kill you but your leaders sent you to war.'

The assault on Falluja coincided with a revolt among the Shia across the south, led by the populist cleric Moqtada al-Sadr after he was clumsily threatened with arrest by the US authorities. It meant a sudden and drastic plunge in security across the country. Dozens of foreign truck drivers and contractors working for the military – Americans, Filipinos, Indians, Japanese, Nepalese and others – were kidnapped and many were murdered. One Sunday morning in mid-April, Asa'ad, one of my translators, received a letter at his home that said simply: 'You will be killed if you continue to work with the English and American enemy.' Several other Iraqi translators working with journalists had received similar threats, some had already been killed. We agreed Asa'ad shouldn't come to work that day. He stayed at home for months and never came back to work for us again.

The next day I decided to leave the house, with its minimal security and dozy guards, and move into the Palestine Hotel for a couple of weeks until the crisis passed. I had already gone to the front desk and paid a bribe to secure one of the last rooms. That afternoon, while my bags were still in a heap on the hotel-room floor, a rocket slammed into the Ishtar Sheraton Hotel, barely a hundred yards away. There was an ear-splitting blast and a shockwave punched through the open window. So I was better protected from kidnappers in the hotel, but suddenly much more of a target for the daily barrage of rockets and mortars around the city. There were American contractors staying on other floors – they wore shorts and flak jackets, carried M16 assault rifles everywhere they went and made little effort to be discreet. Although it was not the Green Zone, there were dozens of American soldiers guarding the hotel compound with nicknames stencilled on the barrels of their tanks, like 'Beautiful Disaster'. Inside my hotel room, the staff had left a faded blue note card from the hotel management on my pillow. It read, 'Nice Dreams'.

It was less than a year since the invasion and for the first time it became truly frightening to work in Iraq. The trip into Falluja the day after the four security contractors had been killed had shaken me and I knew we had been lucky to walk away untouched after our meeting with the gunmen in the village of Garma. This was a war with no front line; you didn't know when it was safe or when it might turn dangerous. The war was everywhere and nowhere. In this, at least, I could understand what the Iraqis were facing. Qais sent me a text message from his mobile phone. 'Tell you what,' he wrote, 'when I am sleeping now, one eye is opened, second is closed, like wolf.'

My fear crept up on me, along with a progressive state of exhaustion. I would leave the country for a couple of weeks and hope that the nagging sense of anxiety would ease up. But, like the tiredness, it never did. It was always there just beneath the surface, as if my nerve for risk-taking was a steadily emptying reservoir. I remember a Friday in May when the price of oil hit $40 a barrel and US Defence Secretary Donald Rumsfeld took responsibility for the Abu Ghraib abuse but refused to resign. That morning I'd planned to drive with another journalist down to Kerbala, a holy city south of Baghdad, where we'd heard the US military was making an assault on Shia rebels. We started later than planned because my friend overslept.

Just after the town of Iskandiriya, we were driving down a dual carriageway when we came upon a blue Daewoo saloon car, the same make as ours, pitched across the centre of the road. The back window had been blown out and there were shards of glass sticking out from the metal surround. There were dozens of bullet holes in the windscreen and a small sticker which said in English: PRESS. One of the back tyres had burst. The pale body of a foreign man lay face down in a stain of blood outside the car. He was dressed in a T-shirt and jeans and judging by the position in which he lay he must have been able to walk a few feet away from the car in the moments before his death. A second foreigner lay dead on the back seat. The driver and the front passenger were gone: we heard later they had been injured and taken to hospital by passing drivers brave enough to stop. The dead, I found out that evening, were both journalists from Poland: one was Waldemar Milewicz, the country's best-known war correspondent, and the second was Munir Buamran, a Polish-Algerian producer. They had arrived in Iraq only a day or two earlier for a short visit and must have looked no more conspicuous than us in their unremarkable car on the same much-travelled highway. Maybe they were spotted and followed a few miles earlier where the road was narrow and the traffic frequently jammed. The injured cameraman said later that a car had come up behind them and opened fire into the back window, forcing them off the road and killing the two men before it sped away. There had been no warning, no reason given. He said only that the shooting went on for perhaps half a minute and that it was followed by a long period of silence. By the time we arrived a large crowd of Iraqis had gathered round the dead. Our car slowed and we saw that the dead men were not people we knew and then we drove on. We didn't stop. We didn't even talk about stopping. That night back in Baghdad I lay on my hotel bed unable to sleep and I told myself there wasn't anything I could have done for the dead. It would have been dangerous to hang around, perhaps there were gunmen still in the crowd. I saw images of their limp bodies and felt ashamed that I hadn't stopped.

12

Playwrights and Poets

The day after the Americans formally handed over 'sovereignty' to an Iraqi government, I went to the theatre. I'd moved back to the house by then and the theatre building was on a roundabout not far away, along a route I took most days. I'd never seen any workmen about so it was a while before I noticed the surreptitious repairs. The building had been looted, like the rest, immediately after the war. But now the wall around it was nearly completely rebuilt, and new black railings had been installed. Every few yards hung a pair of Greek comedy and tragedy masks, bright silver and out of place in the grime of the city. The traffic here was hellish and crawled past oblivious.

Inside, the theatre had a large revolving stage and 1,000 tiered red-velvet seats. It was almost deserted apart from a couple of guards sitting and smoking on white plastic garden chairs at the lobby door. Their Kalashnikovs rested on the table in front of them. They checked our bags, led me into the theatre office and brought tea.

I found a group of playwrights and the theatre director, Menaf Talib, sitting in the semi-darkness looking out into the lobby of the theatre through a small window, like a spy hole. Talib had once been in the national basketball team and now, when he was not running the theatre, he played the part of an insane hospital patient in a television comedy about post-war Iraq. Once, he said, the National Theatre had put on play after play by Shakespeare and had been the pride of the Arab world. In the

Saddam years, though, there had been a distinct theatrical slump and performances were confined to apolitical, low-brow vaudeville acts. They were thought least likely to offend. Actors were all paid government salaries but when sanctions were imposed in the early 1990s those salaries mostly dried up. I had heard stories of those times. Before the war I'd met one of Baghdad's better known actors. He had lost his job and ran a café in a bleak industrial district, a business he financed by selling his house and his car. In a brown envelope in the café fridge he kept a bundle of cuttings: the newspaper reviews of the plays he had appeared in – Shakespeare, Molière and Chekhov. He was a poor and bitter man.

The fall of the regime suggested a new start. Money arrived for refurbishments and the theatre, though still shabby, had just finished a run of a popular new play written by an Iraqi living in exile in Germany. It was called *The Hole* and told the story (which the theatre director insisted was a true account) of a man who had been a member of an opposition political party and was wanted by Saddam's regime. His mother dug him a hole in the garden where he could hide and there he hid for twenty-five years. He went into the hole as a young man and came out after the fall of the regime grey-haired, hunched over and barely able to walk. The play explored how he learned to face the world again.

I found the playwrights oddly optimistic. There were now major suicide bombings across the country several times a week and the death toll of innocent civilians was climbing into the thousands. Few in Baghdad in those days still nurtured hope that life would improve. The playwrights saw it slightly differently: Iraq was a mess and looked hopeless but at least they were not banned from writing about it. Wasn't that something, they asked?

I hadn't been at the handover ceremony the day before, nor

had any ordinary Iraqis. We all watched it on television in the evening and saw the select handful of dignitaries looking embarrassed and confused. No one knew quite where to stand; they stumbled over their words and then paused nervously like schoolchildren before applauding. It was over in a minute or two. They seemed to whisper to one another, 'Is that it?'

It wasn't much of a return of sovereignty given that the Americans had selected the Iraqi government that replaced them. In public they relinquished political control over the country they had invaded a year earlier, but of their military authority they gave away nothing. Now above the Green Zone flew the Iraqi flag: three bands of red, white and black with the words Allah O-Akbar and three green stars across its centre. Iraq's new politicians were full of promises: the rule of law, an amnesty for insurgent fighters and the new dawn of independence. But the return of that flag was about the only change I could see.

Samir Qasim, a scriptwriter for television and radio, thought differently. He said the handover of power was to be celebrated. 'It makes you think optimistically of a better future, more progress, more creativity,' he said.

Qasim had written two radio plays since the war. One was about a man who had suffered under the old regime but was struggling to come to terms with the new order. He desperately wanted the fall of Saddam to herald a bright future, but he couldn't see it. His mind was always 'foggy'. He criticised all the changes in his society, things he said had never been part of Iraqi culture. He criticised the looting, the bombings and the way people's characters changed for the worse when confronted with the new freedoms. These were brought from outside Iraq, he decided.

Qasim's second play was about a woman who was mistakenly sent to jail. After she had spent some time behind bars

171

the authorities eventually realised she was innocent and released her. She went home, took out a key and tried to open the front door of her house but the key didn't fit the lock. As she stood at the locked door she looked back on her life, with moments of comedy and of sadness. Eventually the woman remembered that she had her door key all along, and found it hanging on a string around her neck where she had put it for safekeeping.

I was struck by the similarity of these sparse plotlines. To be released from a life spent in aching repression didn't mean one long celebration. Waking up in post-Saddam Iraq meant loss and disorientation, and it was everywhere I went. The huge changes wrought by the war sowed confusion. Often people would say it made them feel 'tired'. It wasn't usually just a physical exhaustion they were talking about, but a deep mental or emotional weariness. Hopelessness was their sickness. There was nothing to cling to along the way, no hope that the fog would lift and reveal a clear future. You couldn't imagine anything more different from the days of Saddam when life had been carefully, if brutally, defined and directed, when even your thoughts were regimented. It wasn't at all what I had expected to find. I had expected exuberance. I had expected a people determined to live a new life, laden with plans for the future. I had been naïve.

The writers started talking among themselves about the handover and what they could expect from a new, Iraqi government. 'You can't just have a rapid change. First you must relax, and we are anything but relaxed at the moment,' said Talib, the director, from behind his desk. 'It's hard to judge what the new government is going to do because we need to give them a long time to have a chance to change things. We need to be tolerant, but the Iraqis are hot-headed and rush into judgement and that's no good.'

'I want to tell you one thing,' Qasim said, turning to me. 'Before the handover I felt there was a lock on my heart and now I feel relief because that has been removed. When I left the house this morning I felt light, I felt relieved. But I can tell you when the next bomb goes off I will feel just like I used to.'

Some people, particularly outside Iraq, had been anxious that the new prime minister, Ayad Allawi, might prove too much of a hardliner, too much of another Saddam. Allawi was a stocky former Ba'athist who defected and left Iraq in the 1970s. He then lived in Britain and worked for years alongside the CIA and MI6 in opposition to Saddam only to return on the back of the invasion. Qasim thought that since this was Iraq, a fist of iron might not be such a bad idea.

'What Saddam did wrong was to go soft on criminals and hard on politicians,' he said. 'Now we want Allawi to be hard on criminals and soft on politicians. We want him to come down hard on them, even to kill the murderers and looters. We don't want them tolerated at all. We want a strong government.'

So there we were again. Why did it always come back to this hunger for a strong ruler? Was the idea of democracy so alien? Or did they really believe that after thirty years of bitter dictatorship they needed yet another dictator? You can't impose ideas from outside in times like this, however good they may sound. They have no credibility. This is a country steeped in political violence, in military coups, in communiqués from strongmen, in authoritarian governments. There was something in a dictatorship that many people recognised. It was the strength they wanted, for strength was to be admired. Strength was not something they thought could be found in a democracy. Democracies were just a thin curtain that hid nepotism, corruption and prevarication. A dictator could be a good leader, one who would cast his arm around his people, protect them, feed them, regulate them, lead them. At first it sounded foolish and exasperating. Then, after a while, you found yourself seduced by the idea. Perhaps Iraq was so violent, its internal pressures so unwieldy, that just maybe a right-minded dictator was the only remedy. But always the next morning you'd have to shrug off the idea: it was a shallow dream and history always proved it a mistake.

I left the playwrights talking among themselves and walked out into the lobby, through a set of double doors and into the auditorium. A long way below me was the stage, a circular wooden platform with its floorboards opened up so you could see into the workings underneath: pulleys, wheels, ropes, winches. A small group of actors were rehearsing the next play, a production of Iraq's great Babylonian epic, *Gilgamesh*. I watched for a while, trying to decipher their movements around the stage. The actor playing the lead role said he'd spent three months in rehearsals because the part was so difficult to master. He thought his character was not unlike Saddam, a man who desired to be his nation's greatest strongman, even to conquer death.

The poem, several thousand years old and scratched in cuneiform wedges on tablets of clay, tells of Gilgamesh, the tyrannical King of Uruk. It was considered a lesson in kingship and the attributes of leadership and so it was cherished in the libraries of rulers across the Middle East down the centuries.

Two-thirds god, one-third human, Gilgamesh rules his kingdom harshly, forcing himself on every newly married woman, claiming *droit de seigneur*. He leaves Uruk and travels the world, defeating great enemies and building his reputation, to 'establish for ever a name eternal'.[28] Soon victory in battle is not enough and, seeing his companion-in-arms die, he sets out to attain immortality itself. Along the way there are many who warn him of the emptiness of his quest. In one of the finest moments of the story, a wise inn-keeper tells him:

O Gilgamesh, where are you wandering?
The life that you seek you will never find:
When the gods created mankind,
Death they dispensed to mankind,
Life they kept for themselves.[29]

But Gilgamesh disregards what he hears and continues to search. He crosses the Waters of Death to meet the immortal Uta-Napishti[30] to ask him the secret of eternal life. He comes close to his goal but never quite succeeds and is always consumed by his search.

When he has lost all but the last shred of our sympathy, Gilgamesh returns to the walls around his kingdom of Uruk and realises his quest has been hopeless. In his despair he understands he has spent his life forever chasing sorrow, and that it is actually this neglected kingdom and these walls before him that are his legacy.

In the end we are expected to see Gilgamesh as a hero, a man who has seen the depths of the earth and returned humble with knowledge. Gilgamesh is scolded yes, but he is also cast as the victor, as someone who has gained a profound understanding from the futility of his quest and, it is implied, goes on to rule as a just king, hence the lesson of kingship. The conclusion is almost Buddhist: redemption doesn't come by going away to fight against others but by reducing your desires, staying within the community, cherishing what you have at home, loving your family. But it is also a cautionary tale that paints kings in a poor light, as men corrupted by power and arrogance. After all, Gilgamesh's realisation only comes after half a lifetime spent in vainglorious error.

Saddam, of course, was consumed by Gilgamesh's quest and took this further than most, ordering his initials scratched into the bricks of Babylon and filling his cities' streets with huge portraits or statues showing him in turns as president, general, tribal sheikh, devout Muslim, friend of the poor, conqueror of Jerusalem, and defiant challenger of America. His was a personal quest for glory on the back of the suffering of others. Gilgamesh's only salvation is that he worked out for himself the futility of his quest. Most of the rest of us never do.

During these days, in a single-storey building off Saddoun Street that housed the Iraqi Writers' Union, the poets of Baghdad would meet once a week. There were perhaps thirty present on the day I went. Nearly all were middle-aged men and unemployed. A couple wore cream-coloured flat caps, a dapper old fashion hardly seen in today's Iraq, and one had on a tie. I counted only three women, all in headscarves. One of the men was young and wore a black leather jacket, a short beard and sunglasses that hid a cataract in his cloudy right eye. His name was Haitham al-Zubaidi and when I asked what he did he said he was writing a thesis on 'The Function of the Classic Myth in Keats and Shelley'. He was thirty-two and an occasional lecturer in English literature at Baghdad University.

Poetry in Iraq, in the Arab world, is treated with tender reverence. Poems are published daily in the Arabic newspapers and in Arab literary journals, which pay £20 or £30 a piece. The great poets of Iraq have always been respected as national figures alongside kings and conquerors. To speak of Mutannabi, a tenth-century poet from the southern Iraqi town of Kufa, is to conjure a figure of immense national stature, a writer of complex panegyrics but who is as well known as any great caliph or warrior. Poetry carries an emotive power that is part of an Arab sense of identity. Market stalls sell cassettes or compact discs of spoken, improvised poetry, still the most common form. Many are anonymous. Poets are so important that Saddam tried to co-opt them. Those who wrote him eulogies were rewarded with handsome salaries, cars or even comfortable houses.

I first met Zubaidi in the courtyard of the Writers' Union, while we were waiting for the poets' meeting to begin. It was hot and we both sheltered in the doorway of a side building looking for the shade. Before the war, Zubaidi told me, he had found himself in some trouble for a poem he wrote about the collapse of society around him. He called it 'Breaking':

> I hung my heart on a willow tree,
> It broke not because my heart is heavy
> But because it was eaten by moths,
> I hung my heart on a stone,
> It broke . . .
>
> I hung my dreams on a high mountain to save myself
>   from the flood,
> And the mountain broke.

The poem was not published in Iraq, but it did appear in an Arabic newspaper in London. Zubaidi got a call from a government official who was extremely angry about the words 'high mountain' which he believed referred to Saddam.

'What do you mean by this?' the official asked.

'I meant nothing,' Zubaidi told him and he was lucky to get away with it.

'Actually, in everything I wrote I was expressing my dissatisfaction with the regime but I couldn't just announce it,' he said to me. 'You had to use a complicated system of metaphors. Now we can write what we like. My poems have changed radically in tone and subject matter. But some poets haven't written anything yet. They say the events of the war were so tremendous that they couldn't grasp them at first.'

'So what have you been writing about?' I asked.

'Before the fall of Saddam we were not allowed to write about defeat,' he said. 'But I think my generation and my father's saw a very big series of defeats. Now we have a right to say what we want. It may be the only privilege we have got.'

So he wrote a poem titled 'Nobody Told Me We Were Defeated', filled with historical allusions to the wars of the past – a poem that would have been forbidden under Saddam. 'I meant it to be an outcry against all the braggart teachers who kept telling me since my early childhood that I belong to a glorious and victorious nation while in fact it is worn-out and defeated,' he said. 'Nobody told me we were like that until I found out for myself in this war. Saddam kept telling us that we defeated Iran and Kuwait and that we would defeat the USA and its allies, while in fact the grand defeat was shining in the eyes of everybody.'

Another of his poems, 'Wake Up From War', was written one morning during the American invasion, as the tanks rolled into Baghdad. He scribbled it down from memory in my notebook, first in Arabic and then in English.

> This morning passes by my heart in fear,
> Gazes on your face in fear,
> Hoping to see the cavalcade of those who vanished,
> Scrolling their height with mist,
> And those are some deserters,
> A tank-distance behind my house.

I asked if he felt obliged to write about the war.

'A poet differs from other people because of his integrity of self, he cannot divide himself. He writes with his whole heart. And most importantly he should be a poet with his country. No poet approves of war or bloodshed or death,' he said. 'If I didn't write about the war I am not a poet. In all aspects of our life we are living the war and its consequences. You can't just write about flowers and brides.

'One day a student gave me a poem he had written about Beirut, talking about its beauty and feeling pity for the city during war. "Have you ever been to Beirut?" I asked him. "No," he said. "Have you Lebanese origins?" I asked. "No," he said. "Have you been in love with a Lebanese girl?" "No," he said. "Baghdad has received ten times more rockets than Beirut," I said to him, "so why don't you write about your own city? Otherwise what you write is false, it is artificial." A poet is governed by the influences around him. To be a poet is to feel my own misery and then the misery of others.'

He led me into the building. In the entrance hall were black and white photographs of three men: Jamil Sadqi al-Zahawi, Muhammad Mehdi al-Jawahiri and Maroof Abdul Ghani al-Rusafi. These three, dressed in suits and fezzes, were the cornerstones of modern Iraqi poetry, the neo-classical poets of the 1920s and 1930s. Their writing conformed to strict rules and neat rhymes and spoke of the struggle for independence. Of the three, Jawahiri is the most celebrated, perhaps the most highly regarded poet in the Arab world. More recent photographs of him show a white-haired old man, too thin for his suit. He wears thick, square spectacles and a small, patterned woollen cap that clings to one side of his head. It was he who established the Iraqi Writers' Union and chose this building off Saddoun Street as its headquarters. Under Saddam he was forced into exile and died in Damascus in July 1997. Saddam refused to let his family bury his body in Iraq.

Inside the main hall were photographs of the poets who broke the neo-classical mould, men like Badr Shakir al-Sayab and 'Abd al-Wahhab al-Bayati. They wrote intensely political verse, flouting the rules of form. Their words had a startling, sometimes acerbic ferocity. Here is Sayab writing about collaborators:

> I am what you want me to be,
> I am the despicable invaders' shoeshiner,
> Seller of blood and conscience.
>
> For the invaders,
> I am the crow that feeds on pigeon corpses,
> I am the ruin, I am the destruction
> The lips of the whore are more virtuous than my
>   heart
> The wings of the fly are purer and warmer than my
>   hands
> As you wish me to be . . . I am the scoundrel.[31]

The small group of poets sat on chrome chairs above a striped carpet. It was still hot, even though several fans spun overhead. The workmen fitting new air conditioners had taken a break. A man with a microphone took charge of the meeting and announced there would be elections for the Writers' Union the following week and a festival of poetry in Baghdad towards the end of the month.

There were many questions about the procedure for the elections, and little said about the festival. Was the union going to change now the old regime had gone, people asked?

'The elections will be based on the same charter the association had used under the Saddam days. No one will be dismissed from the union,' said the man in charge. 'We will print new ID cards and they will be provided to you. That way there is no chance that outsiders will slip into our group and destroy our aims.'

After the meeting I started talking to another poet in the

hallway outside. His name was Sa'ad Sahib and he was forty-five. He had long hair, which was unusual for an Iraqi, his face was deeply lined and his teeth were dark and rotting.

'My story is a complicated one,' he said. 'I was a prisoner of war in Iran for twenty-one years.'

I had heard stories about the prisoners in Iran but had never met one. They were captured during the Iraq-Iran war of the 1980s and thousands were held for years in appalling conditions in Iranian jails. Some were recruited into the Shia Iraqi opposition party that was based in Tehran and close to the ayatollahs (the Supreme Council for the Islamic Revolution in Iraq) but others, particularly the more secular ones, were released only years later and some only when Saddam's regime fell. They had lived long years in confinement and returned to families who thought them dead and to a country dramatically altered by time and by war.

Sahib was an Arab nationalist and he said this had meant he was held longer than most other prisoners. He was against Saddam but patriotic to Iraq and he was in one of the last groups of prisoners to be released, returning to Iraq just one day before the US invasion. He was a poet before he was a soldier and during his time in jail he continued to write poetry, even though paper and pens were forbidden. It was impossible for him to remember all the poems in his head so he would write on paper he tore out of Iranian cigarette packets. He spent several minutes describing to me an elaborate writing system he and his cellmates had invented. They would dissolve a red antibiotic tablet in water to make a red-coloured liquid, their ink, and used a disposable syringe to write. Once, they tried to fashion a writing board, using empty detergent boxes. They tore strips of cloth from their clothes and sewed them to the board and then covered the cloth in a paste made from detergent and shampoo. They covered the paste with a piece of nylon and

181

would then write on that with a toothbrush and somehow it left a script that was legible to the prisoners.

I asked what he wrote about. Sahib said his thoughts were mostly about homesickness, about being away from his family, and about his desire for a woman. 'Imagine twenty-one years without a woman,' he said. 'Imagine the longing.'

I asked if he could recite one of his prison poems for me. He sat quietly for so long that I thought I had asked too much of him. Then:

> From far, far away I send longing greetings with
>   the wind,
> All my insides are screaming, Iraq, Iraq.
> But who carries the poem to you, my lord,
> Who carries the papers, who carries the
>   recommendations?
> Our days are strange, our clothes are miserable,
> Mirrors are afraid of our faces,
> I lost my soul and it was scattered from my hand
>   in the darkness of the corners.

When Sahib eventually returned home he found his baby sister had grown up and married and his parents were dead. It had been hard for him to adjust to living at home again: he was unmarried and out of work, surviving on a monthly military pension of just 75,000 dinars, around £30. In jail he and his cellmates had tried to encourage each other by imagining what it would be like on the day they returned, all that they would find again, the tastes and the smells. In the end it had been a great disappointment. He was depressed by the Iraq he had returned to. He sensed that the years of sanctions and the recent war had changed the way people behaved.

'People are so tired. Faith is gone, sincerity is gone. The

sincerity between relatives, between husband and wife, it is gone,' he said. 'Selfishness is flooding into our society. I know it is because of the critical circumstances these days, but it is making people greedy. I feel like a stranger here.'

His poetry was still his only therapy. 'Poetry is my way to resist, to fight time and place. I cannot stop writing. It is a curse that fills my head.'

I asked him what he had been writing recently. Again he took a while to remember, then he said he was still dreaming about the touch of a woman and he recited a verse:

> Nothing cures me but the day of meeting,
> The moaning of the soul while we touch,
> Alcohol gives warmth to my heart and repose,
> But lips give a sweet taste.

Some months later, I telephoned the young poet Zubaidi and we arranged to meet for coffee. I liked him because he had no axe to grind. I needed a break from the artificiality of the news reports we wrote: car bomb after car bomb, politician after politician. I just wanted a regular conversation with someone. The only safe place we could agree to sit was in a hotel cafeteria where they had low, round Formica tables, new advertisements for Western beers on the wall and loud Arabic music playing in the background.

A new term had started at the university and Zubaidi was still teaching: drama as well as his regular literature classes, *Faustus* and *Romeo and Juliet*. He talked about the problems at the university – that they were still short of books more than a year after the war and that several professors had been assassinated either because they were former Ba'athists or because they had carelessly spoken out against the more extremist religious parties that were flourishing. A police station had been stormed by a gang of armed men in western Baghdad that morning and other journalists on tables near us were talking about the attack. We spoke in English and Zubaidi liked to add a rhetorical flourish to all his sentences as if life was all one long poem.

'What a pity Iraq is not safe,' he said.

'All our conversations are about security,' I said. 'What have you heard today? Did you hear about the police station?'

'You've got to be careful. Just for the time being,' he said.

'I'm very careful. I feel like I spend most of the time hiding,' I told him.

'Yesterday a friend of mine saw two British people in Karrada, walking around with nobody with them. He said he admired the situation because before the war we used to see foreigners walking in the street all the time. He stopped his car and said: "You are alone and not afraid?" And they said they didn't want to submit to the terrorists. He said: "This is a risk. If you want me to help you I'm ready." But they said no, they said they felt safe.'

'I think it's a little bit dangerous for us to be walking about in the streets now,' I said. Half a dozen foreigners, including journalists, were still being held hostage by different kidnapping groups across Iraq. Two journalists had been briefly kidnapped as they drove out of our hotel. It was getting progressively more dangerous.

'Who is going to help our ailing country?' he said.

When he was a student, Zubaidi and one of his friends, Ali, who was now living in Germany, had dreamed of writing a book mocking Saddam. They wanted to keep a record of all the bizarre and cruel orders imposed by the government.

'Some of the decisions were very strange, like cutting the ear off a deserter or reducing their food rations. Very absurd decisions. Have you ever heard of the sunflower? In Arabic it is called *abad al-shams*, the worshipper of the sun. Once, when he was drunk I guess, Saddam held a meeting and said all people must worship God and God alone so there was to be no more worshipper of the sun. So he changed the name from "worshipper of the sun" to "flower of the sun", *zaharat al-shams*.'

'You had to change your language?' I asked.

'It was his decision and it was listed in the dictionary and the formal writings of the state,' Zubaidi said. 'Imagine, people are hungry and dying and he is ignoring the essential things and only changing our language.'

'That was his paranoia,' I said.

'A friend of mine was a contractor in one of his palaces. After he finished lining one hall with marble, Saddam came and said this was not the design he wanted. Each tiny marble tile cost $30 and my friend said they were all taken out and destroyed. Imagine, each little tile came from Italy and cost $30. Then Saddam went out into the garden and saw a pile of bricks to one side. He asked what this was. The men said the bricks were damaged. Saddam told them: "Be careful. This is the money of the people." As if the bricks were the people's money and the marble was not. We had such duplicity.'

'Did you talk about these things before?' I said.

'There was a sense of sarcasm before. People spoke publicly but not frankly. For example, in matters of love: a man says to his girlfriend, "Do you love me?" and she answers: "Yes, I love you. I love nobody but you and His Excellency." Did you read George Orwell's *1984*? That was the situation in Iraq.'

We talked about his family. He was a Shia from a village in the province of Wasit, south of Baghdad. His village was called Saysabana, the name of an Iraqi tree that opens its leaves with the morning sun and closes them again at dark. His father was a farmer who insisted all his eleven children should go to school. Two were now primary school teachers, others were still at university. One of his brothers was a judge in Ramadi. Ramadi was one of the violent Sunni towns to the west of Baghdad that was still flooded with insurgents. The brother had stayed with Zubaidi in his Baghdad flat the previous night.

'He told me terrible things about Ramadi. He has brought his family out but he still goes,' Zubaidi said.

'Does the court still operate?' I asked.

'He said it hasn't been working for a few weeks: the schools were closed, everything was closed. But tomorrow it's supposed to open again. He likes the life there, the people. He says they are good people but the terrorists are different. The city belongs to the people in the morning and to the terrorists at night.'

'Does he call them terrorists?' I asked.

'No. He calls them mujahideen, because otherwise they would kill him. They don't want to be called terrorists.'

'Now the Americans like to call them Anti-Iraqi forces, even though most of them are Iraqis,' I said.

'Iraqi society is divided into oppressors and the oppressed. The oppressors could not stand losing their authority so they are making the trouble. They cannot be ordinary people living like me and you. For example, if I lose my job at the university I will go and seek other work. That is not the case for those people. They will fight. Already they have shed too much blood.'

I said it sounded like he thought many of the insurgents were Ba'athists. But I thought that the largest element was an Islamic extremist movement that had emerged since the war.

'But also there is a sense of dissatisfaction,' he said. 'Some people cannot stand American tanks loitering here and there. Some people are involved with the insurgents because they have been personally offended. If you kill my brother I take revenge and kill you wherever I find you. And yes, some people find it a religious duty to attack the invaders.'

186

I asked about the Ba'ath. Zubaidi had been in the party; he said he had to join but rarely attended meetings. 'It was a routine job. They said: "If you are not with us you are against us." That was it. I never felt I belonged to it. I am a poet who secretly is in opposition but as a matter of fact being a member saved me from so many troubles,' he said. He was honest about his compromise, able to shrug it off as of no consequence.

Like all young Iraqi men he was also conscripted into the army and he served for a year between 1990 and 1991, during the first Gulf War and the uprising that followed. He was never sent to Kuwait, but stayed in Taji, one of the main military bases north of Baghdad. His camp was bombed by US fighter planes and some of his friends were killed. Then they were sent south to Basra.

'On the way I witnessed the retreat of the Iraqi army. I saw it completely and I lived the experience and nobody told me we were defeated. I saw it myself, the whole scene, the backward procession from Kuwait through the miserable south to our very miserable huts that we call houses.'

I asked about the 1991 uprising. What was it like? He obviously wasn't very sympathetic.

'People unwisely and unsystematically had an insurrection that was doomed to failure from the beginning because it was chaotic, not organised, not well designed, not well led. There was no leadership.'

He described seeing soldiers around him desert, taking off their uniforms, selling their boots, officers peeling off the stars and chevrons of rank from their shoulders.

'There was discontent in the army assisted by discontent in the people and the US let them down. They gave permission to Saddam to fly his helicopters and kill all the rebels. This is why people in Iraq are against the Americans: they don't trust them. They said if they truly desired to help us they should have done it in 1991 when Saddam was about to fall. They needed only assistance from the air. If Saddam had had no helicopters or aircraft things would have been different.'

He briefly left his unit to see his family in their village on the way south. He thought about deserting too, but he was an educated man and the rebels were often not. Besides, he feared his family would suffer. Two of his other brothers were also in the army: one had walked home all the way from Basra, a journey of about 150 miles.

'It was a horrible experience,' he said and he took a sharp intake of breath and stopped for a moment. 'I just didn't want to put my father in a hard situation. Those deserters, you know what happened to them. When I heard that the *intifada* was bombed by Saddam I decided it was over. I joined my military unit again. We went back to Taji.'

Zubaidi heard about some of the deserters who were taken to Harthiya, a military police jail in Baghdad. 'There were so many horrible kinds of torture: hunger, physical torture, they whipped them, they put them in what they called "the corner".' When an officer yelled 'Corner' all the men in the cell had to crowd into the corner, climbing on top of each other so they only occupied a tiny space of floor in the corner of the room, sometimes dozens of men on top of each other. 'It wasn't human,' he said.

'How are these people ever going to reconcile themselves to each other?' I asked.

'I don't believe in reconciliation. They can't leave us alone. Even now they bring suicide cars and destroy our organisations and establishments. They are not ready to be reconciled. And what do you say to the mother whose only child was killed in the *intifada* by Saddam's forces? What do you say to the wife and the children of somebody who was executed? The victim and the victimiser, the prisoner and the jailer, they can never be friends.'

188

13

He Was Our Father

On a Thursday morning in July, Saddam Hussein arrived in chains at a building in the grounds of one of his old palaces in Baghdad, now part of an American military base called Camp Victory. The building, renamed Victory Courthouse, had once been home to the imam responsible for a small, blue-domed mosque next door. Now there were sandbags outside and steel girders on the windows. The walls had been whitewashed and decorated inside with copper and silver trays and paintings of the ancient city of Babylon. A handful of paperbacks in English discarded by American soldiers sat on a shelf.

It was the first time Saddam had appeared in court since his capture seven months earlier and the first time he had been seen in public since television images released by the military showed a soldier swabbing the inside of the former president's mouth with a white plastic spatula. High Value Detainee One, as the prisoner was known to his jailers, was dressed in a new chalk-stripe grey jacket, brown trousers and a clean white shirt that had been bought for him a day or two before. He wore no tie. His hair was dyed dark and since his fall from power he had grown a heavy grey-black beard which had been cut back to a more modest thickness for his appearance today. He was bright-eyed and insistent, in turns pointing his finger, rubbing his forehead, or scribbling on a page of folded legal paper he had pulled out of his jacket pocket. It was the moment so many of his subjects had hungered for and not a few had dreaded:

the dictator supposedly rendered impotent, humiliated and accused before a court of the land. It lasted twenty-six minutes.

The view through the television camera showed only the back of the judge's head and the side of his face. He was too scared to be named or identified. All that was known about him was that he had been a judge in the days of the Saddam regime. He looked young and clean-shaven apart from his dark moustache. He asked the defendant his name.

Defendant: Saddam Hussein, the President of the Republic of Iraq. Saddam Hussein Majid, the President of the Republic of Iraq.

The judge asked his date of birth.

Defendant: 1937.

Judge: Profession? Former President of the Republic of Iraq?

Defendant: No, present. Current. It's the will of the people.

Judge: The head of the Ba'ath Party that is dissolved, defunct. Former Commander-in-Chief of the army.

To the court clerk: Put down 'former' in brackets. Residence is Iraq.

To the Defendant again: Your mother's name?

Defendant: Sobha. May I have a clarification?

Judge: Go ahead, please.

Defendant: You also have to introduce yourself to me.

Judge: Mr Saddam, I am the investigative judge of the Central Court of Iraq.

Defendant: So that I may know, you are an investigative judge of the Central Court of Iraq? What resolution, what law formed this court?

Judge: The coalition forces . . .

Defendant: Oh, the coalition forces? So you are an Iraqi but you are representing the occupying forces?

Judge: No, I'm an Iraqi representing Iraq.

Defendant: But you are . . .

Judge: I was appointed by a presidential decree under the former regime.

Defendant: So you are reiterating that every Iraqi should respect the Iraqi law. So the law that was instituted before represents the will of the people, right?

Judge: Yes, God willing.

Defendant: So you should not work under the jurisdiction of the coalition forces.

Judge: This is an important point. I am a judge. In the former regime I respected the judges. And I am resuming and continuing my work. You, as any other citizen, you have to answer to any accusation or charge.

Defendant: That's true.

Judge: This is an arraignment, a charge . . . If there's evidence, you'll be convicted. If there's no evidence, you will not. Until now, you're accused before the judicial system. So according to . . .

Defendant: So, please let me – I'm not complicating matters. Are you a judge? You are a judge. And judges, they value the law. And they rule by law, right? Right? Right is a relative issue. For us, right is our heritage in the Qur'an and sharia, right? I am not talking about Saddam Hussein, whether he was a citizen or in other capacities. I'm not holding fast to my position, but to respect the will of the people that decided to choose Saddam Hussein as the leader of the revolution. Therefore, when I say 'President of the Republic of Iraq' it's not a formality or holding fast to a position, but rather to reiterate to the Iraqi people that I respect their will. This is one. Number two; you summoned me to levy charges . . .

Judge: No, I . . .

Defendant: You call it crimes.

Judge: If there is evidence, then I'll defer it to a court of jurisdiction.

Defendant: Let me understand something. Who is the defendant . . . ?

The hearing continued like this for several minutes, Saddam weaving the judge ever tighter into a thicket of legal argument. He was not a subdued, humiliated man ready to be mocked by the world, but hectoring and surprisingly agile of mind. For most of the hearing the judge looked his junior: lost and incapable, even unwilling, to rein in his defendant. From the start Saddam had latched onto the illogicality of the moment and it seemed to have struck the judge four-square in the face. He was a judge appointed when the defendant was his president. He had sworn to uphold the dictator's legal system, a legal system that was in large part still valid. Now here was the judge, still a relatively young man, trying to begin legal proceedings that could result in the execution of his president. Who was he to challenge the leader of the revolution, the man all Iraq's children had been taught to obey unfailingly? From the moment Saddam reasserted that hierarchy, the judge was always going to have to take second place to the defendant before him.

But just as Saddam showed his power, he let slip too his delusions. He continually spoke of the will of his people, as if they were just outside the door in their millions, cheering for him. It was as if he had been elected and returned to his throne on a wave of popular support. Perhaps he truly believed it had happened this way. Perhaps he believed that the internal coup within the party that he manufactured in 1979 when he took over the presidency hadn't happened, nor that moment shortly afterwards when he had had dozens of potential rivals executed before him. Perhaps the only way he could ever justify to himself his years of brutality and tyranny was to convince even himself that the revolution, led from the top and unceasingly brutal, was indeed an immutable expression of the people's

192

will, ever eternal. The wonder of propaganda is that, after a while, it convinces even the propagandists.

After some time the judge picked up a single sheet of paper and read from it the outlines of the seven charges that were now to be investigated. They ranged from the general – the killing of political leaders and the killing of religious leaders over the past thirty years – to the specific: the chemical weapons attack on the Kurdish village of Halabja in 1988; the Anfal campaign against the Kurds around the same time; the killing of the Barzanis, the family of a leading Kurdish politician; the repression of the 1991 *intifada*; and lastly the invasion of Kuwait in August 1990. Saddam asked to speak with his lawyers. The judge asked him to sign a document acknowledging what he had been told in court that day and the hearing continued:

Defendant: OK. Let me sign. But you levied charges in my capacity as President of the republic, so don't strip me of that title. The talk about Halabja, I used to hear about that on the radio, attacking Halabja under the regime of Saddam Hussein . . .

Judge: These are only the legal matters, and you have the right not to answer until a lawyer is present.

Defendant: . . . You have to hear me out. And the occupation of Kuwait, charge number seven. It's unfortunate that this is coming from an Iraqi. You are Iraqi and everyone knows Kuwait is part of Iraq. How can there be charges about something that is already ours? In Kuwait I was protecting the Iraqi people from those Kuwaiti dogs who wanted to turn Iraqi women into 10-dinar prostitutes . . . Everyone knows this is theatre by Bush the criminal in an attempt to win the election.

Judge: Don't use foul language and attack. This is a legal session.

Defendant: Yes, I bear responsibility for everything.

Judge: Anything obscene or outside of the norms of a legal session is not accepted.

Defendant: Then forgive me.

They argued the law again for several minutes. Then the judge, now desperate to bring the hearing to an end, asked again if Saddam would sign the document:

Defendant: No, I will sign when the lawyers are present.

Judge: Then you can leave.

Defendant: Finished?

Judge: Yes.

Defendant (to the guards who approach to lead him back to jail): Take it easy, I'm an old man.

The only way I could make sense of what had just happened was to speak again to those Saddam had wronged, so I drove back down to Hilla to find Ali Abid Hassan, the man who had crawled out alive from the mass graves in 1991. I had made an appointment and I sat waiting for him on a sofa in a large office at the Human Rights Association. He walked in with a black plastic shopping bag in one hand and leading his daughter Rania, now three and a half, with the other. She was dressed in a pink shirt and blue jeans and sat quietly next to her father as he spoke to me. From the plastic bag Hassan pulled out a rolled up X-ray of his right leg. You could see the bullet lodged in his upper thigh clearly on the X-ray: a short, sharp and neat white point at an angle in the dark shadow of his leg tissue. It looked quite ineffectual just sitting there deep inside his leg, though it still caused him pain.

When I had met Hassan the previous year, he had talked about his anger at the Ba'athists and the importance of justice and accountability if a new nation was to be built. He had cried when he told me his story but he had also spoken with purpose, with a vision of how the future might look. Now, a year later, he looked a different man. He was listless and sat with his shoulders hunched. He still wanted justice and accountability

194

but now realised they were out of his reach. 'I put my head on my pillow at night wishing that the next day I will see my children and myself alive and safe,' he said.

For the past year he had found no new work and so he still earned money by driving a taxi, an old 1980s Volkswagen Passat, in Hilla. That brought in just enough to pay rent of 55,000 dinars (£20) a month for his small house. The house was near the police headquarters in Hilla and was owned by a former Ba'athist who had been not a low-ranking member but an 'Udw Firqah, a group member, one of the top four positions in the party. This Ba'athist was the manager of the Mahawil brick factory, which was very close to the site of the mass grave where Hassan was nearly executed in 1991.

'I told many political parties in Hilla about him but nobody takes any action,' Hassan said, choking on his words. 'A representative from one party told me: "We are tired of all these things. I know three people who were members of the execution committees." I told him: "If you really know three of these people and you don't take any action that means the same regime will remain in place."'

He said many other former Ba'athists from Hilla were either still employed or had found powerful jobs for their cousins and nephews in the new local administration or in Baghdad. Every time he went to a government office asking for work he would produce the X-ray and a new identity card from the Human Rights Association and explain how he had been a victim of the former regime. Then the officials would politely tell him they could not help, that he was not the only victim. 'Please leave. We all suffered under Saddam's regime,' they would say.

He was indebted to the Americans and the British, he said, for toppling Saddam's regime, but the government that had replaced it reeked of injustice. In the past year his hopes had been briefly raised after he met a handful of aid workers from

195

American organisations who suggested they might be able to take him and his family abroad to live. In particular he met several times with Fern Holland, a thirty-three-year-old American lawyer from Oklahoma who worked on human rights at the Hilla office of the US Coalition Provisional Authority – the occupying power. She had arrived in Iraq a couple of months after the war, to work with the American administration on human rights and women's rights. She had set up a women's rights centre in Hilla and was heavily involved in drafting the first interim Iraqi constitution. She seemed to have offered Hassan the very real possibility of a new life outside Iraq, the ultimate recompense for what he had suffered. He travelled up to Baghdad a couple of times for formal interviews in which he explained in detail his case and gave evidence of what had happened to him in 1991. Then one evening in March 2004 Holland was killed. As she was being driven into Hilla, gunmen opened fire on her convoy killing her, a second American in the car and her Iraqi assistant. Later it was suggested the gunmen were either Iraqi policemen, or dressed as policemen.

'After she died I lost hope,' Hassan said. 'I don't want to live in such a miserable country.'

We talked about the Ba'athists and Hassan said he had thought about finding an investigator and giving information against some of the Ba'athists he knew or suspected had been involved in the graves and other crimes under the old regime. It wasn't that he was advocating their murder; just that he wanted them punished.

'What did you think when you saw Saddam in court?' I asked.

'I could not bear it when I saw Saddam Hussein in such a miserable condition and in a dock facing a trial,' Hassan said. 'He should not be humiliated. After all, he was our president. He was our father.'

'But shouldn't he be punished for what he has done?' I said.

'He deserves the ultimate punishment.'

'You mean death?'

'Yes, death. He executed many of us.'

It was one of the most difficult answers I heard in my time in Iraq. Difficult because here, in stark outline, was what it meant for an Iraqi to see Saddam first captured and swabbed in the mouth like a common prisoner and then in court sitting as a defendant before an Iraqi judge: Saddam, leader of the party, Commander-in-Chief and President for twenty-four years, now on trial for his life. It captured in a few plain words how a man like Hassan who had been shot at one of Saddam's mass graves, who crawled away badly injured but alive, who was arrested and re-arrested countless times in the years that followed and who had lost his own brother in the same graves, might actually feel pity for this reviled dictator. He might actually feel shame for his president's humiliation.

Officials from Iraq's new Human Rights Ministry had visited Hassan asking if he would be ready to appear as a witness in Saddam's trial. It sounded like a chance to take part in the reckoning Hassan had spoken of a year earlier and yet he was reluctant. He was worried first for his safety and for that of his family. He had been promised official protection but, perhaps wisely, he didn't trust the offer. But there was also a reluctance to act against his own president, to play a role in his final downfall.

Despite the fact that the leader of the revolution was on trial in Baghdad, few of his subordinates had been brought to court. It called for a certain confidence in the health of the nation to start arresting and jailing men who, only a few months previously, had been the most powerful in the country, and there was little such confidence in the new Iraq. But in Hilla, more than anywhere else, the crimes that lay buried in the graves had lodged themselves in the soul of the town. So it was in Hilla that the judges and the lawyers tried to dislodge the horror by going to court. It was rushed and confused, compromised and frustrating and it did nothing to ease the pain.

The courthouse in Hilla was a chaotic, noisy place. Outside in the street sat a row of petition writers, often elderly bespectacled men with small tables and typewriters who would write up legal documents and hand out rudimentary advice for the illiterate and the newly litigious. Inside the courtyard were the remains of a crashed four-wheel drive, with bullet holes clearly visible in the doors. An appeal court judge had been shot at as he drove from Baghdad to Hilla a month earlier. He had escaped alive but his driver and police guard had been killed and, for want of anywhere else to put it, the damaged car had been parked here. There was a large crowd in the courtyard, lawyers and their clients, smoking, arguing, pushing and queuing and no one spared the car a second glance.

Inside, one of the prosecutors led me into a courtroom and I sat on a wooden bench so narrow that it forced you to sit uncomfortably upright. There were lawyers next to me, and others who may have been relatives of the victims or the defendants, it was hard to say. There were only three rows of public benches and in front of them a small wooden fence, with a gate. Beyond that sat a clerk at a table, and above him rose a high wooden desk at which the three judges sat. There was no jury. Hanging from the high ceiling were two ineffectual fans twisting slowly in the cloying air. The defendant was brought in and made to stand in a dock to our right. He was in his late forties, tall and neatly turned out, his hair recently trimmed, and he was wearing a smart, grey dishdasha. He didn't look particularly anxious. His name was Jasim Mohammad Hamza.

The judges came in and, without any announcement, one of the three began to read from a handwritten paper in front of him. Because he mumbled and because the tall ceiling carried only the noise of the fans, everyone had to strain forward to hear him. This was case 108/J/2004, he said, and he outlined precisely what it involved. Hamza had been a school physics teacher in Hilla and a Ba'athist, though not from one of the top ranks. A case had been brought against him by a family who insisted that he and a group of armed men had called at their house in the village of al-Husayn, in the farmland just south of Hilla, in March 1991 at the height of the *intifada*. There, they alleged, he had arrested the head of the family, an elderly farmer called Aziz Khadum Hussein, and taken him off to the local Ba'ath Party office. Hussein had never been seen again. According to the judge's statement, his family had found the old man's body when the mass graves of Hilla were dug up the previous year. Not long after that the police had arrested Hamza and charged him with murder though, since it was difficult to prove he had been directly involved in the farmer's killing, the charge was later reduced to unlawful arrest. Witnesses from the family and neighbours in the village had testified that Hamza had indeed shown up at the house that month and led off the farmer. The judge concluded that Hamza had made an unlawful arrest, the charge was proved. It sounded straightforward and fitted a pattern of stories from dozens of families who had lost relatives at that time.

But then the judge noted that an amnesty for all criminals had been introduced by Saddam in October 2002, in the final months before the war. Although the regime was gone, the judge said the amnesty was still technically in force and that meant that there was no way they could convict Hamza.

'All legal procedures should be frozen in favour of the defendant and it is considered that the case is ended,' the judge told the court. A few seconds later he was on to the next case and Hamza was being led out of the court and into the crowded hall outside where his friends were waiting. He seemed not the least surprised and they patted him on the back and shook his hand. Congratulations, they said. It was the second acquittal on this kind of charge that he had enjoyed that year.

I walked out of the courtroom and found Hamza. He was obviously delighted with himself and talked about how pleased he was that these allegations were proved to be false, although that was not exactly what the judge had said. He had already spent eight months and nine days in jail and now he wanted to go home. Perhaps he could even go back to his old job as a schoolteacher. He wasn't in Hilla during the *intifada* of 1991, he said. In fact he had witnesses who could attest that he had been serving in the military in Samawah, another town in the south. And don't misunderstand what the *intifada* was all about, he said. Don't go thinking it had a political cause or that it was just. It was simply looting and fighting against the Iraqi state. These people were robbers, he said. Of course people were arrested, they had broken the law. But no, he couldn't say what had happened to people after they were arrested. He had heard about the graves but no, he said, he didn't know anything about them.

'Are you afraid?' I asked.

'No, why should anyone try to take their revenge against me? I am innocent. I have nothing to do with this. They only brought this case because they knew I was in the Ba'ath.'

I left him and went back to the prosecutors looking for an explanation. The prosecutors said they had to balance the hunger for revenge with the need to demonstrate the impartiality of the court. Their hands were tied by Saddam, they said. On 20 October 2002, Saddam had issued Revolutionary Command Council decree 225, a broad amnesty which opened the doors of the jails to most of the country's criminals. Many were set free, though there were few political prisoners among those released. For years after the decision there was a great debate about the amnesty. Some said it was a sop offered by a desperate man to secure the loyalty of his population with war fast approaching; others, particularly the American generals who were later deployed in Iraq, insisted it was a premeditated attempt to fill the ranks of an insurgency that Saddam hoped would rise up if his regime fell. Whatever Saddam intended, he was again casting his long shadow over the new Iraq. His amnesty was tying the hands of the prosecutors in the new government. The prosecutors insisted that Paul Bremer, the American civil administrator, had expressly ruled that the amnesty still stood, although I could find no evidence of this in any of Bremer's orders. According to the understanding of these prosecutors, the only suspects who were not covered by the amnesty and who could face conviction were those in the top four ranks of the Ba'ath or from any of the ministries, militias or security agencies dissolved by the Americans.

'I'll admit that we are in a situation that I could say is disgusting,' said Khadum al-Taie, the chief prosecutor in Hilla. 'But our job requires us to observe cases from both sides objectively, legally and precisely and to show the legitimacy of a court that is respecting and achieving justice.'

But the more they talked about it, the more it became clear that relying on the amnesty wasn't entirely correct. It was merely a convenient way to deal with the problems of poor evidence and malicious prosecutions. In all the thousands of witness accounts, there were very few who had actually seen the killings and fewer still who could identify those directly involved in the murders. The few who were identified had long since fled. Only the less important grey men were left. I met another prosecutor who acknowledged that the court did not want to unleash a flood of vengeful cases.

'Many people use these cases to get money,' said Mohanad

Fadhel al-Duleimi, the second prosecutor. 'After so many years you can't find good evidence. So what is the solution? It is to say that these people are covered under the amnesty of Saddam. And when we have perfect evidence against the worst criminals, then we prosecute.'

Occasionally senior Ba'athists had been jailed, but these cases were not on a grand scale. I read files about one Ba'athist who had faced the same charge of unlawful arrest. The court heard he too detained a man after the 1991 *intifada,* whose body was later found in the mass grave. However, this time the accused belonged to the National Security Directorate, the Amn al-'Am, and therefore he was not covered by the amnesty. Even so, although he was convicted, he was sentenced to only one year in jail. The family of his victim were incensed.

I left the court building and crossed the road to a shaded but open-air coffee shop. There I talked to Zaidan Hantoosh, who was the lawyer representing the family in the case they had just lost against the Ba'athist teacher Hamza. Hantoosh was a showman and introduced himself, not only as a lawyer, but a victim of Saddam and a leader of the 1991 *intifada*, the uprising that I thought had had no leadership. He was arrested during the *intifada*, escaped from prison, hid in a camp in Saudi Arabia, returned to Iraq, was arrested again, was tortured and eventually released. Now he wasn't interested in forgiveness or judicial balance. He wanted revenge. 'These insects should be taken away to jail or executed. The crimes committed by these Ba'athists would make a human skull sweat,' he said.

We followed Hantoosh outside to his vast, blue Buick Roadmaster. His wife, also a lawyer and wearing a headscarf, sat in the front seat. Hantoosh pulled a Makarov pistol from his pocket and stowed it under the armrest between them. He had stolen the gun, he said proudly, from an Iraqi army

202

colonel during the war. He drove us south out of the town of Hilla and into the village of al-Husayn to meet the family he represented.

The road wound through small villages and past groves of palm trees. But the landscape was odd. On either side, between the road and the trees, ran a 200-metre-wide belt of blackened palm stumps. After the *intifada*, the regime had ordered that palms be cut back in from the road, partly to prevent ambushes and partly as an act of retribution against the rebels, many of whom had been poor farmers.

The family's house was next to a small store which held boxes of white and black grapes, a set of weighing scales and, on one wall, a picture of the Imam Hussain, the grandson of the Prophet Mohammad and the great martyr of the Shia faith. There were portraits like this of Hussain and his father Ali in homes, shops and mosques across the Shia south.

We sat on carpets in the family's front room, picking from a bowl of grapes. A thick curtain closed us off from the rest of the home. Pictures of the family dead hung on the wall, among them Aziz Khadum Hussein, the seventy-six-year-old farmer whom they said the Ba'athist Hamza had arrested back in March 1991. His sons still lived in the house and readily admitted they had taken part in the uprising, attacking the national security and intelligence offices in town. They described how they and their father had hidden in the palm groves behind the house as the Ba'athists hunted down the rebels. Their mother would slip out after dark to take them food and to warn them that Hamza had called at the house many times asking where they were hiding. In desperation the boys prepared to walk south to Safwan, the town on the Kuwaiti border where they knew there was a large British and American military camp and where they had heard refugees from the *intifada* would find protection. But before they could go, Hamza arrived at the house with a group of armed men. Hamza searched among the palm trees and found the boys' father.

The sons escaped with hundreds of others through the desert to the west and across into Saudi Arabia. Many months after the war they came back home, but still their father had not returned. It was hard to look for him when the regime was still in place and had its eye on the former rebels, but after Saddam fell they scoured the graves and the prison cemeteries looking for a trace of his body. They never found him, although there was no doubt by now that he had been executed. In order to bring a case against Hamza, they had to present a death certificate for their dead father and for that they needed his body. In the end, because they could not find his corpse, they bribed an official to give them a death certificate and brought the case. The family had also lost a young cousin, Dinar Jabbar, who was arrested and executed and whose body they did find in the graves. In total, thirty-six people from the village went missing in March 1991, including two men from the house next door. Most of the other families also blamed Hamza for the disappearances. He had taught in the village school, his house was just down the road. In a few days he would be back here, living among them again. The sons were furious and began to talk of revenge.

14

Re-education

A year or so after the war, it became clear to the American administration in Baghdad that their campaign to 'extirpate' the Ba'ath from Iraqi society, or to 'put a stake through its heart' as the official had described it, was far too severe and was simply playing into the hands of the insurgency. They began, instead, to talk about 'reforming' the de-Ba'athification laws, and 'revisions to the implementation process'. In effect it was a broad reversal of policy. Now senior Iraqi military officers could return to the army, and the blanket ban on senior party members returning to work as teachers or other government officials would be lifted. When, in June 2004, the handover of power brought Ayad Allawi into government as Prime Minister, the issue was revisited again. He had been a Ba'athist in his youth and over the years in opposition he had brought many defecting Iraqi army officers to his side, men who believed in the Ba'ath but believed too that Saddam had poisoned their party. As Prime Minister, he insisted de-Ba'athification should be relaxed further and talked of an amnesty for some of the insurgency. The De-Ba'athification Commission, run by Mithal al-Alusi, the former prisoner from Germany whom I had met at the start of that year, was still operating. But now it was ordered to change tack. No longer was it charged with wiping out the Ba'ath; instead, its task was to determine how much of the party could now be forgiven. Given the fact that the insurgency was burgeoning you could understand, even applaud, the relaxation of the de-Ba'athification agenda but at the same time it left Alusi and his deputies in the commission in unscripted territory.

Alusi's commission exercised great power and saw no danger in that. They decided to begin running courses for Ba'athists to prepare them for a return to work in the new Iraq. Re-education, they called it, and it was fraught with difficulties. In the end there was only ever one re-education course, a series of eight lectures over a month for around a hundred middle-aged men and women who had been senior Ba'athists, mostly teachers, and who wanted to go back to work. They were a reluctant audience but they had been told that if they sat through the course and signed papers renouncing their party, they would receive a letter of recommendation that would greatly increase their chance of going back to work.

On the days that I attended, the course was led by Abdul Karim al-Khafaji, an exile who had been jailed in Germany along with Alusi for attacking the Iraqi embassy. He had only returned to Iraq a few months earlier. He began with a register, going through the list of names on the paper in front of him and ticking off all those who attended. Any who skipped a class lost their chance of a recommendation letter.

'We ask you to put your hands with our hands,' he told the audience in a lecture theatre in the sports department at Baghdad University. 'We are not here to fight you or cut off your source of income. Our purpose is to build Iraq by co-operation between every single Iraqi who wants to help. You are people who work in education, we cannot just dismiss you.'

This went down well and several people in the crowd were nodding silently in assent. Then Kafaji introduced a colleague who would be delivering today's lecture which was, he said, about 'rewriting history'.

The lecturer, Yassin Khudair, stood up and looked up at his

audience. He was bearded and wore a plain blue shirt. 'We have to write a clean account of our history,' he announced. 'What happened before is that the former regime fabricated history. They marginalised the truth. The reality is that there were a lot of mistakes committed in our past, especially in the last decades.'

He said that the party had distorted the country's history to further their own ambitions, claiming, for example, that the monarchy was a mere agent of the colonial powers. Saddam, he said, had even re-written his own family tree to try and prove he was descended from the Prophet's son-in-law and leader of the Shia faith, the Imam Ali. He talked about the regime's misleading accounts of its attacks on the Kurds, the war with Iran, the repression of the Shia and the invasion of Kuwait.

The audience listened quietly until he came to the coup of 1941, an event the former regime had described as a 'revolution' and a proud moment of Arab nationalism in an Iraq slowly breaking free from colonial and monarchical rule. That interpretation of the coup was quite wrong, the lecturer said. 'In fact, its leaders were Nazis.'

Everyone took a sharp breath.

'This is the first time I have heard these people were Nazis,' one man shouted. 'My father died believing the 1941 revolution was led by nationalists. Is this not right?'

'This is a problem. I know you don't agree with this but if you look in the history books or go to Europe you will find the real facts,' Khafaji said from the front.

The men from the commission didn't have any history books to hand and when I checked later I found that even modern historians seem to disagree on the extent of the involvement of the Nazis in the 1941 coup. It was true that its leader, Rashid Ali al-Gailani, had seized upon the divisions in Europe as an opportunity to squeeze out British influence in Baghdad, but how far he was allied to the Nazis was debatable.

In 1940 Gailani was Prime Minister. Although not expressly pro-Nazi, he had rallied a tide of anti-British sentiment to his nationalist cause and in doing so fell out with the British-backed regent, 'Abd al-Illah. In January 1941 the regent told Gailani he had to resign. Gailani did quit but on 1 April he and the acting chief of the army led a coup against the regent, forcing him to flee the country. It was the first time a coup in Iraq had been directed specifically against the monarchy, rather than against a rival prime minister. Gailani suggested deposing the regent and replacing him with his more amenable cousin, and parliament agreed unanimously. But the new regime was short-lived. Britain refused to recognise Gailani's government and in early May sent troops to force him from Baghdad. Gailani asked Germany for help and though Germany and Italy sent some small arms and warplanes to Mosul in the north it was too little too late. By the end of May, Gailani's government had collapsed and he had fled abroad, not to return to Iraq until the monarchy finally fell in 1958. Some of his time he spent in exile in Nazi Germany. Some historians have since emphasised Gailani's connection with the Nazis during the coup, others suggest he was actually trying to carve a neutral path between the British and the Axis powers.[32] His was a disputed legacy and a tricky place to begin a 're-education' programme.

'How can you describe nationalism as Nazism? How can you prove it to us?' shouted a second man from the audience. 'You are criticising the former regime for rewriting history but you are doing the same. I hope you are not being too hasty.'

'I insist,' said the lecturer Khudair. 'These people had tangible links with the Nazis. Their ideology was a Nazi ideology. These are the facts.'

'We have an ideology and you have an ideology. I respect

your point of view but we have two different opinions,' said the man in the audience.

'No, these people had tangible links with the Nazis,' said the lecturer.

'Where is your evidence?' asked the man in the audience.

'Their ideology was the Nazi ideology.'

'I need some evidence. I want to read it for myself.'

'These are facts.'

'No. I can't accept them as facts. Show it to me in a book.' But the lecturer had no book and his audience was unconvinced.

What had begun with promises of co-operation and togetherness had degenerated quickly into a dogmatic dispute. The men from the commission did not seek to persuade, but to command and so proved themselves little different from the Ba'ath that had gone before them.

After the class I introduced myself to the man who had argued so much about the 1941 coup. He was tall, with a heavy grey moustache and his name was Muthanna Ibrahim. He was sixty-one and said he had been a member of the party for forty years. He had joined as a young student and then spent his life as a teacher, a small cog in the Ba'ath system. In the final years before the war he moved to the Education Ministry where he worked as an adviser. Immediately after the war he went back to work, expecting to pick up where he had left off. After ten days he was dismissed and had not been offered work since.

'I find this very difficult,' he said. 'The Ba'ath Party represented a national ideology: Arab unity, freedom, socialism. It was what the Arabs stood for. It was quite clear. But this course is an attack, an ideological attack. They want to remove from our memory what we believed in for more than forty years in a course of just eight lectures. They are just talking about the negative points of the former regime, but you know in the end there was a difference between the regime and the Ba'ath Party.

The faults were with the regime, not with the party. The invasion of Kuwait, it was the regime's fault. The Americans came to war with our country to topple our regime, to topple a national regime. They don't want the Ba'ath, but this is also why we believe in the Ba'ath. I believe in Arab unity. It is our ideology. It runs in our blood.'

I asked what future he saw for his country.

'For now it is vague, it is very unclear. If we want stability, the American forces should leave. The Iraqis can live together, it just depends how you make it work. In Iraq there were millions of Ba'athists. Were we all wrong?'

Around the time that the re-education classes began, Mithal al-Alusi was sacked from the De-Ba'athification Commission. He had travelled to Israel, using his German passport, to take part in a conference about combating terrorism. He had spoken publicly in praise of the American invasion of his country and said how important he thought it was for Iraq to open diplomatic relations with Israel. It caused a small storm in Baghdad. Iraqi politicians simply didn't travel to Israel. It was illegal in Saddam's Iraq and regarded as an extremely high-risk adventure after the war. The government in Baghdad was incensed and issued an arrest warrant for Alusi demanding he be jailed or deported. He had visited an 'enemy state'. In the end he was sacked from his job, kicked out of his political party – the Iraqi National Congress led by Ahmad Chalabi – and lost his official team of bodyguards. He now lived in his rather ordinary house in Baghdad and worked from an office in a second, newly rented house in a district of the city called Yarmuk. He was plotting his comeback as the head of a new political party.

The offices were low-key, with surprisingly little security. A large generator sat on a trailer in the garden next to a row of fuel barrels. In the reception inside there was a line of yellow plastic chairs against the wall, a solitary guard smoking and a

210

television switched to the news in the corner: there had been another car bomb that morning, near a police station in Baghdad. Alusi came in carrying an expensive leather briefcase and several packets of cigarettes. He looked tired. His dark silver hair was thick and his face was puffed out with two deep lines running down through his cheeks either side of his mouth. One of his sons, Jamal, came in briefly and brought him some papers.

Alusi began to speak but he was so angry that his line of argument was difficult to follow. He was infuriated with the religious Shia parties, who looked most likely to dominate the first elections, which were planned for January 2005. He seemed to accuse them of recruiting into their ranks large numbers of former Ba'athists who made a show of repenting their support for the party. I said I thought it most unlikely: most of the people in these parties seemed to be those who had been in exile during the Saddam years or had been persecuted by the Ba'ath. He said no, that there were now many ex-Ba'athists filling their ranks. Then he said the Sunni parties wanted to give up on de-Ba'athification completely and just allow the Ba'athists to take up their places in society once more. It was the only chance the Sunnis had for the future, he said. Everywhere he looked he saw the complex issues surrounding the Ba'ath disappearing for the sake of political exigency. The legacy of the party was being forgotten too quickly, as if the past thirty years hadn't taken place or hadn't really been that bad. What had happened to the original idea to exclude the most senior Ba'athists from public life? It was being diluted, he said, and it scared him. Criminals from the most senior ranks of the party were going back to work.

I said the time was coming when the Iraqi government would have to start talking with the insurgents, as the British had done with the IRA. Alusi said it was unthinkable.

211

'Here there is no way to have a political dialogue,' he said. 'Here you are dealing with killers, people who have killed women, children, the elderly. The solution here is that we have the law and we should give no chance to the killers, no repentance, no reduction in sentences. If you start a dialogue that means accepting that some of their points are right.'

I asked him why he travelled to Israel and he explained about the anti-terrorism conference and how important it was to acknowledge that Iraq was now the 'centre of terrorism in the Middle East'.

'Iraq and Israel are two very parallel nations,' he said.

This was an extraordinary statement from an Iraqi. You couldn't possibly underestimate the bitterness against Israel that seeped through this country. Many believed that the Israeli intelligence service, Mossad, was somehow responsible for the September 11 attacks; that it was Israel that had pushed America to invade Iraq; that even now there were hundreds of Mossad spies crawling through Baghdad conspiring in the country's downfall; and that Israel coveted all the land between the Nile and the Euphrates, meaning most of Iraq. Alusi couldn't fail to understand quite how far he had stepped beyond the Iraqi consciousness.

'In this country, people who say they are with Israel are treated as if they are crazy,' said Alusi. 'I know people will try to kill me for this but I don't agree with our approach. I think you have to open the door, to break psychological taboos.'

His new party – the Democratic Party of the Iraqi Nation – didn't have a specific programme, other than generally trying to follow his vociferously anti-Ba'athist approach. Of course, every other political party was just as short on policy, so Alusi wasn't alone when he talked in generalities of a political programme that would 'polish the Iraqi character' and 'try to find policies that will put our people in a safe position'. How

212

could anyone not want to see Iraq polished and made safe?

At times Alusi sounded inflexible, talking about the importance of 'fighting terrorism' and 'not negotiating with killers' and painting a future shaped by a worldwide battle against fundamentalists demanding an Islamic revolution. At other times, though, he sounded like one of the few people in the country who appreciated how to reckon with the past. Alusi was correct that many of those who had committed atrocities were slipping through the judicial net and, whatever you thought was the answer to the insurgency, the evasion of justice on such a large scale was hard to excuse. But then, given the enormity of the problems the new Iraqi government had to face, perhaps it was understandable that the past should cede to the present.

I had kept in touch with Hajim Hassani, the man I had met in April when he was negotiating with the insurgents in Falluja. I saw him again in mid-May, an hour or two after the president of the Governing Council had been assassinated in a huge suicide car bomb. I found Hassani remarkably relaxed considering he had narrowly missed being caught in the same bombing. He had been stuck in the same traffic queue as the council president, Izzedine Salim, and was just a few minutes behind him when the bomb went off. It was the same road he used every morning and you could see why the bomber had chosen it. The road led to one of the main gates into the Green Zone and was used by most of the members of the Governing Council. With their large four-wheel drives and the cluster of security guards around them, they stood out as an inevitable target as they waited patiently in line while the cars ahead of them were slowly searched at the checkpoint. At the hospital one of Salim's drivers told me that as they were queuing he saw a Volkswagen Passat car cut straight into the line of traffic and detonate just in front of the politician's olive-green Toyota Land

Cruiser. Salim was tossed onto the road by the force of the blast and he was still gasping for life as he was brought into the hospital. A few minutes later he died. Salim's nephew, two of his bodyguards and another of his drivers were also killed. I didn't need Hassani to tell me what was rapidly becoming obvious to us all: that senior Iraqis working in the government were now open targets for the insurgency and that the violence was only going to get worse as the handover of power at the end of June approached. He was worried that in the face of an unrelenting security crisis, the Americans would be reluctant to cede any more power to the Iraqis. Now there was talk that the first elections might have to be delayed because the violence was so bad. This, he said, really scared him. The longer the authorities in Baghdad remained exclusive, not inclusive, the worse life would get. 'As long as you try to exclude people there will be violence,' he said. As far as the Sunni community went, almost all their political representatives were now being excluded, except for Hassani's Iraqi Islamic Party. The Sunnis' sense of injustice only grew as the months went by.

It had been a mistake, Hassani now accepted, to have appointed the Governing Council in the first place. They should have been elected in some way at the very beginning. The council should have included groups or parties with real support among the Iraqis to balance the domination of the exiles, he said. And where were the parties founded on policies, not on sectarian divides? There were none. The council was torn by the same confessional rifts that became so entrenched in the Balkans and in Lebanon. Positions were given out not on the basis of merit, but in accordance with formulas intended to balance rival ethnic or religious groups. It was hardly a solid foundation. 'I don't want that kind of Iraq,' said Hassani. 'I don't want to be involved in the kind of Iraq that is divided in the way it was in the past.'

When the handover took place in June, Hassani was rewarded with a post in the new government, becoming Minister for Industry. A few weeks later I went to see him in his new office. The ministry, like others in Baghdad, had been comprehensively looted after the war. There were workmen still on the site trying to repair the damage: in some parts of the building the first few floors had been completely burnt out. You could see the black scorch marks curling up through the window frames onto the outside wall. The building was of a peculiar design: heavy and with few windows. Beams of concrete jutted out in a regular pattern along the sidewalls. It wasn't a handsome building, but heavy and monumental in that grey Soviet style. There was a large garden spread out beneath it, but it hadn't been tended for many months. One part of the building had been cleared. There was a large waiting room downstairs, where guests had to leave their pistols and their mobile phones, and on the first floor a narrow strip of red carpet led to the one corridor where the minister and his aides worked. It was sterile and quiet: new doors, new brass handles, few visitors. In Hassani's office the television set was switched to al-Jazeera, the volume off. There were new shelves but no books and a plastic flower display on the table in front of us in garish purples and pinks. The curtains were gold and from the floor above came the whining of a drill so loud that at times we could barely hold a proper conversation. A large Iraqi flag hung loosely on the wall behind his desk. That morning a mortar had landed inside the grounds of the ministry, though it hadn't hit the building and had done little damage. 'Security is always a problem,' Hassani said.

Even though he had his government position he still wasn't entirely happy. There had been protracted talks about how the ministries would be divided up and he admitted he had hoped for a security ministry, perhaps Defence or Interior: something

215

that wielded real power. The Ministry of Industry wasn't particularly glamorous and he hinted carefully that he was disappointed. But the job was still a colossal challenge. The Iraqi government owned fifty-nine large, industrial companies and most were hugely inefficient and over-staffed. They were now his responsibility. Hassani reckoned of the 150,000 staff employed at these companies only half were needed. But he could hardly institute a regime of redundancies when the security situation was so precarious. It was widely acknowledged that demobilising the army the previous year, thereby sacking hundreds of thousands of soldiers, had only added fuel to the insurgency. Now there were thousands of people dismissed from their government jobs during the Saddam years who also wanted to come back to work. The talk of a quick reconstruction of Iraq looked ever more far-fetched.

In the early days after the war there had been pressure from some among the Americans to push ahead with a massive privatisation programme. An investment law was introduced allowing foreign firms the right to full ownership of Iraqi companies, save in the oil, gas and mineral industries. Corporate tax was set at just 15 per cent and there was no restriction on how much of their profit they could repatriate. Iraq was to be wide open to foreign buyers, far wider of course than in the days of Saddam, but also far wider than most developing countries. Many were anxious about this, including Hassani. Through his time with the Governing Council he had heard the Americans proposing their privatisation initiatives and he was reluctant.

'We thought it would be rushing things and I think ordinary Iraqis would not accept that,' he said. 'I believe in a market economy but where we differ is how to achieve it. It is going to take some time and you have to improve the quality of the factories and you have to get the private sector ready to compete.'

In the end, questions about privatisation were postponed until after the elections. Iraq was no longer an easy goldmine for foreign investors. So in the meantime Hassani thought he should encourage foreigners to invest in the upgrading of state industries rather than selling them off outright. In the year before he took the job, the Industry Ministry had received only $66 million to rebuild state-owned factories. He estimated it would cost at least $500 million. He hoped to lease out a handful of industrial plants to foreign firms for periods of up to twenty years. Contracts would have to stipulate that employees could not be sacked, he said. Not every industry was in a slump. Some, like petrochemicals, steel and cement, did make a profit and could perhaps be leased out. But then there was the question of security. Hassani had struggled to find anyone prepared to take the risk of investing in Iraq. 'There are many firms who want to come but the security situation is making people hesitate. I told them the courageous ones will win,' he said. He talked like a good salesman but Iraq was a hard sell.

After I talked to Hassani I went to some of the state-owned factories to see how bad the problem was. In the 1 May plant of the State Company for Woollen Industries I found one mechanic who had been there for twenty-nine years. He worked a six-day week and earned only a modest salary, but had a small apartment nearby at a peppercorn rent. Now though, because of the power shortages and the drop in demand, the factory was running at only half-capacity. Rather than employees being laid off, most of them, the mechanic included, were working only a three-day week. They still received their full salary for working half the time but they knew that this couldn't last. They had already been told that soon they would have a fifth of their salaries deducted to cover the cost of their housing. They could see redundancies beckoning. At the other end of the scale was a man called Ali Salim Omar, the director of the State Company for Construction Industries. His firm made bricks, plastic piping and gravel, and should have been prospering in the rebuilding of Iraq. But power cuts, the increased cost of fuel and security problems meant his factories were seriously affected. Of his 3,000 staff, at least 700 were at home being paid not to work. Staff salaries were doubled by the government shortly after the war and now his balance sheet was heavily in the red. The Americans had given him $500,000 to repair his factories: it cost him $400,000 just to install one power supply at one plant. There wasn't much about this situation that was likely to change quickly or easily.

'If the job is so difficult, why are you still doing it?' I asked.

'Somebody has to do it,' Hassani said. 'For thirty-five years we were sitting outside Iraq criticising what was happening and saying it has to be changed and then the day arrives when change happens and somebody has to step in and make some sacrifices. If nobody does it then Iraq will be in chaos and it will get more difficult. Somebody has to take a lead.'

There were sacrifices. Hassani lived in Baghdad with his wife, his son, aged nine, and two daughters, one six and the other two and a half, but he had little time to spend with the children and worried that the schools in Baghdad were not good enough. He was thinking of sending them abroad but to one of the Arab countries nearby, not back to the States. Even when they were living in the States he and his wife had made sure the children kept up their Arabic, at least at home. He didn't want them to grow up cut off from Iraq.

We talked a lot about religion. Iraq was becoming very publicly religious: much was made of going to the mosque, or of fasting during Ramadan, or of invoking God's word, or dressing according to strict religious instructions, the outward signs of the faith. But unlike others, Hassani didn't wear his religion for all to see.

218

'Religion is different from the way we portray it,' he said. 'I think Islam is a very beautiful religion when you really understand it. I would definitely consider myself a religious person. But to me religion is principles and values that you want to instil in society. That does not mean I want to have a state ruled by religion. Whether you pray or fast is between you and your God. Nobody should judge others. This is how I understand the Islamic religion.'

He said Islam had been distorted, partly by its own extremists, but partly also by the West. 'To tell you the truth the West also played a role in creating these monsters we have today,' he said. 'The other part we are responsible for. We need to properly present religion to the people in the right form.'

He was concerned about the role of the clerics in Islam and against the idea that there should be people in society judging whether or not he was a good Muslim. He believed fervently in the separation of religion and state, which immediately cast him in a much more moderate position than many other politicians then in power in Baghdad.

'If you are going to have a democracy in the right way then everybody should contribute equally and nobody should be appointed a judge to tell you whether or not you are a good Muslim. The mistake of the clerics is that they appoint themselves judges in the world.'

'You sound like someone asking for reform in the Catholic Church,' I said.

'We probably need another Martin Luther King,' he said and began to laugh.

219

15

A Bridge to Paradise

Weeks went by when it felt as if there was no time to breathe between the car bombs, the assassinations, the new military operations: an endless flow of blood. For a while I tried to dismiss it. However bad it was, I told myself, this violence wasn't everything. It obscured more than it explained. I would do better listening to the other stories people had to tell about their lives, even if they were just stories of getting by in difficult times. The wonder of violence is not the bullets or the blood. It is how easily we come to accept it and live with it, with just a shrug of the shoulders. We adapt so quickly.

But however much I wanted to reason it away, the violence of the insurgency was inescapable. It defined so much of what happened in the new Iraq. It painted our landscape. In the end no one could escape the fact that while the occupiers in Baghdad promised democracy and justice, thousands of young Iraqi men were taking up arms against them in a brutal guerrilla war. So I began to seek out the rebels. In the height of the summer of 2004 there were signs of a second revolt among the Shia. It began in the hours before dawn on a Thursday. A group of fighters from a militia loyal to the cleric Moqtada al-Sadr attacked the main police station in Najaf. In a panic, the provincial governor called in the US Marines who were based in the desert outside the city and there was a protracted gun battle. Within a few hours the Americans claimed 300 rebels killed, although they could provide no evidence. The

Americans called them 'anti-Iraqi forces'. The rebels, all but a handful of whom were Iraqi, called themselves the Jaish al-Mahdi, the Army of the Hidden Imam. I spent a week among them.

Sadr's principal mosque, his stronghold, was not in Najaf but in the nearby town of Kufa. The day after the gun battle he was conspicuously absent from the mosque for the Friday prayers and another cleric read out his message in which he described America as the enemy and exhorted his followers to fight. 'Heaven doesn't come without a price,' he said. His audience understood this meant there would be a rebellion.

On that Friday I was in Basra, another fierce Sadr stronghold at the southern tip of Iraq. Even in the hotel there were rumours that the militia had already set up road blocks outside the city. We drove to a mosque run by Sadr's people. There were police checkpoints and a couple of British Army Land-Rovers parked a discreet distance away, their occupants watching as a large crowd swarmed into the compound for lunchtime prayers. In the corner was a heap of stone ruins, perhaps the remains of an older mosque, and above them loomed two large, sandstone domes decorated with blue tiles. Armed men from the Sadr movement took up positions on the ledges of the domes. Beneath them a small circle of men stood arm-in-arm chanting songs about Sadr and his opponent, the pro-American Prime Minister, Ayad Allawi. Others walked through the crowds handing out small, wrapped sweets and pastries or posters of Sadr himself. The moment of rebellion was starting to feel like a festival. They were chanting.

Who do they think Moqtada is?
He is the son of the man who never seeks a seat.
Not like Allawi who came only for a seat.

221

Moqtada, Moqtada,
Moqtada is a bridge to paradise.

To one side of the courtyard was a space for prayer, a large expanse of concrete covered with deep, red carpets and protected from the sun by a flimsy corrugated iron-roof. Several metal water containers stood at the side, each with a cup attached by a chain. A man drank eagerly. As the crowd grew, each man unrolled his prayer mat and placed before him a small circle of clay where he would rest his forehead as he knelt in prayer. Hundreds of men packed into the small space and a suffocating, sweaty heat swelled out from the crowd. Even the local Iraqi policemen, wearing thick woollen balaclavas to disguise themselves, raised their hands from their rifles and joined in the chants to Sadr. Perhaps they were truly with him, perhaps they were too scared not to be. Behind them hung a newly painted banner which read: 'Death to the governor of Najaf, that criminal and shameless traitor, and his police.' The several senior police officials who were kneeling in the front rows of the congregation pretended not to notice.

Even sometime into the prayers, the sheikh in charge was having trouble controlling the crowd. As he preached his sermon they would interrupt one at a time and shriek: 'To jihad, to jihad.' He told them the time to fight was near, but they should wait. He ridiculed the 'great devil America' and said there were many out there intent on destroying Islam, these people must be fought. 'We don't want American Islam,' he shouted to the crowd. They roared back in approval. As I drove back into Basra that afternoon I passed a sign on the road in English and Arabic which read: 'New Iraq, New Life, New Basra'.

I drove back up to Baghdad and on the Monday I headed to Najaf. The commanders of the revolt – young men in unkempt clerical beards and neatly wrapped turbans – were running the most important of their several frontlines from a small courtyard office at the shrine of the Imam Ali. The thickly carpeted room was air conditioned and the walls were covered with images of Sadr. There was a metal-framed sofa under which were stuffed several Kalashnikov rifles and a pair of umbrellas, and in the corner was a roll of mattresses on which the sheikhs and their followers slept at night. Before them was the gold-domed shrine in its magnificence, resting place of Ali, son-in-law and cousin of the Prophet Mohammad and father of the Shia sect of Islam, the holiest site in the Shia faith. The shrine was a place of prayer and pilgrimage; the mosque around it served many more functions: it was a place of study and instruction, of meetings and respite, of eating and drinking and, now, of planning a battle and tending the wounded. The large outer courtyard was two storeys high with recesses every few yards, decorated with tiled mosaics of brown, green, gold and white in geometric patterns. The teardrops, hexagonals, kite-shaped trapezoids and intricate curlicues were so carefully formed it was as if the mathematics within them was the greatest beauty man could offer to his God. Around the main gates in each of the outside walls were exquisite turquoise arches inscribed in calligraphic Arabic with the ninety-nine names of God (Allah, The Compassionate, The Merciful, The King, The Holy, The Source of Peace, The Guardian of Faith, The Protector, The Mighty, The Compeller . . .).

The frontlines at Najaf were commanded by a thirty-four-year-old sheikh whose name was Ahmad al-Shaibani. He had a long, handsome, sunburnt face. His skin was stretched taut over broad cheekbones and slid under a thick, dark beard. He wore an immaculate white turban, which signified he was a properly qualified cleric but that he was not from a family that traced its ancestry back directly to the Prophet: they alone, like Sadr himself, were allowed to wear the black turban. He carried a small mobile telephone, through which he communicated with his fighters, and wore a pair of old metal sunglasses that, although they protected his eyes from the painful midday glare, meant he looked neither particularly clerical nor austere. In previous months he had been the chief judge at an illegal Sharia law court nearby that handed down tough punishments in the name of God. His men called him Maulai, a term of exaggerated religious respect.

Shaibani was standing in the courtyard talking to a handful of other men, mostly fighters. None were armed – they had left their guns leaning in a row against the wall by the main gate to the mosque. 'I need a hundred fighters. We want a battle in the Sharaka neighbourhood,' he told them quietly and they disappeared, nodding at his command. A few minutes earlier the man he followed so loyally, Moqtada al-Sadr, had appeared briefly at the mosque to defend his 'honest resistance' against the Americans.

'We don't want anything more than independence, freedom and democracy for our country,' Sadr had said. He had been standing in front of a poster of his father, Ayatollah Mohammad Sadeq al-Sadr, a white-bearded, respected man who had preached moderation and advocated reform of the Ba'ath and paid for it with his life. The poster showed the ayatollah wrapped in a white sheet and sipping a glass of water, in the background a saccharine-sweet scene of the sort I had seen in many clerical offices: a verdant bunch of pink flowers, a deep blue sky and the Imam Ali mosque glinting in the sun. The young Sadr was careful always to have his father's image nearby for in that lay his greatest strength.

Sadr's political programme was crude and pragmatic, not based on the intellectual reasonings of his father or his other clerical ancestors. Though he didn't oppose the idea of elections, he wanted a leading seat for himself at the table and an Islamic government that ruled under his conservative vision of Islamic law – veils for women and bans on alcohol and cinemas. He called for an immediate American withdrawal, or at least for the Iraqi government to be given overall command of the US military units operating in Iraq. Often when he spoke, he sounded more like a petulant adolescent than the calculating leader of a ruthless guerrilla army. His fight was quite different from the Sunni insurgency that the Americans were already facing in Baghdad and in cities like Falluja and Ramadi to the north and west. In fact there were two separate rebellions under way. Sadr's was a more cohesive revolt but from a bedraggled and poorly equipped army who didn't always seem committed to dying for their cleric. The Sunni fighters, on the other hand, while split between dozens of separate and unco-ordinated militias were far better trained and armed and most of them intent on fighting to the death.

Najaf is perched on the edge of a deep, flat desert that leads on without respite across the west and into Saudi Arabia. Pilgrims from the Shia world flock here in life to pray before the shrine of Ali; the most fortunate are buried in the crowded ranks of the cemetery of the Valley of Peace, just a few hundred yards from the mosque. To be buried here, they say, means to rise with Ali on the Day of Judgement.

The militia had taken over the narrow streets of the old city surrounding the mosque. There was heavy fighting between the rebels and the Marines by now, but it was a mile or so away and centred around the cemetery. The fighters deployed in the city stood or sat in shaded passageways, singing occasionally, joking with each other and every now and then jumping to attention when one of their kind shouted 'Sniper, sniper' or 'Aircraft, aircraft' as the helicopters approached. Most wore green strips of cloth tied across their forehead, a religious symbol of martyrdom. The religious context pervaded even their speech.

'Peace be with you,' one fighter said to another.

'Ali be with you,' the other replied.

'Ya Moqtada, Ya Mohammad, Ya Ali,' the first chanted back, as if at prayer again.

The young commander Shaibani was born in a small town near Diwaniya, a rural province a few minutes drive to the east of Najaf. One of his neighbours, he told us with a smile, was now the Minister of Defence in Baghdad who was leading the fight against the militia. After school Shaibani studied at a teaching institute and began teaching Arabic in the local school. When he was twenty-six he came to Najaf to study for the clergy at the Hawza, the Shia religious seminary that was at the heart of the city's Islamic heritage. He studied under Sadr's father, Ayatollah Mohammad Sadeq al-Sadr, and, once qualified, returned to his hometown to preach the Friday sermon. After the ayatollah was killed, Shaibani transferred his allegiance to the younger son, Moqtada, even though Moqtada was only in his early twenties and not nearly as qualified a cleric as his father had been. It was not an automatic choice. Many Sadr followers, particularly the better-educated, middle-class faithful, considered a much more senior cleric, Grand Ayatollah Kadhem al-Husseini al-Hairi, to be the rightful heir. Hairi was born in Iran. He worked for a while with the Dawa party in Iraq until the 1970s when he was forced to return to Iran. There he stayed, remaining outside Iraq even after the fall of Saddam. Moqtada, however, was inside Iraq and free to claim the family legacy which he did remarkably swiftly.

The younger Sadr's movement was quite distinct from the clerical traditions of his family. The Sadrs had long been known as intellectuals, moderates and reformers. Not only was there his father, Mohammad Sadeq, but before him was an uncle,

Mohammad Baqir al-Sadr, a celebrated intellectual of Islamic thought and a leading figure in the Dawa party. Mohammad Baqir wrote extensive critiques of Marxism and capitalism as well as highly-regarded essays on Islamic banking and democratic Islamic government. He too demanded reforms of the Ba'ath and, after several spells in prison, was executed with his sister in April 1980. It was Mohammad Baqir who began the activist, or what was known as the 'spoken' school in Najaf's Shia clerical community, advocating an Islamic state through revolution. He challenged the quietists who thought the clergy should confine themselves only to the acts of God.

If the Sadr family had a reputation for social activism, the youngest heir sought to pursue it much more aggressively. In doing so, he was rebelling against more conservative, educated seniors and placing street activism before ideology. While the other senior Shia clergy either worked with or acquiesced in the occupation, the younger Sadr gradually rallied a significant force against the American military, drawing the younger clerics to his side and thus cementing his own new power.

The strength of Sadr's militia was not in its political argument but its size. Hundreds of young Iraqi men who had little else to live for supported its cause. I asked why they came to fight and their answers were almost always the same. Most came from the poor, urban working class. Many had been soldiers in Saddam's conscript army and were now unemployed and frustrated that the invasion had brought nothing for them.

'There are three kinds of job you can get now: a guard, a janitor or making sandbags for the American camps,' said one man. 'And then there's the new Iraqi army. They are fighting alongside the Americans and tomorrow they might fight Iran or Syria. How can we join our hands with them?'

I found him sitting on a pile of fishing nets in a dark, brick basement. He was with a group of other men all from Khalis, a small Shia town just north of Baghdad. They had come to Najaf to fight four months earlier and had stayed together as a unit. This was how the fighters were often divided: into small platoons from their hometowns. There were dozens of little groups like this positioned across the old city: the men from Khalis, from Amara, from Kut, from Basra, from Baghdad. The leader of the Khalis platoon said his name was Latif. Under Saddam, he had spent his life running from military service and had been sentenced to death four times for suspected membership of the opposition Dawa party. Several others in the group said they too had been in Dawa and were unable to find work before the war. One was an electrician, others were daily labourers.

'We had this happiness at the beginning then the Americans came and they didn't fulfil anything for us,' said Latif. 'All the rich people in the West came and started taking money and contracts in this country. The wealthy people in the West didn't think of the poor people in Iraq.'

I spent the day moving from one group of fighters to another, trying to assess how close the US Marines were. At one point a fighter began to lead us across a broad, open road. I stopped beside a building, unsure if it was safe to cross. The fighter came back laughing, took my hand in his and led me across the road like a child. We went on and peered round corners looking into the cemetery. The frontline was some way ahead and though I could hear the fighting I could see no sign of the Marines.

Later in the afternoon, after I had returned to my hotel on the newer side of Najaf, the local police chief summoned all the journalists in town to his headquarters to insist that he wanted peace and stability restored to the city. He also wanted to show off a couple of hundred suspected militia fighters his officers had arrested since Thursday. They were sitting in a large hall in the basement of the police station and before we were allowed in we heard the unmistakable sounds of men screaming as they were beaten. Inside, row upon row of young men sat cross-legged and facing towards a sidewall. Around one corner were several plastic water bottles filled with urine, the stench clogged the air. The police chief wanted to show how diligent his men had been in rounding up the fighters, but it turned out that most of the men in this hall were policemen. They had switched sides to join the Sadr militia as soon as the revolt began and were arrested at checkpoints as they tried to drive into Najaf from the surrounding towns.

By early on Tuesday morning the Marines had completely encircled the old city. From 8 a.m. the sound of heavy machine-gunfire echoed across the vast cemetery that began a couple of hundred metres from the mosque's wall. A couple of Marine Humvees were driving around Najaf just beyond the range of the militia, issuing messages in Arabic telling people to leave: 'This is the last warning to the armed militia. This is your last chance to drop your weapons and to leave Najaf peacefully or death will be your penalty.'

I was with two other journalists, one British, one Iraqi, and we worked together for the next few days. Qais had also come down to join me in Najaf, but I thought it was too dangerous to bring him with me to the mosque and the frontlines so he spent the days in the hotel on the other side of town waiting for news. That morning, on the way towards the mosque through the old city, some of the fighters begged to borrow our satellite phones to speak to their families and we listened as they tried to downplay the imminent American assault. However much they vaunted their courage, they sounded scared.

'I'm fine,' one said. 'Don't send anyone down to bring me back. I'll come back on my own when I'm ready.'

229

'I'm OK,' said another. 'There's no fighting around me. They gave me a rest. You can hear shooting? That's far away. Don't worry.'

At the mosque, Shaibani was in his office telling us about the latest position on the frontlines. He had many of his men deployed in the cemetery. The gravestones were not in serried ranks. The land was uneven and sprawled for miles past graves and tombs and shrines, criss-crossed by a network of roads. Sadr's militia had mined it heavily, and a stream of dozens of brightly coloured wires led in long, straight lines out of the graveyard and up to command positions in the alleyways where the blasts could be easily detonated. Shaibani was angry because his men had found letters written by the Najaf police chief to Baghdad recommending that the water and electricity supply into the old city be cut off. But he was encouraged by a second letter which suggested large numbers of Iraq army soldiers from units in the Shia south had deserted rather than face the militia. I only later found out that Shaibani had retrieved the letters from the police chief's car when his men had held it up and kidnapped the driver, who was also the police chief's uncle. The old man was held hostage for several days and beaten before he was eventually released.

I asked Shaibani if he had a military strategy for facing down the most powerful army on earth. He said he wanted simply to show how his ragtag band of fighters were 'humiliating' the great American army and called his fight 'our Islamic resistance'. There was something desperate, almost pathetic in his plan and it seemed likely that, eventually, his clerics would sign another peace agreement. This was more about a show of force, a fist slammed on the table, than a fight to the death. It was about street power, rather than an act of serious resistance.

Shaibani kept insisting, however, that their movement had much more support than we could possibly imagine. By way of example, he told me that two young British men had come out to Iraq expressly to join the rebellion. It seemed an idle boast until a few minutes later he led them into the small office and they sat before us and explained, in startling London accents, what had brought them to fight in Najaf.

The men were dressed in simple robes like the others around them and wore their hair short and their beards trimmed. Both had been born in Iraq, one in Najaf and the younger in Baghdad, but had been taken abroad by their families when they were young. They grew up in London, went to school and college there and had British passports. The elder of the two was twenty-three and more confident. He worked in a London supermarket. The second, aged twenty-one, was his nephew and had been studying to be a computer teacher. They told us they had come to Iraq through a 'not legit' route and that although they had talked to others in London about travelling to Iraq to fight only the two of them had gone. 'We told them: "Our brothers are fighting down there, they are not eating well, they are not sleeping well, we have to be in the same place as them, the same position as them."'

The other militiamen had given them a rudimentary training in how to fire a Kalashnikov and to use the cumbersome and weighty BKC machine-guns that the fighters relied on, as well as mortars and rocket-propelled grenades. There was little in the way of provisions and no comfortable shelter. We asked where they slept at night and the elder man said simply: 'We believe Najaf is a holy city so wherever you are in it you will just chill out and sleep.' The younger nodded and said: 'There is no salary. The food is simple, no barbecues or anything. Just a simple sandwich of bread and nothing else. But we believe that if you see your brothers and they have problems and someone is killing them and it is not fair, then you have to stand with them.'

231

We asked why they had come to Iraq and they complained bitterly about the Americans. 'They were wrong to come to our country,' said the younger man. 'They said they came for chemical weapons and they didn't get permission from the UN so they attacked Iraq for no reason.'

'It's pride my friend. It's pride,' said the elder. 'If someone wants to step on your head I don't know if it would be accepted in Europe or England . . . Bush said you are either with us or against us. We had to decide either to be with him or against him and we are against him definitely.'

They posed for photographs for us outside the door of the mosque, their faces wrapped in scarves and heavy rifles resting awkwardly in their arms. A few days later the pair were seen, battling alongside the militia in the graveyard, but we heard no more of them after that. Perhaps they survived and made their way home, perhaps they did not.

As dismal a military outfit as Sadr's militia looked it had put up a strong fight in the cemetery. Several American soldiers had been killed and one of Shaibani's aides brought us what they had collected that morning from the battlefield. He carried two magazines of M16 rounds marked 'Center Industries Corp., Wichita, Kansas', a box of 5.56 mm rounds, a green US military T-shirt and the helmet belonging to a US Marine whom they claimed to have killed. His name was marked clearly on the back: Reynoso. The aide, himself a cleric, laughed as he showed off his trophies. Others in the courtyard gathered round to look for themselves. The loudspeakers from the mosque, which had been exhorting the fighters all day, issued another message: 'God Bless you who are carrying the banners of the Prophet Mohammad and defending Islam. God is great.'

Later I learned that the helmet had belonged to Marine Sergeant Yadir Reynoso, who was twenty-seven and from Wapato, in Central Washington. He had joined the Marines out of high school and served for eight years, becoming a mortar specialist. He had been killed outside Najaf on the previous Thursday, the first day of the rebellion and the official Department of Defence announcement said simply he had died from 'enemy action'. He had a four-year-old son.

By Wednesday there were reports on the news that the pro-Sadr clerics further south were proposing that southern Iraq should cut itself off from the rest of the country and continue life as a separate, wholly Shia, state. Shaibani said the movement denounced the idea and had no wish to see Iraq dismembered by its own people. The idea of a Shia state in the south never disappeared though: it had been discussed briefly in some of the think-tanks in Washington and London just after the war and it reappeared the following year in the desperately tortuous negotiations to write a new constitution.

The atmosphere in Shaibani's little room was more tense than before. The Americans were moving closer and closer to the old city and jet fighters and attack helicopters had flown several sorties overhead.

We walked through the alleyways outside the mosque until we reached a small group of fighters standing in the shade just a few yards from where the cemetery began. They were from Amara, a Shia town in the south where hundreds had risen up in support of Sadr. The newest volunteer among them was called Ali and was twenty-six. He had arrived seven days earlier and wore a green canvas ammunition pouch on his chest on which he had written neatly in pen his name, address and telephone number, like a schoolboy's satchel. 'In case I die, so they can reach my family,' he said.

He was a bright biology student who said he had come to Najaf to fight 'for the defence of Islam'. He hadn't always followed Sadr. In the first months after the war he had allied himself to a popular local warlord named Abu Hatem, a tribal

233

leader from the marshlands of southern Iraq who had fought for many years against Saddam's government. However, when Abu Hatem was chosen to be one of the twenty-five Iraqis in the Governing Council, Ali and his friends began to turn away from him. They thought it was a betrayal for him to work alongside the occupation and, once they saw how he started to fill the local police force from the ranks of his own men, they were quickly disenchanted. Sadr, on the other hand, was one of the few who had refused to co-operate with an occupation that was now so clearly failing and for that he had their support. Ali thought of Sadr as a 'nationalist' and idolised him as a 'lion'.

For a couple of hours I stayed with Ali and his companions in their narrow shaded street. There was a sniper lying by a window in the building above them and occasionally he would fire out a round into the cemetery, making the alleyways around us shake in the deafening echo. Sometimes an American attack helicopter passed overhead and the fighters would dash out of the shade and inexpertly fire off their Kalashnikovs or machine-guns, as much for our benefit as for their own. One man on the machine-gun boasted to a fellow fighter: 'Do you think I aim when I shoot? All this is done by the Imam Ali. All I have to do is carry the thing and pull the trigger and he will help me with my aim and bring down the helicopter. It is not me that does these things.'

None of them had actually brought down a helicopter, but this mystique of their cause was a palpable comfort. A few minutes past 1 p.m., the loudspeakers in the shrine issued the call for prayer and the fighters carefully laid down their guns, peeled off their ammunition belts and knelt to pray on strips of cardboard placed on the floor. Later someone brought up plates of rice from the mosque and a cool-box full of grapes and they sat back in the shade joking among themselves as the afternoon stretched on. More than 2,000 Marines gathered at the other side of the cemetery that night making their final preparations for an assault.

I woke in my hotel room on Thursday to find the US military had poured into Najaf before dawn and had set up a cordon of tanks and armoured personnel carriers around the mosque and the old city, isolating the militia from the rest of Najaf. I drove up to the cordon and at first it looked as though I and the two journalists with me might not be able to get back to the mosque at all, but eventually some locals directed us through the back streets past the American barrier. It was a long walk and a couple of hours passed before we reached the militia's frontline in the old city. We had passes: notes scribbled on scraps of paper by Shaibani or other clerics, which we hoped would be enough to let us through. They were accepted, but only with reluctance. Where before the militia had welcomed us without question, this time they were on edge and much more aggressive. Some of the clerics we had met before were privately extremely anxious, asking if we could smuggle them out past the American positions. Their only protection was the sanctity of the mosque itself, which they judged the Americans would be loath to attack. This was a hope to which Shaibani clearly clung more easily than most because when we found him he was dozing on a mattress in his office. He had been up early that morning trying to encourage the militia's resistance to the overnight American push and still he received text messages on his phone from commanders in the field. The loudspeakers started issuing ever more vigorous exhortations to the fighters: 'God is greatest. God bless you. God make your feet steadfast. God make you victorious.'

Shaibani put on his sunglasses and wandered into the court-yard, trying to sound bullish. 'We have been expecting this moment. It is either a massive attack or a massive withdrawal,' he said. 'We expect the latter. There is a lot of political pressure

235

in Baghdad.' Other clerics were meeting in private inside the mosque, appealing to the UN and pursuing last-minute negotiations. I heard one senior cleric bawl into his mobile phone: 'Just please ask the American forces to pull back from the old city until the negotiations have finished. Then they can do what they want.'

But of course this was a war and there was always a price to pay. Throughout the day more and more injured young men, wrapped in bandages, were carried into the mosque. On one side of the courtyard, far from Shaibani's office, was a small makeshift hospital with two metal beds and a stack of drugs and bandages. On the opposite side was another room, now a crowded ward chilled by two water coolers. The doors were always closed and a pile of clothes stained with blood soaked in a metal bath outside. Sitting in the sun was a young man named Hassan Liwis. He was twenty-six and a student of oil engineering who had left his final exams to come to Najaf to fight. He spoke English and was eager to talk to me even though half his body was swathed in bandages. He had been badly burned in the face and on his arm when a helicopter fired a rocket at him as he stood holding a rocket-propelled grenade.

'You know I saw my face in the mirror. I know how it looks. But we believe if you are injured then the Imam Mahdi will appear,' he said.

The fighters loved to talk of the mysterious Imam Mahdi, as if the promise of his return was a collective solace. Technically Shias believe the Imam Mahdi – the Guided One – was a man named Mohammad al-Mahdi, who was the twelfth and last imam, or leader of the faith. He was born in Samarra, a few hundred miles further north in Iraq, but at the age of five he disappeared, or, more strictly speaking, went into occultation. He became the Hidden Imam who is predicted to re-appear just before the day of resurrection to conquer the world and install a new government of peace and justice. Since then several men have claimed to be the Mahdi or have been seen as such by their supporters. Among them was Mirza Ghulam Ahmad who was born in the Punjab in 1835 and founded the Ahmadiyya sect of Islam, which survives across the world today. Another was Muhammad Ahmad, the Sudanese religious leader who rallied an army that defeated the British in Khartoum in 1885 and beheaded General Gordon on the steps of the city's palace. For the Shia in Najaf, though, the Mahdi was still hidden and eagerly awaited.

I asked Liwis why he had come to fight. 'Because our leader is here,' he said. 'I find myself able to do anything to defend my leader, the Imam Ali and my religion. We will do anything to stop the Americans and to defend Moqtada.' He lowered his voice. 'We know they have sex and drinking and other things and we don't agree with this.' He had left three small children at home, the youngest he had just named Moqtada, after his cleric.

The loudspeaker started up again. 'In the name of God, peace be with you. Imam Ali, peace to you. You the loyal people of the imams, God bless you, you who are defending the Imam Ali, prince of the faithful. Help them protect your shrine, help them protect your holy city.' There was a pause and then a few minutes later. 'Be patient and fight, God bless you. Victory will be yours with the help of God. Ya Mohammad, Ya Ali.' Some minutes later, now in the sleepy heat of the afternoon, it started again. 'Fighters return to your positions. The enemy is running away. Go to your positions immediately.' And so it went on.

Later that afternoon I was in Shaibani's office as he and his men sat discussing the US military strategy and insisting it would surely fail. Every few moments Shaibani sent text messages on his mobile. Another in the room sat in the corner spraying breath freshener into his mouth. A fighter came in and reported that a friend of theirs had just been brought to the hospital, a young man named Haider, who had been shot in the head by an American bullet and was barely alive. For a moment the room fell silent.

It was now too dangerous to walk back to the hotel and so I and a couple of other journalists spent that night sleeping on a carpet under the night sky in the courtyard of the mosque. Shaibani brought us water and bread and cans of tuna fish originally donated by the Iranian Red Cross. One of his friends walked around feeding the pigeons that flocked to the courtyard with grains of wheat. After dark, the fighters came back to the mosque and spent several minutes washing their feet, arms and faces in the bathrooms before heading into the shrine to pray. Occasionally helicopters would fly past in the distance but there was little sound of any fighting and we passed a peaceful night.

I woke just before 5 a.m., when the floodlights snapped on, bathing the courtyard in a beautiful yellow luminescence. Dozens of fighters wandered back into the mosque to wash and pray and to collect plates of food and plastic tubs of water. In the dawn half-light they chanted incantations to Sadr and later we followed them back to the frontlines. Already in the distance was the deep rumbling of American tanks moving quickly from one position to the next, closing in gradually on the old city.

I came to a group of fighters hiding in a building. Some were apparently experienced and unperturbed by the fighting, others much younger and palpably afraid. 'Ali be with you,' they said to each other in greeting. The Americans had attacked a position nearby early that morning and there was still occasional fighting up ahead. As a militiaman in a nearby building fired off his gun the others would cheer their support, 'Allah O-Akbar' or 'Ya Ali, Ya Ali', and then shout instructions from the street to the rooftops and back again. Heavy rounds came in from the Americans, shaking the buildings and filling the streets with clouds of smoke and it continued like this for more than an hour, the two sides trading machine-gunfire and lobbing mortars. A militia sniper shouted down from a building above us: 'One of their tanks is on fire!'

The others cheered. Then a heavy round pounded into the building where he had been hiding. The others scurried away quickly, ducking behind the walls or down into the basement. Moments later the sniper was brought hurriedly down the stairs, badly injured and holding his head in his hands. Two friends lifted him into the back of a pick-up truck and raced back to the mosque.

One of the men who had been with him, a young man of only twenty-two and dressed in a T-shirt printed with the words 'O Hussain, O Martyr', came over towards us. He was covered from head to foot in concrete dust and described how the room in which they were hiding had taken a direct hit from a tank round. He stopped and took apart his machine-gun, using methylated spirit to clear the dirt from it. The others took out cigarettes and started smoking.

They were not called upon to go back into battle that day. While these men were fighting, Sadr's clerics had been negotiating hard and had won a pause in the battle. The Americans pulled back from their positions and asked Sadr's fighters to withdraw from the mosque. All around us, the militia began to celebrate a victory and the clerics, in palpable relief, said they had only ever wanted a peaceful settlement. A procession of thousands of Sadr's supporters drove down from Baghdad, bringing with them food and medicine, some of it even given by the Sunni guerrillas of Falluja in a remarkable cross-sectarian display of loyalty.

That afternoon as I walked back to our hotel through the old city the people of Najaf were starting to return to their homes. The streets that had once been the frontline were abandoned by the fighters. We passed a small market with street stalls selling a handful of vegetables. Other houses nearby had been destroyed by the fighting, large roadside bombs still lay in place every few hundred yards with wires trailing from them. As soon as we were only a mile or so from the mosque, all sympathy for the fighters began to evaporate. 'Why do you come here to see the misery in Najaf?' one woman shouted. 'May God take his revenge on the one who is responsible for this.' Another man ran up to me and said: 'Moqtada and his thugs are outlaws. They are criminals and not from Najaf.'

That night at the mosque, Sadr appeared before a crowd of hundreds of his rebels to denounce the Americans and the Iraqi government and to claim victory. Shaibani and the other young clerics stood proudly before the cheering crowd. I watched one cleric I had met before whose name was Qays al-Khazali, a young man but one who was very close to Sadr. He stood by the main office of the shrine on a wooden dais, dressed neatly in his unspoiled gowns. He kept studiously still before the chanting hysterics of the fighters. He was so still, with such unashamed hauteur, that he seemed to disdain their screaming. Then one poor man dressed in a dirty shirt and trousers rushed forward, clasped the cleric's head in his hands and kissed him loudly on the cheek before slipping back into the crowd.

16

Haifa Street

Haifa Street is one of the main arteries of Baghdad in the heart of the old city. It runs parallel to the river, passing five bridges before it arrives at the old palace compound, now the Americans' Green Zone. In Haifa Street was the old British embassy, a large Ottoman brick building on the river bank with courtyards and wide green lawns. Here too were rows of apartment blocks and behind them on either side was a web of narrow streets, crowded with houses, small groceries and car workshops. Spaced between them were several mosques, all large and well maintained. Like Adhamiya, a few miles to the north on the opposite bank, this area was a Sunni quarter and, because of its narrow streets, had become a natural place of refuge for the insurgents. There had been many car bombs and ambushes on passing American army and Iraqi police patrols.

In December 2004 I made contact through a friend with the commander of a cell in the Sunni insurgency who was prepared to meet me. I was told to drive to a mosque at the northern end of Haifa Street, now one of the most dangerous places in Baghdad. Just a few weeks earlier, an American armoured vehicle had been ambushed on the street and, in retaliation, a helicopter had opened fire into a crowd. Among the dead was a correspondent from al-Arabiya television, who was killed as he stood at the scene speaking into his camera. The shocking images, played repeatedly on the television, underlined just how tenuous was American control over a main road only a mile or so from their political headquarters.

In the end, we drove through easily, as if it had been any other area in Baghdad. There were no signs of the insurgency, just the usual vitriolic graffiti on the walls (in English: 'American army go to hell' and 'Down USA. No USA'). The only signs that this was a place somehow apart from the rest of the city were the dozens of new potholes in what had been a modern and serviceable road, and the unusual number of men standing idly on the streets watching the traffic. At the mosque a young man promptly arrived and climbed into the front of the car, greeting us all with a handshake and advice for the driver that he should take care to avoid the potholes, most of which were wired-up artillery shells buried beneath the road surface for future ambushes. He led us back down Haifa Street for a few minutes and then off in the direction of the river and into the driveway of an old school building. In the days before as the meeting was being arranged, our contact had insisted that I and the two Iraqis coming with me would have to change out of our clothes and into dishdashas once we arrived. He said it would ensure we had no weapons or any tracking devices. After some hours of anxious discussion among ourselves we finally agreed, but in the end we were never asked to change. Later, after our meeting, when we asked why, they laughed and said we should understand it was only their little test.

It didn't look as if there had been any schoolchildren in the building for months. It was mid-morning and the place was deserted. The man who gave his name only as Abu Mujahid, sat at a table that was covered in a plain white plastic sheet. On the wall a cheap clock chimed the half-hour and a handful of chairs and metal cabinets in the corner were the only other furniture. One of his assistants brought in a tray with glasses of sweet black tea and a plate of freshly washed bananas.

The man was in his thirties and wore a thick, black beard. He had on a waistcoat over his robe, a red and white keffiyeh neatly folded around his shoulders and a pair of black-rimmed spectacles. Before he began to speak he whispered quietly under his breath the small prayer that begins each Sura of the Qur'an: 'In the name of God, the Compassionate, the Merciful.' He claimed to have been a labourer before the war, although that was perhaps an evasion. He seemed better educated than that and spoke good Iraqi Arabic, his sentences laced self-consciously with religious references. He said he had been jailed four times in the days of Saddam because of his adherence to the strict Salafi school of Islam and because he had attended secret religious classes and discussions. He was only released in the last year before the war.

Salafis are conservative Sunni Muslims who seek to follow the 'pious predecessors' or the first three generations to follow the Prophet Mohammad. The movement emerged more than a century ago as a reform of the faith but in recent years has become an extreme school that rejects Western cultural influence.[33] Although in his final decade Saddam had started what he called a Faith Campaign and turned even further away from the Ba'ath's socialist tradition in an attempt to embrace Islam, he still treated the Salafists as a subversive threat. 'As you know, the Iraqis then were not that powerful and we couldn't go up against Saddam's people,' the man said. 'Now, we are fighting against the unbelievers and that is why the fight represents jihad. We are fighting now against the unbelievers and against the government too because they are not following Islamic precepts. We fight those who fight us and those who support them.' He said he believed one of the reasons that brought the Americans to his country was a Western war against Islam.

'Did you fight during the invasion?' I asked him.

'I never fought. I stayed at home because I didn't want to fight. Why should I fight? If you fight for Saddam and he wins, you are not winning. If America wins, you are not winning,' he said. 'They freed us from evil but they brought more evil to the country.'

He held a brown handkerchief as he talked and, even when he began to speak about the failings of the Americans and his war against the unbelievers, he never once raised his voice. He spoke instead in long paragraphs, barely pausing for breath.

The fight back did not begin immediately after the war, he said. There was a pause. At first, there was no properly organised resistance. However, gradually over the weeks that followed, the preachers in the mosques in his area began to encourage young men to take up the fight against the occupation. 'We had Islamic people telling us to go to jihad and we were eager.'

Some of his friends had agreed to join him, others said they were against the idea or thought it too dangerous. He said that hadn't particularly bothered him. He simply thought they were wrong and that he was right. He was doing what the clerics at the mosque had told him was God's will and that this was a fight for God and for his religion. That had given him immunity from criticism and he could do no wrong. It was comfortably simple and allowed no room for debate. Nor was it really any different from the reasons given by the young Shia fighters I had met in Najaf. Sunni and Shia would never have accepted such comparisons and, in the months ahead, they went on to fight not just the Americans but each other in a bitter war of sectarian vengeance. Both were absolute adherents to the same faith and yet divided by that faith.

What was even more striking at the time, however, was the disparity between the official understanding of the insurgency and the reality on the ground. Military commanders and

Western politicians tended to emphasise the role of former Ba'athists – whom they called at first 'dead-enders' and later 'former regime loyalists' – and foreign fighters: young Arabs from Saudi Arabia, Syria, Yemen and elsewhere who had come to Iraq to fight jihad against the Americans. What they were far more reluctant to acknowledge was that, although these two groups certainly existed in the insurgency, they were not the majority. In fact large numbers of young men among the Sunni communities fought for simpler reasons of nationalism or honour, perhaps their brother or cousin or a member of their tribe had been killed and they wanted revenge, or else they felt simply the humiliation of occupation. To admit this would be to admit the failings of the occupation. Then there was the newer group represented by this young bearded man before me – Iraqis who fought for a religious conviction and who had never been Saddam loyalists. In the early months it was the Ba'athists who dominated the fight, with their networks of intelligence and security officers still largely intact. But soon it was the Islamic groups that came to dominate the insurgency and cast it in their own mould. They fought not because they wanted Saddam back, but because they wanted an Iraq free of Western influence and cast according to their own Islamic vision. The authorities were slow to acknowledge their dominance of the battle since it suggested the insurgency was not an evil relic clinging to a Ba'athist past, but a new movement set loose by the occupation itself. In the American vocabulary of war, the insurgents were always belittled as 'anti-Iraqi forces' or 'dead-enders' in much the same way that British generals during their occupation a century earlier called Iraqi fighters 'semi-savages'.[34]

I asked the man to tell me what precisely his men had done in their fight, but he would give little detail. He said they had no heavy weapons, but had still ambushed tanks or fired at helicopters in and around Haifa Street. We heard the sound of an American helicopter flying past in the sky, high overhead.

He said there were three groups operating in the area. One was 'Tawhid and Jihad', one of the names given to an extreme militant group thought to be led by the Jordanian Abu Musab al-Zarqawi.[35] It was this group that had brought the most horrific element to the insurgency – suicide bombings, kidnappings, videoed beheadings, street executions. The second was the Islamic Army, another organisation with an extreme anti-Western agenda and a propensity for turning its murders into professionally-crafted video footage posted on the internet. The third group he simply called 'jihadis', unwilling to give their name. I presumed, only for the fact that he was prepared to sit and talk to a Westerner, that he was not extreme enough to be a member of the first two groups, though he would not begin to consider criticising their tactics.

I had met a handful of other rebels in previous months and while all had spoken intently about their reasons for fighting, none had really articulated a vision of a future Iraq. This man was different and said he wanted Iraq to become a conservative Islamic state.

'We fight for our land, against those who are fighting Islam, for our country and for our women. Our goal is to fight whoever fights us and not just the Americans. We want this country ruled by the Tawhid and Sunnah and if, in the end, it is not then that means all of us will be dead because we will have fought until the last breath.' The Tawhid and the Sunnah were the central pillars of this fundamentalist vision, a return to the essentials of the faith that has been common to radical Islamic movements for decades. Tawhid meant monotheism or unification, a reaction against the worship of Islamic saints, or pilgrimages to Sufi shrines, and Sunnah meant to follow the ways of the Prophet, the acts Mohammad carried out while on earth.

246

There were now more regular sounds of helicopters criss-crossing in the sky above us and though the man appeared not to notice, his assistant in the corner of the room was growing restless. I asked if he envisaged a state like that set up by the Taliban in Afghanistan and he seemed rather affronted to be compared to the Afghan mullahs who had tried to drag their country back hundreds of years into the past.

'God willing, in future we will make a better state,' he said. He wanted his vision of an Islamic government to spread beyond Iraq to the rest of the Arab world. 'It took the Prophet twenty-three years to spread Islam and so we are very far from the end. We will keep on going until we have spread Tawhid and Sunnah.' He stood up and said that because of the helicopters overhead he had to leave. Before he went, he shook my hand. We were led back to the car, driven again to the mosque and from there we made our way out of the Haifa Street area. By now there were several helicopters circling in the sky, the beginning of another military operation.

It wasn't enough for these men just to fight. They had to win others to their cause and so they began to produce short home movies which you could buy for a few hundred dinars in market stalls across the country. I watched many of the films and they are all similar. I'll describe two.

The first is produced by Tawhid and Jihad, the extremist militant group. It was filmed in a small room somewhere in western Iraq, probably in the city of Ramadi, the provincial capital of al-Anbar. At the beginning, as always, words appear on the screen: 'In the Name of God, the Compassionate, the Merciful.' Then follows the text of two verses from the Qur'an sung by a voiceover. They warn of terrible punishments for those who fight against God but also offer room for forgiveness.

Only, the recompense of those who war against God and his Apostle, and go about to commit disorders on the earth, shall be that they shall be slain or crucified, or have their alternate hands and feet cut off, or be banished the land: This their disgrace in this world, and in the next a great torment shall be theirs –

Except those who, ere you have them in your power, shall repent; for know that God is Forgiving, Merciful. (5:37-38)[36]

On the screen appears an image of a grey globe, an open book, a Kalashnikov rifle and a hand with a finger held aloft, with the words 'Tawhid' and 'Jihad' stamped across it in gold letters. This is the symbol of the group, a group as brand-conscious as any Western company. The film is titled: *Al-Anbar Governor Repents* and, as it suggests, features the unhappy provincial governor of al-Anbar who has been kidnapped and who makes a public offer of repentance in return for his life.

At first we see only a still photograph of the governor dressed in a suit and dark sunglasses, standing next to an American army officer. Behind the two men are three flags: the Stars and Stripes, the flag of the 82nd Airborne Division, and the Iraqi national flag. The camera pans back, showing that the photograph is in a frame at the feet of the governor who is dressed in white and sits dejected before a white wall. He wears black leather shoes and a leather watchstrap on his wrist. Above him is a sign in golden Arabic letters that reads: 'There is no god but God and Mohammad is his Prophet.'

The governor, his shoulders hunched, begins to speak, introducing himself as Abdul Karim Birji. 'I hereby declare my repentance to God before you for any act I have done against the mujahideen or any other work being done with the infidel Americans. I announce my resignation from my post from this moment and state that I shall not return back to this post. And I shall not give any information about the mujahideen or any Muslim to any side. I call all the governors and officials who work with the infidel Americans to quit their jobs as this job is against Islam. Almighty God said that the people who work with the infidels are one with them.'

He appears again, some time later, now wearing a keffiyeh held carefully in place on his head with a black circle of rope. Two of his sons are brought in one after the other and they embrace him until they sob in one another's arms.

A voiceover begins in the background: 'Governor, your repentance was much more lovely to us than killing you. We are not seeking blood. We do not love killing and we shall not accept any moral corruption to betray the Ummah (the Islamic nation). We do not seek life on this earth and we do not sell our principles . . . All that we hope is that your repentance will be a symbol and a scene to be followed by those earthly pleasure-seekers who sold their religion and supported the infidel occupiers. And we give them the warning that we have already killed the president of the Governing Council, Abdul Zarar, followed by the Deputy Minister of Interior. The Minister of Justice survived, but we killed the Governor of Mosul, and we captured the Governor of al-Anbar. A list has started from the beginning but the chapter has not ended. Take care of yourselves and once you are captured in our hands we shall not be merciful and we shall not be cheated by false repentances.'[37]

The victims on the list represented a few of the senior-level Iraqis within the government who had been assassinated, or nearly killed, in some of the insurgency's more high-profile attacks of the early years. Many more would die in the months and years to come.

The film ends with a warning to Ayad Allawi, the then Prime Minister. As the leader of the appointed Iraqi government, he had taken on particular importance for these propaganda-minded rebels. As far as they were concerned he was the ultimate symbol of collaboration and he found himself frequently denounced in their diatribes.

In its final moments, the film cuts to footage in black and white of Allawi giving a speech at a podium. It must have been a speech or press conference recorded from the television, though it is hard to tell precisely the occasion. Gradually as he speaks, a wave of graphic, orange flames that has been superimposed onto the image pours in from the four edges of the screen, filling the picture and consuming the image of the Prime Minister.

'Be sure that for you there shall not be anything from us except the sword and the sword will not be satisfied except with your blood,' says the voiceover. In the background is the sound of an explosion as the screen goes black.

Occasionally, when I was away from Baghdad and back in London, I would go to the British Museum to spend time walking through the quiet corridors of ancient Iraqi sculptures, pictures of an age that seemed grander but just as violent. Many of the stone panels record the acts of war and domination that marked this land for so many hundreds of years. One, in particular, seemed to me not so very far removed from the carefully programmed video denunciation of Allawi as a collaborator of the occupying powers.

It dates from 660–650 BC, during the Assyrian empire when a man named Ashurbanipal was king of a land that stretched from Egypt into modern Iraq.[38] The frieze celebrates the routing by the Assyrians of the men of Elam, a small independent state on the empire's eastern border in what is today southern Iran and their appointment of a puppet ruler, a pro-Assyrian Elamite refugee. In the carved scene, an Assyrian adviser, distinguishable by his pointed conical hat, stands before a crowd of the defeated Elamites who bow to the floor in supplication to their conqueror. With the tendons in his arm flexing, the adviser holds the appointed ruler by the wrist and introduces him to the people. Because of the way he holds him, the moment is an almost forcible act of violence. The Assyrian is standing bolt upright, the puppet ruler is a step behind him, meekly bent forward. In the river beneath them, flow past the bodies of soldiers and horses killed in the battle. The message of power and dominance is overwhelming.

Some time later, though, there was a revolt among the Elamites against their puppet ruler. When you look at the frieze today, it is almost perfectly preserved. The only damage is to the puppet ruler's face, which has been gouged out of the rock in an act of iconoclasm by the rebels, an iconoclasm that was no different from the toppling of the statue of General Maude in the 1958 coup, or of the statue of Saddam in April 2003, or the orange flames that consumed the American ally Allawi in the insurgents' video a few months later.

The second film is from a compilation of short movies called *Winds of Victory*. It begins in the darkness, a poorly lit scene somewhere outside. A man wearing a headband and a white shalwar kameez stands before a circle of men. He glows in the light of the camera and reads quickly from a paper held in both his hands, sometimes stumbling over his words. His Arabic accent is not Iraqi, but perhaps Saudi. He is young and has a slight beard. His sleeves are neatly rolled up to his elbows. The men behind him have their faces covered in what look like white scarves, their eyes reflecting the bright light of the camera. Most wear ammunition pouches strapped across their chests, some hold rocket-propelled grenade launchers over their shoulders, but the man himself is not armed.

'Praise to the God of all the universe and peace on the leader of the mujahideen, Mohammad the messenger of God and all

251

his Companions,' the young man says. On the screen his name appears: Abu Al-Harith Abdul Rahman al-Doseri.

'To my father, to my mother, to my wife: peace from God be upon you. I will not forget you. I loved you a long time. For days and nights I have thought about you. I did not leave only in response to God's call for jihad. How can I be pleased with my life? The unbelievers are touring through our country and they are disturbing our sanctuaries and humiliating us. How can I live and how can the others live? And what of our sisters in the American prisons in Iraq? The women are crying: "Oh you mujahideen." The sisters call us to kill them and they say that will be a mercy for them. We are all responsible before God. My heart is broken just to be away from you.

'You will hear strange words about us from the evil clerics. But according to the holy Qur'an don't consider that those who killed for the sake of God are dead. They are alive. God bought the hearts of the believers so they may enter heaven. Those who remain behind, if they knew how prosperous we are they would wait no longer.

'In every step we make we see death. It is sweeter than stepping towards you. Oh my brother, come for jihad and support your brothers in every place. And let your tongue say: "Oh my soul if you are not going to be killed then die."

'And finally I tell my family and all my friends: If we are not going to meet again and death separates us then our appointment will be in the paradise of Eden.'

The man's voice begins to weaken. 'Say God willing.' And the men around him repeat: 'God willing.'

A man from the crowd leads him away, at times almost pushing him forwards. The others around him are chanting songs: 'Martyr of the banner, you are going to enter paradise.'

The young man walks slowly, a slight smile on his face, but he doesn't look scared. The men walk with him, encircling him as if to protect him and then each steps forward to embrace him. He kisses them on the cheek. 'We are saying farewell to you,' they chant. 'The cup of death is separating us. We will have our appointment tomorrow in the house of the immortals.' The ceremony is slow and deliberate but few other words are said. Some hug him briefly, others who seem to know him better hold his embrace for several seconds. But still he doesn't seem nervous. He stands strong and smiling. By now the light of the camera shows behind him the cabin of a truck, the driver's door open.

Finally, the young man waves his right hand and climbs two or three steps up into the truck, closing the door with his left hand. It is a large truck, perhaps a fuel tanker although it is so dark it is difficult to tell. The camera moves in closer to the driver and using a torch the young man shows the seat next to him on which there are several wires and a large black button held in place by a black strap.

'In the name of God, the Compassionate, the Merciful,' he says in a low voice. 'This is it. This is a button. Only by pressing here and by saying "There is no God but Allah" then I leave this world and do what I am supposed to do as God ordered us.' He turns to look into the camera lens. 'Don't forget about us. We will miss you.'

Now the truck is driving away. The camera follows from a car. Dawn is breaking. Now we see the truck from a distance. It is on the other side of a river and is approaching a large bridge. The camera shakes and the picture is unclear. The truck drives steadily up to the bridge and there are three or four sharp cracks and bright flashes, perhaps the gunfire from the guards on the checkpoint, then a moment later there is a huge explosion and a bright torrent of flame billows up into the sky with a deep roar. There are secondary explosions, more deep roars and the car drives away.

There is a pause and now the camera shows the head of a dead man. He is wrapped in a blanket but his face is clearly visible. There is blood, but no injury. One eye is closed, the other half open. His teeth are bright white, the rest of his body is hidden by blankets. It might be the same young man we have been watching, it is impossible to tell. There is a voiceover, low and rhythmic as if chanting a holy verse: 'You really are Abu Harith, God keep you. Your soul left your body through the big, three-and-a-half-tonne explosion which blew up the infidels and crushed them all. May God keep you clean in body. You only have slight injuries. Here you are after ten days as if you are already coming to life with a fresh strong body and hot blood, perfumed blood. May God have mercy on you and grant peace on your soul among the immortals.'

The attack shown in the film took place on Saturday 24 January 2004, when a suicide bomber at the wheel of a large truck drove into an American military position at a bridge in Khaldiya and detonated his explosives. Three soldiers were killed and another six were injured in the blast. By this point, over 500 American troops had been killed since the invasion a year earlier.

And then there were the execution videos. I thought by now I would have erased them from my mind but I cannot. The scene was always identical: a victim kneels towards the camera in front of a line of armed, masked men. The victim begs, then one from among the armed men speaks to the camera, his voice gathering pace and rising in tone. His words become more and more insistent, more abusive, more threatening and finally, as he begins his last sentences, he reaches for a long-bladed knife hidden beneath his belt and holds it up to the air for a second. He pauses then stretches down. He twists his victim to the left, it is always to the left, and slices into his throat. It is never clean or surgical and sometimes the victim appears conscious, other

254

times not. It always takes many seconds and then the head is raised up and placed on the back of the fallen, bloodied body. The men chant. The video ends.

Was the point just to terrify? Or was it a boast of their bloodlust? I think it probably harmed their cause among many ordinary citizens who were otherwise frustrated and bitter about the occupation but could never associate themselves with suicide bombings or such acts of sheer horror. But perhaps it mattered little. The power of the Sunni militant groups was growing unchecked.

I should describe the effect of seeing a film of one man killing another in this way. It is not like standing on a battlefield as soldiers fire their guns at each other. It is not like being there when one man shoots another at close quarters. There, the noise of the weapons is overpowering. It steals your senses from you and leaves you with only the sounds of the guns: the whoops, the cracks, the whistles, the rushes. The bullets, the rockets or the mortars move too quickly for your eye and so you are left with only the anticipation and the effect. And once you realise you have not been hurt yourself, there is also exhilaration.

The execution by a knife to the throat is altogether different. It is intimate. You wish for a deafening sound, something so overwhelming it might mask the chanting of the killers and the gargling of the last bubbles of air venting from the victim's throat. It is an act of tremendous raw power, so much more physical than popping a mortar into a tube, or squeezing a trigger. If you watch, even on a video, it is deceptively traumatic. It feels like a hand of ice touching your heart and, where it touches, a small part of you freezes and dies.

17

A Razor Blade in Your Throat

For many weeks the Americans had been warning that they
were about to launch a second assault on the city of Falluja,
which by now had fallen completely under the control of the
Islamic insurgency. Civilians were encouraged to leave and the
majority had, living in makeshift refugee camps or sleeping on
the floors of distant relatives. Mohammad Hassan al-Balwa, the
Fallujan businessman, property owner and one-time council
leader, was luckier than most. He had borrowed a friend's villa
in Arasat, a wealthy district of Baghdad, and now lived there
with his family. I went to visit. Balwa was standing on the
pavement waiting for me, looking more anxious than usual. The
house was modest compared to some villas in Baghdad and was
partly hidden from the road by a privet hedge, behind which
was a small green lawn and a BMW parked in the drive. Balwa
led me inside and upstairs to a sitting room, where the television was already on in the corner. There was little furniture,
apart from a pair of grey sofas and a Chinese screen in the
corner, and it looked as though it had hardly been lived in.
There was a faint smell of incense.

The television was tuned to al-Hura, 'The Free One', a new,
American-funded Arabic news channel. That surprised me.
The channel was set up to provide a pro-Western alternative to
the popular and highly critical al-Jazeera and al-Arabiya but I
didn't think many Iraqis watched it, least of all someone like
Balwa who, by now, was quite outspoken about his frustration

with the Americans. I asked how the situation in Falluja had been when he left. 'Everyone was listening to what the mujahideen *shura* said,' he replied bluntly.

The *shura* was a council set up by the insurgents – he called them the mujahideen – to run the city in the weeks after the first American attack. It contained around twenty people, some clerics, others commanders in the different militant groups. One of them was Abdullah al-Janabi, the cleric who had sat with Balwa on the city council and whom the Americans had tried to arrest in the spring.

The *shura* ruled by a mixture of punishments and ad hoc religious edicts. It was a quite extraordinary situation: a small town just forty or so miles outside Baghdad which the US military could not enter and which had become an independent fiefdom under the most radical of laws. The local police force established by the Americans had soon disintegrated, leaving parts of the city under the complete control of the insurgents and other areas patrolled by police units who sympathised with the militants, or were too scared to confront them. There were several accounts of people being executed for crimes like theft and stealing cars. Edicts had been issued against all criminality and several gruesome videos like the many I had watched were being filmed and distributed by way of warning. The deputy provincial governor was kidnapped, the provincial police chief arrested by the US military for defecting to the insurgency and the head of the city's Iraqi National Guard unit murdered.

As we spoke, it was clear that Balwa was appalled by the latest American offensive. I had expected this, but not the way that even he, an educated moderate, now spoke freely of his sympathy for the insurgents and showed few misgivings about the Islamic extremists among them.

'How did you find it living in a Falluja like this?' I asked Balwa.

257

'That was the best possible situation,' he said. 'When the mujahideen *shura* were in charge there were no robbers, nobody was being arrested and no Americans were going in.' And then he offered a slight retreat. 'We didn't have any other choice. It was not the best thing we could get, it was the best thing we had. The people of Falluja don't want to be separated from the rest of Iraq. They want to live their own lives like other people, but this was the only way they had.'

Although the family was fasting for Ramadan, his eldest son Hassan brought in a plate of baklava and cans of Pepsi for me. By now the television was showing scenes from the fighting in Falluja – smoke rising from the city, aerial bombing by the Americans, angry Iraqis in front of the cameras.

'If the Americans were not in this country,' said Balwa, 'we wouldn't have heard of Tawhid and Jihad or seen on the television what is happening now. But the pressure that the Americans brought on the Fallujan people is what made them so tough and created Tawhid and Jihad.'

There had been several days of negotiations before the latest attack began, but Balwa said he thought the Iraqi government and its American allies didn't give the talks a chance. To him it seemed as if they were intent on attacking the city from the start. He was probably right. Tremendous pressure had built up on the American military to correct the mistakes of the spring when they left behind a tremulous ceasefire that only emboldened the insurgency. Balwa said it had become an irredeemable disaster. But it was also true that there had been dissension within the Falluja *shura*. The men from Tawhid and Jihad, the most extreme of the radical groups, had been opposed to negotiating while most others on the council wanted the talks to go on.

'Do you really want to have Islamic clerics running your city, issuing these fatwas, holding these executions?' I asked him.

'In my opinion Islamic leaders are for the mosque only. They are not educated to be leaders in the country or politically. They should be people that we ask for advice.

'I really want to make this point clear,' he said. 'For four months I worked with the Americans: I and a lot of doctors, technical people and educated people. But they couldn't do anything for us.'

Sometimes as he talked he seemed to slip into the phrases that I had heard repeated so many times by the die-hard opponents of the Americans. The coming elections were a 'lie' he said, there were no candidates who represented the opponents of the Americans and now the insurgents were preparing a 'black day' for the Americans.

'After this attack, the resistance will build up its strength again and they will fight in another way and keep fighting and resisting until the Americans get out of this country,' he said. He hadn't been this dogmatic before and I was taken aback. What had intrigued me about him when I first met him, how he danced that careful line between collaboration and resistance, had disappeared. Now, although he was still polite and courteous he was also bitterly angry. He could see what was coming to Falluja, everyone could see that much. This time the city was going to be completely crushed by the American attack, this time there would be no half measures.

I had coffee one afternoon in the hotel café with an Iraqi friend, a young man in his twenties whose English was good and whom I had known for a while. His house was just round the corner from mine, though he was from a wealthy family that lived near Falluja. His father and uncles ran a construction company that had been successful in the Saddam years but had taken little part in the post-war reconstruction, such as it was, because they were worried that to accept a lucrative contract from the Americans would damage their reputation.

My friend was depressed. Two of his cousins had died in the latest fighting in Falluja – both were with the insurgency – and a third had been killed on the way to check on his wife's family, who were in Ramadi, the next-door town. The way he told the story, his cousin had stopped at a US military checkpoint and got out of his car as instructed and was then shot in the neck. Eight days later, he died. He had been married six months and his wife was pregnant.

I asked my friend whether he had ever thought of becoming a fighter along with his cousins. He laughed at me. 'I'm too broadminded for that,' he said. 'The fighters have minds that are closed like fists.'

He told me his cousins had originally joined the fight on tribal grounds. One of their brothers – another insurgent – had been killed fighting the Americans. So their motivation was largely for revenge. But, my friend said, the clerics had got to them and began to convince them that it was much more worthy to fight for their religion. He said there was a distinction to be made. These men couldn't be said to be fighting under the tribal codes of honour and revenge because the codes put a limit on how much revenge you could take. If one of your family or tribe was killed by another you had permission to kill one of the other's family. But a fight against occupation was something different. 'There's no limit,' he said. 'You fight until you feel you have got your satisfaction.'

He thought most Fallujans wouldn't return to the city. He felt some of them were finally angry with the mujahideen for what had happened. 'My uncle said that if he saw a mujahid he would slap him on the head with his sandal for destroying Falluja,' he said. 'People are still against the occupation, of course. But now some of them are thinking that it can't be defeated. It's like having a razor blade in your throat. You can't cough it up or swallow it without hurting yourself. We know

260

the Americans aren't going to leave Iraq – they've built bases that will be here for years.'

Around this time I went back to see Najwa al-Bayati. You still entered her house through the kitchen, but now the front door was permanently locked. She had lost the key. There was a four-wheel drive Toyota parked in the small courtyard, but otherwise the house was the same. Inside, it smelt of roasting chicken and kitchen detergent.

Najwa was sitting in an armchair smoking her Pines cigarettes. Two of her sons were there: Omar, the eldest, now sporting a wiry and slightly adolescent beard; and Ashraf, the youngest. On her lap, Najwa cradled her new joy: Omar's son and her first grandchild, a blond-haired, blue-eyed boy, one month old, named Azad, after her late husband. Pinned to the baby's clothes was a small, tear-shaped gold brooch holding a simple, turquoise stone – a protective charm to watch over the child.

She spoke the absurd greetings which tended to begin most conversations you had these days: Wasn't it terrible that execution two weeks ago of the kidnapped aid worker? She was slaughtered like a sheep. Did you know that a roadside bomb exploded near the boys as they were walking to school last week? They had to run into a field to take cover. All these bombers are Ba'athists, I hate them. Have you heard how much a bottle of cooking gas costs these days? It's up to 10,000 dinars for a single canister.

In the half-year since I had last seen her, Najwa had finally got her job back. After collecting numerous letters of support from her friends at the Communist Party, the Agricultural Ministry had made her assistant to the head of the central veterinary laboratory. Her salary was 400,000 dinars (£150) a month, a lot more than she had earned when she last worked at

261

the government labs. But then, there was more risk involved these days. One of the party officials who had helped her with the letters had been killed two weeks earlier. He had been driving with his bodyguards north from Baghdad when they were ambushed and he was shot dead. I'd seen a condolence book set aside for him in a corridor at the National Assembly offices inside the Green Zone. His assassination barely made the news. Around the same time, Najwa's office had received a letter from an insurgent group called the Islamic Army. The typed letter told the head of the lab, Najwa's boss, that he should give up the position and return to an ordinary staff job. It was unclear exactly what was behind this, but it seemed to fit a broader pattern in which radical groups were targeting mid-ranking and senior officials and bureaucrats across the political spectrum simply to immobilise the government, which they saw as a puppet of the occupation. The laboratory director was, understandably, terrified. He had gone straight home on the day the letter arrived and hadn't come back to work since. Najwa had effectively taken his position.

She was determined not to be intimidated. Not long afterwards there had been a visit to the laboratories by a group of American officials and soldiers. The Americans parked five Humvees in the courtyard and the officials in civilian clothes told Najwa they were vets from America who wanted to assess the state of the laboratories and see what was needed. She showed them round and listed the vaccines, drugs and equipment they required for their work. She explained to her American visitors why the director of the lab was at home.

'Why aren't you afraid like him?' one of the Americans said to her.

'I am a brave woman. I believe only in God and if He wants to end my life in any way then He can,' Najwa told him.

Later that day some of her colleagues berated her. 'How can

you make a tour with them and drink Pepsi with them?' they said to her. 'It's too dangerous. You shouldn't have done it.'

'They're civilians. They wanted to bring equipment and drugs to help us. What was I supposed to do?' Najwa told them. She ignored her colleagues and ignored the Islamic Army's warning. She didn't even bother to tell the police about the threat – 'What can they do?' – and so she carried on with her new job.

When I had stayed with her in the spring, Najwa had taken me to see some other vets at a meeting of what was left of the Iraqi Veterinary Union. They were decent, well-educated men who hungered for recent copies of any veterinary journals from the West and who seemed to meet more to keep each other company than for any other reason. The organisation was a hangover from the days of the regime when everything in society was neatly organised into committees and unions and associations: writers, actors, artists, doctors, vets. Since the war, there hadn't been anything to put on the agendas for their meetings and they continued to convene in their fractured way – the slow unsticking of the last threads of glue of the old days. And in the twisted logic of the guerrilla war, the men who now led the unions and associations were targets. So, two months earlier, Turki Jabar al-Saadi, the head of the veterinary union, and one of the men we had met in the spring, had been killed. He was driving home from his clinic in Abu Ghraib, in western Baghdad, when he was shot dead in what looked like a targeted assassination.

Then there was the story of Haider Peugeot, the taxi driver and the house comedian. His twelve-year-old brother had been kidnapped on his way home from school one day. No one knew why they picked on this little boy. His family wasn't particularly rich, after all Haider was the taxi driver who never seemed to have any passengers and who always had plenty of time to sit

263

about, eat and laugh. The kidnappers called Haider's family to say they wanted $100,000. It was more than they could possibly afford to pay so for the next ten days they negotiated the price down. They argued and argued, and occasionally they were allowed to hear the boy crying over the phone as proof that he was still alive. In the end, they brought the ransom down to just $2,600 – a testament to the family's resilient negotiating skills and perhaps a sign that the kidnappers were no more than petty opportunists. Haider sold his taxi, the car he had lovingly washed every day and had adorned with furry toy animals, and the family got the money together. His brother was returned. He had been beaten, but was not seriously hurt.

The violence seemed to be creeping closer and closer to the family and to Najwa, and yet it didn't seem to shake her. She kept telling me how she was strong and not afraid of anyone. I didn't know whether to encourage her or chastise her for being naïve.

On a side table next to her chair she had pulled out two large sheets of white paper, electoral registration documents printed neatly in Arabic, to show me that she thought the elections due to take place early in the following year were important. Each family was to collect their registration documents and check that the names of eligible voters were accurate. It was the first opportunity Iraqis had ever had to vote freely. The Americans trumpeted it as a crucial milestone on the way to peace and democracy, while the insurgents stood against it. Anyone could see it was no quick fix and would not mean an end to the occupation but it was something to cling to none the less, a momentary breath of fresh air in a whirlwind of chaos.

The electoral system was to be quite simple. The country of Iraq would be treated as one electoral district. Each voter was to select the party they favoured and the parties with the largest share of the votes would win a proportional number of seats in parliament. The seats would be allotted in descending order from the list of candidates each party submitted. Najwa herself had been chosen as a candidate by the Communist Party and was fiercely proud of it. She had perhaps benefited from the new voting procedures (drawn up under American oversight) in which every third name on the list of candidates had to be that of a woman, forcing the men who dominated Iraq's fledgling, patriarchal political parties to make a desperate search for female candidates. Given that Najwa was about two-thirds of the way down the Communist Party list, there wasn't a chance that she would win a seat, but it was the principle that mattered. As if to demonstrate her loyalty to the Communists she pulled out a party leaflet from 2001. It had been secretly printed and it had been a huge risk for Najwa, at that time, to possess such a document. She told me with pride how five of her friends from work had recently joined the party under her influence.

At this point, running a party wasn't so much about having a programme of policies, as presenting a list of respected names and asking the voter to trust them. As a result Najwa's pitch for the Communists was quite straightforward: 'We stand for educated people. Everybody can see the people on this list are special people, with good personalities. And they haven't taken a single dollar from the Americans.' The Communists were one of only a couple of parties offering a non-theocratic agenda, which might have been a strong point in her favour.

Of everything that had happened since the spring, Najwa and her family were most upset by the story of their young friend, Saira, the twenty-six-year-old translator who had fallen in love with an American soldier. Although I had been pessimistic when she first asked my advice about getting a visa to join her soldier, she had succeeded and had been elated to find a way out of Iraq and into an entirely new, American world. Saira's parents were no longer alive and she had been living with her sister and her large family. This would be her escape: she could join the lucky ones who didn't have to live through the chaos that was swallowing up their country.

Towards the end of the summer, about a week after she got her visa, Saira was driving to work as normal when she ran into an ambush. She must have known the risks – dozens of Iraqis working as translators for the American military had been killed. They were one of the prime soft targets for the insurgency, especially those like Saira who lived outside the Green Zone and drove to work every day. Najwa said the gunmen were armed with a BKC, a large, Russian-made heavy machine-gun. They tore her car apart in a volley of bullets. Saira died instantly.

By the time I went back to see Najwa, we'd moved out of our house for good. We made the decision suddenly one morning. The day before, two Italian aid workers had been kidnapped in daylight from their office, not far from our house. Four cars had pulled up outside the building, filled with gunmen in smart suits. No one put up a fight and within a couple of minutes the two women were being driven away. In the end they were not freed for many weeks and went through a harrowing ordeal. At our house the two or three indolent guards we employed spent most of the time asleep or arguing with each other and clearly weren't going to offer much in the way of protection. So I went back to the Hamra Hotel, where I had stayed when I first arrived after the invasion. By this time the hotel compound was surrounded by tall blast walls, metal gates and teams of armed Iraqi guards. I found a room on the top floor, with a view across to the university and the river, but it felt like a defeat: that we had tried to live among an Iraqi community as ordinary neighbours and had failed, retreating behind the concrete walls that at once protected us and cut us off.

On Christmas Eve, the residents of Falluja were allowed back into their city. The attack was over but American troops still surrounded the place and the roads leading in were still dangerous. I tried several times to hitch a lift into the town with the Iraqi Red Crescent, a well-connected charity, but it never quite seemed safe enough. A French journalist had just been kidnapped after she spent a morning talking to a group of Fallujan refugees camped out in a mosque in the grounds of Baghdad University and that was only five minutes from my hotel. Other French journalists had been told to leave and Jacques Chirac had appeared on television to reinforce the order to go home: 'If there were fewer journalists, there would be fewer risks. It is not reasonable,' he said. Falluja may have been technically pacified by the might of the American military, but it was too dangerous for me to visit.

Balwa had driven back to Falluja on Christmas Eve after being told the city would open at 8 a.m. He left his family in Baghdad and took one of his assistants as a driver. They spent four hours in a queue of cars, waiting. Each car and each person was meticulously searched, their documents carefully studied (identity card, food ration card, business card, everything in his wallet). Once inside the town he was allowed to go back only to his house but to no other district. A curfew was set for 5 p.m., so by then he would have to decide whether to remain in Falluja overnight or return to Baghdad.

When Balwa got to his house, he found that an artillery shell had ripped through the outer wall and into the kitchen and the large reception room, where I had slept. The furniture in the rest of the house had been upturned, suggesting the place had been searched. Balwa, it turned out, had left several weapons in the house, a rifle and several pistols (including one belonging to his young boy Hassan) all of which had now been taken. His new, half-built house was also badly damaged, as were several

267

other of his properties across the town. There was no electricity or water. He didn't spend the night, but drove straight back to Baghdad. 'Falluja is now a city of ghosts,' he said.

We sat talking in the same empty room as before, with the television on again in the corner. Since Christmas Eve, he'd driven up to Falluja again to look at his properties. A large red cross had been sprayed on the outside wall of his main house, indicating it had been searched. He couldn't think of living there again for now. 'I passed the cemetery and I really envied the dead,' he told me, 'because they didn't see what has happened to Falluja.' Then he produced a tray with bowls of cakes and a brightly coloured trifle which he insisted I eat as we talked. He didn't touch his bowl and sat there explaining how angry he had found everyone in Falluja, how much tougher this attack had made them, what a great mistake the Americans had made. 'Have more trifle,' he said.

He didn't want to return. His children were now at a school in Baghdad and he wanted them to complete the year. For the first time they were mixing with children from other backgrounds, with Shias and with Christians. It had been difficult at first for them to make friends, it sounded as though the boys from Falluja had been teased by their classmates, but they were bright children and had settled in quickly.

We went back again over the period shortly after the war, when he had been on the council and involved in discussions with the Americans. I suppose this was the time when he felt he had played the most important role in his town and it was something he wanted to revisit again and again. He produced piles of papers that he said showed the suggestions he and others had made, about how the Americans could build a relationship with the city without being heavy-handed. All of their offers had been ignored.

'So who was to blame for the destruction of Falluja?' I asked

Balwa. 'It wasn't just the Americans, was it? If the mujahideen hadn't taken over and run your town, this wouldn't have happened.'

'Anyone who looks at this will see the Americans already had a plan to destroy Falluja, it was part of the plan of occupying Iraq,' he said. 'The resistance withdrew from the city before the attack. The full responsibility of the destruction of Falluja is with the Americans and the Iraqi government. It is true, though, that there are some people who think the mujahideen are partly responsible because they gave the government the chance to implement their plan of destruction.'

Didn't I realise, he said, that this attack would only embolden the insurgents once again? Because they had pulled out of Falluja with most other people before the attack, there were now many more incidents elsewhere, in Baghdad and in Mosul further north where dozens of police stations had just been attacked in a co-ordinated and effective campaign to immobilise the town. 'The Americans always take to power and leave behind logic and reason,' he said. 'They didn't read the history of this region and the customs of the area and so from the beginning they made mistakes.'

18

A Passage to India

The second American attack on Falluja, in the autumn of 2004, left Hajim al-Hassani in a difficult position. Until now it had been possible for him to reconcile his membership of the Sunni Iraqi Islamic Party with his position in government, as Minister of Industry. However, the second attack on Falluja pushed many of the Sunni leaders into an even more irreconcilable position. The hardline Muslim Clerics Association, which represented thousands of mosques across the country and had strong links with much of the insurgency, ordered its followers to boycott the coming general elections. Then in mid-November Hassani's Iraqi Islamic Party said they were pulling out of the government. Hassani could not accept that, so he kept his ministry and quit his party.

'I think everybody in the government from the President to the Prime Minister wanted to solve the issue of Falluja in a different way than using force but in the end there was no choice,' he told me on the phone the next day. He still hoped that the Sunni community would take part in the coming elections, but he admitted it would depend how the operation in Falluja developed.

'Ordinary Iraqis are frustrated and they want peace more than anything else,' he said. 'We need tremendous help from our friends and we need to build up a strong Iraqi police and to control the borders. There is nothing else that can be done in Iraq if we can't do that.'

By the time I saw him again, about a month later, he had formed a new political party with the then Iraqi President, Ghazi al-Yawar, a moderate Sunni from one of the country's biggest tribes. We were in his office at the Industry Ministry and he sat dressed in a shiny grey suit in his large, leather armchair. A selection of mobile telephones was laid out on the desk before him. On the way in I had passed several American Humvees, guarding the building, one with the words 'Madd Dawgs' stencilled on its side. A beige carpet marked with dirty footprints was rolled out from the lobby of the ministry directly to Hassani's Toyota Land Cruiser, which had brown tinted windows.

Hassani had just come out of a meeting with the ambassador of Sudan. He was still struggling with the huge portfolio of lumbering state firms and his plans to lease out some of the companies hadn't yet produced any results. Investors continued to be hesitant, he said. The problems of over-employment hadn't yet been tackled and, if anything, they had got worse. Some of the former Ba'athists who had been sacked after the war had now been allowed back to their jobs, swelling the numbers even more. Nothing was moving as quickly as he had hoped. The electricity supply was so bad that now he was importing massive generators to support some of the state factories.

I asked about Falluja and why he had decided to quit. He said he had taken a different view from others in his party. 'My thinking is that no matter what happens you should not be out of the political circle because that is where you can affect the decisions. Once you are out, they will barely hear you.'

'Was it right to attack Falluja?' I asked.

'It is very difficult to say whether it was the right thing to do. If it was up to me probably I would have found some other solution. Falluja was out of control. The people were sick and tired of their city being hijacked. Then a military decision was made and I think the city suffered tremendously. I think you need a military solution in parallel with a political process and it seems that the second part is still missing.'

It also needed an economic solution, he said, a programme that would provide thousands of jobs to young men who otherwise would be drawn to fight against the occupation. It was an economic solution that, like the political process, was still missing.

Hassani seemed always to take conflicting positions. He had spoken against the first attack on Falluja and then decided not to resign in protest with his colleagues at the second attack, saying that, although the operation was wrong, there had been few other realistic options. He said elections would be difficult without security, but, unlike most Sunnis, he still thought the vote should be held and he wanted to contest a seat.

Confronted with each of Iraq's many pressing difficulties he laughed at the impossibility of it all. 'I blame the Americans,' he said. 'OK, that's only a joke.

'Right now you have to go through these impediments we are facing, that are working to divide the country and the land and the people,' he said. 'We don't want the country to be divided by sects, or nationalities. This is the most important goal we want to achieve. I think we need to talk right now as one community that everybody should be involved in.'

He was still inside the political circle, as he called it, because he believed that to exclude and ostracise the Sunni community even more was a mistake. The more isolated they became, the more dangerous for the entire country. Many Iraqis were talking about the onset of civil war. Would the different sects and ethnic groups take up arms against each other? Was it happening already? Attacks on specifically Shia mosques or Shia leaders were beginning, as were assassinations of Sunni clerics or tribal leaders.

I sat with Hassani as we ate lunch at a large conference table next to his office. It was too dangerous to go out to eat, so one of his staff had ordered in kebabs. Security was as tight as ever. The day before, Hassani's driver had been gunned down outside his home in southern Baghdad.

I asked about reconciliation. Could he see a time when people would come to terms with the crimes committed against them and their families and friends?

'The suffering was too much,' he said. 'The political parties didn't help much. Reconciliation should come from the leadership. Once they lead the people onto that path I think people will go along with them. But when your campaign is not to accept that these people should be brought back then you will keep the fires burning. It's not good for this country. You cannot eliminate that number of people without creating holes in the society.'

He believed there were great divisions in Iraq that were still unresolved, differences that went back well beyond Saddam's time and back to the early years of the Islamic faith and the sectarian divide between Sunni and Shia. 'If we cannot get over that then I think we cannot work out the problem of Iraq. History is gone and those of us who are sincere should work to the future.' He thought this was a rare moment to overcome these sectarian divides, although on the ground the fractures in society only seemed to be growing broader.

'I'm going to say something you probably don't hear from a lot of people: democracy is something that came to us from heaven. It is the process that will solve our problem,' he said. 'I think there are a lot of Iraqis that don't understand that because they are still living under the illusion of occupation or they want revenge on each other.'

'But the signs of sectarianism are everywhere and I don't see much sign of unity,' I said.

'It's going to take some time. You have to educate the people.'

'Do you think the occupation is part of the problem or part of the solution?'

'It's still a problem. I think the solution is to hurry up and build up our forces and get the troops out of the major cities. I think that will minimise the friction we have that affects our society tremendously. The dilemma is that if you want the troops out of the cities you've got to have enough forces to control the security in these places. It's a Catch 22. The Americans didn't trust anybody and, you know, if I was an American I would have been the same.'

Siham Hattab Hamdan, the English lecturer and councillor from Sadr City I had met in the spring, had not put her name forward to be part of the Iraqi government at the June handover. By then she had received a couple of serious, threatening telephone calls from men allied to Moqtada al-Sadr. Even though she was religious, conservative, wore a hijab and was equivocal in her support for the occupation, they didn't want her working on the local council. She had stopped attending council meetings in Sadr City and only travelled with one of her brothers as an escort and protector. By this point she had also given up teaching at the university. Instead, because of the connections she had made, she was able to spend the summer that year studying literature in Illinois, in the US, on a scholarship programme. There she gave interviews on radio and television, always dressed in her hijab and speaking her confident English. She was asked why she covered her hair (a personal choice made by many Iraqi women, she said) and whether she was married (no, she said) and she told her interviewers how much she wanted change in her country and how little she sympathised with the insurgency.

While she was there she had sent me an email. 'I am now in

Illinois University and I can only hear the news from afar. Anyway, I feel happy that Iraqis received power, it is a small relief. I am sure that they will work hard to make the best of this chance. They have no other choice.

'As for Moqtada I think he can have a chance especially with the popularity he has and with the many young men following him. I am not sure if he has a certain agenda but who has?

'I try to call people at home and they say that things are OK. What do they mean by this OK? I only wonder. Salaam.'

Now I received another email: 'Back in the wounded Iraq. It seems that I cannot get rid of it. It is a destiny,' she wrote.

We agreed to meet in an office in central Baghdad because she still felt threatened in her own neighbourhood. A few weeks before, another woman on her council in Sadr City had been kidnapped by what appeared to be a criminal gang. They asked for a ransom, there was a brief period of negotiation and then she was murdered.

In the main offices of the municipality, the Baghdad City Council was holding a meeting. It was a monolithic structure served by a pair of tiny lifts that took an age to reach the top floor. Here there was a vast council chamber that took up nearly the entire length of the building, its darkened windows offering a broad view across the city, over the river and beyond until you could make out the remains of the fields of palm trees that once stood where the dense suburbs now began. A wooden eight-pointed star was embedded in a dome above us, surrounded by silver and gold mirrored tiles. From the ceiling hung dozens of fluorescent tubes flickering uncomfortably, and an array of plastic tubing that dangled down like licks of hair. The wall was adorned with a large map marked 'Comprehensive Development Plan of Baghdad 2000'. One day officials from the Ba'ath had met here, and the next they were gone. The room and its peculiar décor had simply been appropriated by the new authorities.

I found the lobby crowded with visitors each holding a file and hoping to petition the city mayor who was hiding in a back office. There was no queue and none of the petitioners seemed to be having any success so they simply stood and smoked. Three men were mopping the floor around them, dressed in starchy new orange jumpsuits, oddly like the ones worn by hostages in the insurgent propaganda films. To one side of the crowd was a noticeboard with a couple of newspaper profiles, the biggest in Dutch, about one of the members of the council. Someone had scribbled 'hero' underneath his newspaper picture. Someone else had drawn a line through it.

By the time the meeting began, there were thirty or forty councillors in the room sitting behind a circle of new wooden desks. Each had before them one of the room's original microphones, none of which worked. I took a seat in the corner, on one of the row of chairs occupied by uniformed American soldiers and staffers from the State Department who wriggled uncomfortably in their body armour. To begin the meeting, the man in charge announced a moment of silence and reflection while he read from the Qur'an in memory of one councillor who had been gunned down outside his home that week. He was the third or fourth to die since the council had been set up.

I had spoken briefly to Siham before the meeting started. She had told me about her trip to America, about how she was the first Iraqi academic to take part in the seminar, about her visits to Chicago and her cruise along the Mississippi. She had been flooded with questions about life in Iraq and wasn't quite sure how much to tell them. 'I tried not to give them a flowery picture, but at least a realistic one,' she said. 'I told them it was going very badly.'

While she was away in the States, I had been in Najaf watching as the whole of southern Iraq and Sadr City rose up in rebellion against the Iraqi government. It was quieter now, but there was no sense that the radicalism of Moqtada al-Sadr had in any way dampened. Siham was no supporter of his and said he needed to become 'more sensible'. She was a gradualist but then she added, as an afterthought: 'We need this kind of radicalism, but not now.'

'What do you mean you need radicalism?' I said.

'It will be a last resort when all the choices have finished and there is no other alternative. But on the political scene we still have many choices and I feel sorry to see the bloodshed of so many hundreds of young men. These are our brothers and sons who have lost their lives and what have they gained?'

We talked about the elections, which were still several weeks away, but which were being heavily promoted by the American and Iraqi administrations as a signpost towards the future. Siham took the position of most other Shia, that while the elections weren't perfect they were a step forward. It didn't have to be spelt out, of course, that since the Shia were in the majority any vote would surely bring a Shia government. For the first time in Iraq's modern history the tradition of rule by the Sunni minority would end and the Shia would finally come into power. 'We have to start somewhere – a new government can't just come out of a vacuum,' she said. 'And we can't live like this for another year. Things will only get worse.'

I wasn't sure how much it mattered. Of course each election, each of the several steps in the political process, was important. But there were two different realities. Inside the Green Zone and in the political party offices across the city, you had diplomats from the US and Britain and Iraqi politicians arguing out the detailed texts of interim constitutions and election laws and the intricate process of forming a new government after the vote. This was one Iraq and you could be persuaded into thinking that it was an Iraq that was moving forward, however slowly. Then there was a second, much-larger reality, which was what was happening on the streets outside. There the picture wasn't nearly so good and progress wasn't inevitable. In fact, in many areas things were getting worse. This was why my security had become so bad that I'd been forced to leave the house. It was why Siham had received threats from Sadrists in her neighbourhood even as she travelled to the States enjoying her new freedoms. It was also why, since she had returned from the States, she spent her time pressing the Americans on the same old questions: why weren't they clearing the rubbish from Sadr City, or fixing the sewage pipes, or providing employment in large public works projects?

'I came back to find the place drowned in hills of trash and sewage. The municipality officials said they couldn't get into the area because of the fighting. So if it was bad before, now it's even worse,' she said.

As the short prayer for the councillor was being said I had a call on my phone. I slipped outside the chamber. Three Westerners had been kidnapped that morning from Mansour in western Baghdad. I noted down the scant details we had: a time, an address and an approximation of one of their names. In the weeks ahead the three – two Americans and a Briton named Ken Bigley – were shown on television with gunmen from Zarqawi's Tawhid and Jihad pleading for their lives. Then they were beheaded.

By the time I got back to the chamber an American official was addressing the meeting, saying something about the free American mobile phones everyone had been given a year before and how these now had to be registered or they might be turned off. Then the councillors began to raise their own points: one wanted a fund set up for people working for the city who had been killed in the violence, another wanted to know why stocks of butane and kerosene were still so low, another complained that the councillors had only just been given an agenda for the meeting and hadn't had time to consider the issues. One of the men in the small group with Siham asked what compensation there would be for the ordinary people of Sadr City whose houses and cars were damaged in the fighting over the summer. The governor of Baghdad said he had asked for a fund of $1 million for compensation, but he had had no reply from the government. Another said that people from other parts of Iraq should also get compensation for damage, not just in Sadr City. The electricity cut out for a few minutes and the councillors carried on their debate in the darkness.

'We should take care not to compensate the men who have weapons. They are terrorists. We cannot compensate people who are destroying houses with mortars,' said one man in a white shirt.

'We should sit with Sadr's people and listen to their demands. They are not flesh-eaters, we should listen to them,' said another. The temperature of the debate rose sharply.

'This is a people's uprising,' said a man wearing a black and white keffiyeh on his head. 'And Mohammad Sadeq al-Sadr, the father of Moqtada, was a cleric who rose up against Saddam Hussein and against Israel and the Americans and we should respect the Sadr movement and compensate their people.'

'This was not a real uprising,' a woman in green shouted back. 'An uprising is only against a dictatorship and that is not what we have now. Whenever we try to solve this problem people call us agents of the Americans and that is wrong. We are patriots.' The chairman banged his wooden hammer heavily against the table and shouted for silence.

After the tensions of the council chamber, Siham's other life, as a lecturer in English literature at Mustansiriya University, felt like a respite. The campus was on the eastern side of Baghdad on a crowded plot of land marked with a large arched entrance gate. It had been rebuilt in the oil boom after the fall of the monarchy, and although it had been allowed to run down since, it still retained a series of colonnades that wove their way through the buildings from one department to the next and protected you from the glaring sun.

At the gate, where armed guards checked for weapons and strangers, I joined crowds of students, some of the women wearing a hijab over their hair, others not. Most of the students were Shia and there was considerable support here for Moqtada al-Sadr. Posters of the cleric and his father were glued to the walls in the street outside – along with a large poster for Peace 106FM ('Music is Freedom'), a radio station that encouraged its listeners to call up the police with tips about terrorists.

Siham's office was in the heart of the campus and up a flight of stairs. Outside I found a young man desperately flicking through his copy of *Great Expectations* trying to skim the hundreds of pages he was supposed to have read. Inside, Siham was sitting with three of her female colleagues taking a break between lectures. All her classes were taught in English and nearly all the authors she taught were British. This year they were trying to introduce modern American literature to the curriculum, starting with *The Scarlet Letter* and *The Great Gatsby*, but it was proving difficult. At first, Siham blamed this on the lack of new textbooks. Then after a few minutes, she and her colleagues began to admit that it wasn't simply a shortage of books, books could always be found and photocopied for the class. There was a broader reluctance to accept anything American.

'Still students ask me: "Why are you teaching American literature now? Is it because of the occupation? Is it imposed on us?"' said Siham. 'Some of them exploit this and say we are making them study American literature so that they accept everything American. These issues seem somehow childish, but this is what they ask about.'

280

'So what do you tell them?'

'Sometimes our answers don't convince them. We give an academic answer: we choose to teach them American literature not because of the occupation but because we have the opportunity now to add to the curriculum. I told them we were occupied by the British but that doesn't stop us studying British writers.'

Before the war, the curriculum had been a sensitive matter, something ordained from the state that could not be added to at the whim of an academic in her classroom. It wasn't just American literature that found itself on the banned list. There were many forbidden books, from Shia religious texts to *Animal Farm* and the works of Abdul Rahman Munif, a Jordanian-born former Ba'athist turned Saddam critic who fled Baghdad for Damascus and became one of the finest novelists in the Arab world.

Siham collected a pile of books and papers under her arm and went to her next lecture, on the Metaphysical poets. I had been ordered to sit for tea with the head of the department and so I didn't catch up with her again until she was halfway through a lecture on John Donne. The classroom was large, one wall covered by an old, scratched blackboard and the floor crowded with wooden chairs each with a fold-out writing desk on one arm. There were about thirty young men and women sitting there, some sharing books, most with their heads down staring intently at the pages in front of them trying to avoid her questions.

'Can you give me any reason why John Donne had never written a completely faultless poem? What do you think?' Her questions almost always met with silence.

'He was interested in what? In thoughts, in the content and so he forgot about the form of the poem, right?' More silence. She tried again.

'He was a priest. So what kind of poetry did he write?'

'Religious poetry?' said one loud student from the back.

'Right,' said Siham, with some relief. 'And what else?'

'He wrote a lot of works,' said the loud student.

'OK,' she said and on she went, talking about form and content and poetic conceit and the class whispered among themselves, half an eye on the clock. 'So next week I want you to pay attention to Francis Bacon and we are going to talk about the authorised version of the Bible and then we go directly to Milton. John Milton is very important because he was the writer of? Of? Of what?'

There was no answer. It was almost the end of class.

'He was the writer of *Paradise Lost*. Don't ever forget it.'

It didn't matter that Siham might as well have been talking to herself, that the students barely seemed to register a word of what she was saying. A few minutes in that classroom felt like an injection of sanity after the failing politics and bloody vengeance that filled the country outside the door. But at the same time, I was awed by what Siham was undertaking. I remembered how as teenagers my friends and I struggled with Donne and yet that was thousands of miles away at a good school in London where English was our first language. I wondered at the huge gap the students were trying to bridge, between the chaos of post-war Iraq and the complexity of seventeenth-century Metaphysical poetry. Would they find something that resonated in the literature classes, something that taught them how to face the world outside, how to challenge the new strictures of their lives? If they could then that would really be something.

Siham and I talked a lot about this, about how far removed these literature classes were from the reality of Baghdad. Her great obsession was E. M. Forster and she was due to teach *A Passage to India* later that year. It was this book, she said, that came closest to capturing their dilemma in Baghdad. She talked

282

about the sense of foreign occupation in the novel, the delicate balance of relations between the British and their Indian subjects, and the relationship between Aziz, the Indian doctor, and his English friend and supporter Fielding. After Aziz is wrongly accused of assaulting a young Englishwoman in the darkness of the Marabar Caves, he is brought to trial and his relationship with Fielding collapses as the chasm between occupied and occupier stretches too wide.

'Forster was trying to establish such an intimate relationship between the two, a personal relationship, not a public one,' said Siham. 'They agree on a personal level but when they come into conflict on a national level they are separated and they cannot continue this kind of friendship. But at the same time Forster has some hope that one day, when the bad feelings have disappeared, these two peoples and two countries can reach a point where people forget their animosity and their hostility and these matters of superiority and inferiority.'

'Does the novel reflect similar problems in Iraq today?'

'Ordinary Iraqi citizens feel that sense of foreign forces on their land, that this is an occupation. Sometimes you can justify it, but you cannot accept it. At the beginning we thanked the British and Americans for getting rid of Saddam but again we cannot accept them as a reality. It is difficult to decide between them. This is the better of two evils, but it is still an evil.' The final scene in Forster's book, she said, captured exactly what she wanted to say.

I went away and some weeks later I re-read the novel. In the final scene Aziz and Fielding are out riding together, reconciled as friends but conscious that this is their last meeting. They discuss the past and then start arguing about politics:

And Aziz in an awful rage danced this way and that, not knowing what to do, and cried: 'Down with the English anyhow. That's certain. Clear out, you fellows, double quick, I say. We may hate one another, but we hate you most. If I don't make you go, Ahmed will, Karim will, if it's fifty or five hundred years we shall get rid of you, yes, we shall drive every blasted Englishman into the sea, and then' – he rode against him furiously – 'and then,' he concluded, half kissing him, 'you and I shall be friends.'[39]

19

An Election and a Funeral

In the New Year, two weeks before the elections, I was sitting in my hotel room early in the morning when there was a powerful explosion outside. The blast was heavy and close enough to shake the windows. For a few seconds there was silence, and then the sound of gunfire from the policemen stationed just across the road. After a few minutes that stopped too and there was only the roar of a generator and the faint sound of sirens in the distance. The Iraqis living in the apartments opposite the hotel stood on their balconies and pointed towards a column of dark smoke rising into the sky a mile or two away. I thought how strange it was that, although my neighbours and I hardly ever spoke, we now exchanged familiar looks, all of us sharing the same apprehension and relief, breathing in the same distant smell of burning car tyres. A suicide car bomber had driven into the entrance to the main office of a Shia party, the Supreme Council of the Islamic Revolution in Iraq. Two guards had died. A few minutes later there was another, even deeper explosion somewhere else in the city, and more sirens and gunfire. Then two American observation helicopters, small glass globes powered by a frenetic, high-pitched buzzing, started circling in the sky just a mile or so away. It was still before 9 a.m. I looked out of the window and a man in the flats opposite stepped onto the balcony in his underwear. Oblivious of the gunfire and panic around him, he collected a pair of socks from the clothes rack where his laundry was drying and walked back inside.

The next morning just after 7 a.m. there was another explosion, this one so huge that I felt it deep in my chest before I heard it. I shot bolt upright in bed and got dressed quickly. It was the loudest, longest and closest blast I'd heard yet. This time the smell of burning tyres was thick in the air. My neighbours on their balconies were pointing to a spot very close to the hotel, their eyes wide. I waited for a few minutes and then, with a friend, started to walk slowly through to the other side of the hotel. There were broken windows everywhere, debris in the lobby and in the swimming pool. A suicide car bomb a hundred yards away had hit a tall, half-built tower block used as a base for Australian troops. Though the Australians were well protected and hadn't been hurt, two Iraqis had been killed and several others injured.

I went down into the street where the shops opposite the Australians' building, including the Milky Way ice-cream parlour, had been torn through by the blast. An American Abrams tank sat blocking the road. It had 'Hell Yeah' printed on one side of the barrel and 'Heavens No' on the other. Two Apache helicopter gunships circled overhead as American soldiers inspected the wreckage. A crowd of Iraqis looked on, one man wearing a burgundy dressing gown and plastic slippers. It was the first time I'd been able to stand out in the street in the open for months. The next morning I woke again at 7 a.m. waiting for the sound of another explosion, but nothing came. I was so tired but I couldn't sleep.

The day of the first elections finally came, at the end of January 2005, and although there were mortars at dawn and bombings at some polling stations there was less violence than I had expected. With all the roads closed and police everywhere, I was able to spend the day walking through the streets talking to ordinary people without feeling at risk. The district around the hotel was heavily Shia and so there were many people voting, and long queues at the polling stations. Children raced past on bicycles, their parents walked behind often smartly dressed and clutching their voting cards. Neighbours set up plastic chairs in the road, drinking sweet tea from thin glasses and showing off their inked index fingers, the indelible mark of the voter. Several of the parties had formed alliances among themselves, and put their candidates forward in a joint list of names. The Shia religious parties, including representatives from Moqtada al-Sadr's movement, had combined to form one list, supported by Grand Ayatollah Ali al-Sistani, the leading Shia clerical authority. It was called the United Iraqi Alliance, or known by its number: list 169. There was great pressure on the Shia voters to support this list. As well as large cloth banners hanging outside the polling stations on the day, there were even exhortations from Sistani himself. On the walls near the polling station there was crude graffiti: 'Saddam is a dog and a disgrace,' read one. 'Saddam is a coward and a dishonour,' read another. In other parts of the city and in the Sunni towns like Falluja, of course, it was quite different. In those areas there were few voters and a lot of intimidation. The boycott was enforced.

I walked along Amar Bin Yasir Street, a main road that led on to our old house near the bank of the Tigris, and I sat on a white wooden bench at a teashop. There were perhaps half a dozen men sipping tea from glasses and flicking their prayer beads as they watched the voters walk past. There was a large clay water jug on the pavement near them and two American military Humvees blocking the street not far away. Most of these men had voted for the Shia alliance, although at least one admitted he had voted for the incumbent Prime Minister, Ayad Allawi. To a man they cursed Saddam and the Ba'athists and spoke proudly of the election.

'They said that anyone who goes to vote would get shot but just look at the streets, even women and children going to vote,' said the first man, a former factory worker named Tariq. 'Enough is enough. Now it is time for the Shia to rule this country.' A police car drove quickly past us.

'Even if we just have 40 per cent of a democracy this time, then next time it will be 80 per cent and it will get better and better,' said his friend Abdul, a labourer and, like many, a deserter from Saddam's army. 'The Americans did us a favour.'

'But we are against the occupation and the Americans should leave,' Tariq said to him.

'But if the Americans didn't topple Saddam he would have ruled us for generation after generation,' his friend replied. 'They did us a favour, now they should make a timetable and then leave.'

The Shia alliance, list 169, won that first election and it was one of their leaders, Ibrahim al-Jaafari, head of the Dawa party, who became Prime Minister.[40] The Kurdish parties also did well and this was reflected in the appointment of Jalal Talabani, a Kurdish politician, to be President. Few from the Sunni community voted and so few of their leaders were elected. Hassani, however, did manage to win a seat and some weeks later was named Speaker of the National Assembly, a position of much greater prestige than Industry Minister. Najwa al-Bayati, as expected, did not win her Communist Party seat. Ahmed al-Barrak, the human rights lawyer I had first met in Hilla shortly after the war, had also stood as a candidate but he had not won a seat either and he was disconsolate.

I saw Barrak again a week after the elections. The Governing Council on which he sat had been disbanded at the 'handover' but, because his seat on the council had made him a high-security risk, he now lived in a well-protected compound of houses near the Green Zone. Barrak's house – a comfortable two-storey building with new furniture and central air conditioning – had once been the home of a member of Saddam's Presidency Council, a fact that rather embarrassed Barrak.

We met in the Convention Centre, a large building inside the Green Zone used by Iraqi politicians and the US military and administration. Barrak was angry about the Shia alliance, which he thought had unfairly monopolised the vote. At first he claimed that this was because it was too religious and was led by people who wanted a theocratic government. But as we talked some more it became clear his objection had nothing to do with these criticisms. In fact he had been offered a place on the alliance's list. He had refused to take it because the position they offered him was only 190th on the list and he knew that there was slim chance that this would bring him a seat. There had followed a negotiation in which he was offered 157th, 120th and finally 96th position, but it still wasn't good enough for Barrak so he walked away. In the end he joined a much smaller party, the Movement for a Democratic Society, led by a couple of his colleagues from the former Governing Council. This time he was a big fish in their small pond and was given second place on their list. But the party was small, and had done little campaigning even in the south where they thought they could count on a good reserve of guaranteed votes. By the time it came to election day, the powerful Shia alliance had done so much campaigning, with posters and clerical endorsements, that the little parties struggled to stay afloat. Barrak's party didn't even win enough votes to qualify for one seat.

The low point came when Bassam, Barrak's brother-in-law who lived in Sweden, called him just after the elections to congratulate him. It was an awkward telephone conversation.

'Ahmed, congratulations for the big success,' Bassam had

said. And after they talked for a few minutes: 'I voted for 169, you know.'

'What? Why did you do that?' said Barrak. 'You know I wasn't on that list.'

'No, I knew you were on that other list. But I voted 169 because I follow Sistani, he is our leader, our authority, and I couldn't go against his decision.'

'But, Bassam, you live in Sweden, you know full well what is going on. You know my thoughts, my education, you know that I have degrees in law and economics, you know I am qualified to represent you in parliament and still you voted for the 169 list?'

'Ahmed, it's a democracy.'

'But democracy means you choose the right person to represent you in parliament. That is democracy.'

I was due to leave Iraq in two days. It was nearly two years since I arrived and by now I was worn-down and scared. I bought a plane ticket, packed my bags and went to a last funeral.

Someone had been trying to assassinate Mithal al-Alusi, the former De-Ba'athification chief, for months. He'd had mortars fired at his house and gunshots aimed at his car. Now there had been another shooting: gunmen had opened fire on his car just as it pulled up to his house one morning. Yet again, Alusi escaped unhurt. He'd been inside the house at the time. But in the car were his two sons, Ayman and Jamal, who worked as his drivers and assistants. They had come that morning, like most other days, to pick him up and take him to the office of his new political party. When the gunmen opened fire on the car, the two boys hadn't stood a chance. They were both killed. Ayman was thirty and had a wife and three young children. Jamal was twenty-three. Today was the second day of mourning for them. A black banner on a street corner in Jamia, a mixed Shia and

Sunni area, announced their funeral: 'We are of God and to God we will return,' it said.

A large grey and yellow tarpaulin tent had been set up on a patch of land opposite Alusi's house. Inside were two long rows of white plastic chairs and a table on which stood a tape recorder playing a reading from the Qur'an. It was early afternoon and there was still a dull winter chill in the air so heaters had been positioned down the length of the tent. There were brass trays laden with packets of cigarettes, several different varieties, each packet unwrapped, opened and laid out in a circle.

There is a certain, unspoken choreography to an Iraqi funeral that makes it both public and yet very personal. Qais and I walked in and saw dozens of other guests sitting down. If this had been an ordinary occasion, we should have shaken their hands. We did not. Instead we found our own seats, sat down and Qais raised his hands palm upwards and silently mouthed a prayer, the Fatiha, the opening verses of the Qur'an. He spoke a couple of sentences and then brushed his palms across his face and sat back in silence. We sat for about thirty minutes, talking quietly to each other. Occasionally another visitor would enter, sit and mouth the Fatiha and everyone would pause for a moment and then acknowledge them quietly. It was only men that came into the tent, most dressed in suits, a few in dishdashas. Women were directed inside the house where there was an area set aside for them. After a while Alusi came in. He was smoking heavily and looked drawn and tired. The Qur'anic tape was still playing, low and rhythmic.

Alusi came over and sat next to me. I said I was sorry that his sons had died. I said I hadn't known them, though perhaps I had met one briefly in his office a few months back. I asked what had happened. He described how he had heard gunfire in the drive. Fetching his Kalashnikov he had run into the streets. By then his two sons were dead and the gunmen had gone.

291

He seemed to have some information that suggested the attackers belonged to Ansar al-Sunna, one of the more extreme Sunni Islamic groups in the insurgency. He was sure they had been trying to assassinate him. 'It is another proof that the terrorists mean to kill every human being,' he said. It made him especially angry at those within the government who had begun to argue that the only solution to Iraq's violence was to start negotiating with the rebels. The rebels were simply terrorists, he said. It was wrong to consider making deals with them, or to give them any sort of political credibility. As far as he was concerned they were killers and needed to be arrested and, at the very least, jailed.

I said I found this difficult to accept. Of course I hadn't suffered as he had, but still it seemed reasonable to me that the only chance of a decent future was to begin to talk to at least some of the rebels, if not the most extreme among them, then certainly those who claimed to fight a resistance in the name of Iraqi nationalism. Surely the one lesson of guerrilla wars the world over was that an iron-fisted military solution never worked. Only with a political dialogue could a path to peace be found. Alusi was not in the mood to accept this. I asked him what future he saw for Iraq.

'It is either terror or democracy, one of them has to win. The violence will continue like this unless we build quick alliances between Iraqi democrats and liberal people across the world to fight against terrorism.'

He hadn't managed to convince many that he was the right man to build these alliances. His party hadn't won a single seat in the elections a week or so before. In fact, they'd barely taken 4,000 votes across the entire country.

As we were speaking, an old man stepped forward in front of us. Alusi stood up to acknowledge him. The old man moved closer. 'You really are brave,' he said as he shook Alusi's hand.

'You have proven you are a strong man and this is an honour for you as an Iraqi.' He placed his hand on Alusi's shoulder and then walked away.

Alusi sat down again. 'Everybody has to understand that making politics doesn't mean making a copy of Saddam's regime. We don't need a strong man in Iraq. We need a system. They have to understand the difference. The liberation started on 9 April 2003 and it is not finished. We will need much more time.'

We talked some more and then I stood up to go, shaking his hand. I said the formal words of condolence that I had memorised before the funeral: 'Al-baqia fi hayatak' – 'May their lives come into yours.' And then I walked away into the cold spring afternoon.

Epilogue: April 2006

Ali Abid Hassan, the survivor of the mass grave at Mahawil, is still living in Hilla and working as a taxi driver. He has yet to find the body of his dead brother.

Ahmad al-Barrak, the human rights lawyer from Hilla, is now living in Baghdad. Having failed to win a seat in the first post-war election in January 2005 he was appointed as head of the Iraqi Property Claims Commission in July of that year. The commission is responsible for dealing with claims of property confiscated, seized or forcefully sold since the Ba'ath revolution in July 1968. So far the commission has received nearly 130,000 claims. Barrak stood as a candidate for the National Assembly a second time, in December 2005, but again failed to win a seat.

Mithal al-Alusi, the former head of the De-Ba'athification Commission, continued his political campaigning and in the December 2005 elections he finally managed to win himself a seat in the National Assembly.

Najwa al-Bayati, the widow and housewife, is still living at her home in Baghdad with her three sons, her daughter-in-law and her grandson. She is working as a department head in a government veterinary laboratory where she has become a specialist in searching for cases of bird flu. She has received several threats recently from an armed gang who have visited her house complaining about what they say is an old property dispute.

Siham Hattab Hamdan, local councillor and English literature lecturer, is still living in Sadr City and still working on the local district council, where she is now an advocate for women's rights.

Mohammad Hassan al-Balwa, the businessman from Falluja, has now moved back to his home city with his family. He has closed the office of his trading company in Baghdad and his work has ground to a halt.

Hajim al-Hassani, the former internet entrepreneur and Minister of Industry, took up his job as speaker of the National Assembly. It was a high-profile but largely powerless position, although he was involved in negotiating the passage of the bitterly-disputed constitution which was approved by the assembly in October 2005. He was re-elected in the December vote.

Haitham al-Zubaidi, the poet, has been trying to leave Iraq. He found work with a Western company in Baghdad for several months, which although it gave him a regular salary also made him a possible target for insurgents. He spent three months in Jordan and was then offered a job running an Arabic website in Washington. He is waiting for his visa to come through.

Qais, my guide, translator and friend, is living in Baghdad with his wife and son. He is still writing his poetry.

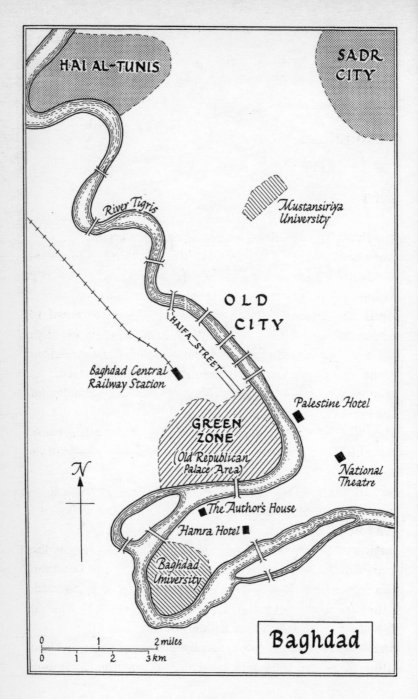

HAI AL-TUNIS

SADR CITY

River Tigris

Mustansiriya University

OLD CITY

HAIFA STREET

Baghdad Central Railway Station

Palestine Hotel

GREEN ZONE

(Old Republican Palace Area)

National Theatre

N

The Author's House

Hamra Hotel

Baghdad University

0   1   2 miles
0   1   2   3 km

Baghdad

Chronology

2003

March 20: The American-led war against Iraq begins.

April 9: US troops help a crowd of Iraqis topple a statue of Saddam Hussein in Firdous Square in Baghdad. The Iraqi regime collapses twenty-one days after the invasion.

April 28: American troops in Falluja fire on a crowd of demonstrators, killing seventeen and injuring more than seventy. Two days later at a second protest in Falluja, American troops shoot dead another two people and injured sixteen.

May 1: US President George Bush announces an end to 'major combat operations' in Iraq.

May 16: The American proconsul in Baghdad, Paul Bremer, signs his de-Ba'athification order and a week later demobilises the Iraqi Army.

July 13: The Iraqi Governing Council holds its first meeting.

July 22: Saddam's two sons, Uday and Qusay, are killed in a gun battle with American troops in Mosul.

August 7: The first major suicide bombing in Iraq targets the Jordanian Embassy in Baghdad, killing eleven people. Less than two weeks later the UN headquarters in Baghdad is bombed, killing at least twenty people including the UN Special Representative Sergio Vieira de Mello.

August 29: A car bomb detonates near the main mosque in Najaf killing more than 100 Iraqis, nearly all of them Shia, including the leading Shia cleric, Ayatollah Mohammad Baqir al-Hakim. He had returned to Iraq three months earlier after living in exile for twenty-three years in Iran.

September 14: Baha Mousa, a hotel receptionist in Basra, is arrested by British soldiers and later dies in custody.

December 13: Saddam Hussein is captured by American troops in an underground hideout on a small farm near Tikrit.

2004

February 1: A double suicide bombing in the Kurdish city of Irbil kills sixty-seven people and injures more than 250 others. The two bombers wear explosives packed with small ball bearings.

February 10: A suicide car bomber attacks a police station in Iskandiriya, killing at least fifty young men queuing to join the police force.

March 1: The Governing Council announces a new interim constitution.

March 31: Four American security contractors are killed in an ambush in Falluja.

April 4: A Shia uprising begins in eastern Baghdad, Najaf and across southern Iraq.

April 5: US troops launch a major assault on Falluja.

April 29: Photographs emerge showing American troops abusing Iraqi prisoners at Abu Ghraib.

April 30: US troops pull back from Falluja after striking a deal with guerrillas and installing a local security force to keep the peace.

May 11: The first insurgent video showing the execution of a Western hostage is posted on the internet. It shows the beheading of an American businessman, Nick Berg.

June 6: A two-month standoff with Shia rebels ends when American forces pull out of Najaf.

June 28: America transfers power to an interim Iraqi government. The Governing Council is disbanded.

July 1: Saddam Hussein appears in court in Baghdad for the first time.

August 5: Another Shia uprising begins in Najaf. Shia rebels clash with American troops.

August 20: Two French journalists are kidnapped on the road to Najaf. They are held for four months. An Italian journalist kidnapped at the same time is killed a few days later.

September 7: The number of American soldiers killed in Iraq reaches 1,000. Two Italian aid workers are kidnapped in Baghdad. They are held for three weeks.

September 16: Ken Bigley, a British contractor, and two American colleagues are kidnapped in Baghdad. All three are later killed.

October 6: In Washington the Iraq Survey Group says in a final report that it has found no evidence that Saddam Hussein had significant weapons of mass destruction before the war.

October 19: Margaret Hassan, a British-Iraqi aid worker who runs the Care International office in Baghdad, is kidnapped as she leaves her home. A month later she is killed. She had lived in Iraq for thirty years.

November 8: American troops launch a second offensive on Falluja, after weeks of air strikes.

December 24: The US military encourages Fallujans to return to their homes, although sporadic fighting in the now largely destroyed city continues.

2005

January 19: Five car bombs explode within a few minutes of each other across Baghdad targeting a police station, a bank, the international airport, an army base and an Australian military building near the Hamra Hotel. In total around twenty-six people are killed and dozens injured.

January 30: Iraqis go to the polls in the first general elections for decades.

February 13: First results from the elections show that an alliance of Shia parties won just under half the votes, allowing them to dominate the new government. It is the first time the Shia have ruled Iraq for centuries.

Notes

1   There shouldn't be any room for doubt about what exactly President George Bush senior said and whether he really did encourage a revolt. On 15 February 1991, Bush gave two speeches, one at the American Association for the Advancement of Science and the second to employees at the Raytheon Missile Systems Plant, in Andover, Massachusetts. In both speeches he referred to the latest news from Baghdad and both times, using the same phrase, he said: 'There's another way for the bloodshed to stop, and that is for the Iraqi military and the Iraqi people to take matters into their own hands to force Saddam Hussein, the dictator, to step aside and then comply with the United Nations resolutions and rejoin the family of peace-loving nations.' The official texts of both speeches are reproduced on the website of the Federation of American Scientists. See *www.fas.org/news/iraq/1991/910215-172746.htm* and *www.fas.org/spp/starwars/offdocs/gb910215.htm*.

2   There are good accounts of the 1991 uprising in Human Rights Watch, *Endless Torment: The 1991 Uprising in Iraq and its Aftermath* (Human Rights Watch, 1992), and in chapters one and two of Andrew Cockburn and Patrick Cockburn's excellent modern history of Iraq, *Saddam Hussein: An American Obsession* (London, Verso, 2000).

3   Faleh Jabar, 'Why The Uprisings Failed' in Micah L. Sifry and Christopher Cerf (eds.), *The Iraq War Reader: History, Documents and Opinions* (New York, Touchstone, 2003), p.113.

4   The divisions of the Republican Guard were adorned with heroic names that were supposed to highlight their elite status: Hammurabi, Nebuchadnezzar, Madain, Tawakalna. Above the Republican Guard was a much smaller, even more loyal force

called the Special Republican Guard which was founded in 1995 and commanded by Saddam's second son and heir apparent, Qusay. It had the task of protecting Saddam and dealing with any rebellion or coup and was the only significant Iraqi military force allowed into Baghdad. Both were regarded as the military elite and were feared by the Iraqis, yet when it came to the final fight they folded quickly in the face of the US invasion in March 2003.

5   In the 1980s as many as two million Egyptians were encouraged over to Iraq to work and had earned a reputation for often taking on the manual labour that the Iraqis themselves would not do. Many of the Egyptians who came at this time still remain. Several witnesses at Mahawil told me they believed the drivers of the mechanical diggers on the nights of the executions were Egyptian labourers and that they too, as witnesses to the crime, had been shot and buried in the graves.

6   Headquarters United States Central Command, News Release, 29 May 2003, Release Number: 03-05-110, *Alleged Murderer Mistakenly Released from U.S. Custody*.

7   *Iraq: A Tourist Guide* (Baghdad, State Organisation for Tourism, 1982), p.35.

8   There were several ranks in the modern Ba'ath, ranging from the junior position of *'Udw*, meaning member or comrade, to the four senior levels within the party whose members were now banned from public office which were, in ascending order of importance: *'Udw Firqah*, group member, *'Udw Shu'bah*, section member, *'Udw Far*, branch member, and *'Udw Qutriyya*, Regional Command member (the region under command was Iraq, a region of the much larger planned, though not yet realised, pan-Arab nation).

9   The figure comes from an estimate drawn up by Human Rights Watch shortly before the war. See: *Justice For Iraq: A Human Rights Watch Policy Paper* (Human Rights Watch, December 2002) and *Iraq: State of the Evidence* (Human Rights Watch, November 2004). The disappeared include 100,000 Kurds who were killed between February and September 1988 in the Anfal campaign; between 50,000 and 70,000 Shia and Marsh Arabs arrested and probably killed in the south during the early years of the Iran-Iraq war; 8,000 members of the Barzani clan disappeared

304

in 1983 from resettlement camps in Iraqi Kurdistan; at least 10,000 men separated from their Feyli Kurdish families who were deported to Iran in the 1980s; around 50,000 opposition activists, including Communists, leftists, Kurds, other minorities, and out of favour Ba'athists, disappeared in the 1980s and 1990s; and around 30,000 Shia men disappeared after the 1991 uprising was crushed. In its paper *Justice for Iraq*, Human Rights Watch wrote: 'The importance of justice for Iraq cannot be over-emphasized. Should crimes such as those discussed above go without prosecution, or should perpetrators find their way into a new government in Iraq, the stage would be set for such crimes to be repeated... In order to provide foundation for a government that respects fundamental human rights, the most serious criminal offenses must be prosecuted. Amnesties for such crimes would not only contravene international law, but would fail to provide such a foundation.'

10 See Hanna Batatu, *The Old Social Classes and the Revolutionary Movements of Iraq* (London, Saqi Books, 2004), pp.722–48. Batatu was a respected Palestinian historian who, around a decade after the Ba'ath revolution, wrote a commanding history of the politics of mid-twentieth century Iraq, a monumental work based on extraordinary access to rarely seen Iraqi government records. It can be an impenetrable read but its heavy detail is balanced with Batatu's gentle and sometimes frank tone. He dissects Aflaq's thinking and is tough on the young ideologue. He argues that his theories were confused and rarely thought through and that the party remained elitist, resorting frequently to violence to maintain control even in the early years. Even in July 1968, Batatu says, the population of Iraq was unimpressed by the sham talk of revolution. 'The people met the change of government with utter indifference. They had grown tired of communiqués no. 1, and their wearisome and tasteless rhetoric. The whole thing seemed so distant from them, from the difficulties of their everyday life and the general conditions of the nation. They were simply unable to see the point of it all.'

11 Jawad Salim, the artist who created the Freedom Monument, died from a heart attack from the stress of the work just as it was being completed in 1961. The woman who represents freedom in the

frieze is shown with legs that end without feet. 'Feet stick to the ground; I wanted her to soar high,' Salim is reported to have said. There is more on this sculpture and others in Iraq, in Kanan Makiya, *The Monument: Art and Vulgarity in Saddam Hussein's Iraq* (New York, I.B. Tauris, 2004).

12 See Said K. Aburish, *Saddam Hussein: The Politics of Revenge* (London, Bloomsbury, 2001), pp. 170.

13 Coalition Provisional Authority Order Number 1 De-Ba'athification of Iraqi Society. The full law is available on the CPA's original website at: *http://www.cpa-iraq.org/regulations/ 20030516_CPAORD_1_De-Ba_athification_of_Iraqi_Society_.pdf*.

14 Coalition Provisional Authority Order Number 2 Dissolution of Entities. See: *http://www.cpa-iraq.org/regulations/20030823_ CPAORD_2_Dissolution_of_Entities_with_Annex_A.pdf*. You get a sense of how quickly and under how much pressure these orders were written when you notice the glaring spelling mistakes that there wasn't time to correct: in the title of the document: 'suthority' and 'dissoulution'.

15 Some of the best analysis on the question of tackling a country's dark legacy has been done by the historian Timothy Garton Ash. His writing is drawn from the experience of Central and Eastern Europe in the 1990s. The fall of these paranoid, security-obsessed, former Communist states perhaps offers the best parallel to the challenges Iraq would face after the fall of Saddam. In particular see his book *History of the Present* (London, Allen Lane, 1999), pp. 294–314.

16 See: *Dissident Iraqis seize embassy in Berlin*, Kate Connolly, the *Guardian*, 21 August 2002; *German police free embassy hostages*, CNN, August 20, 2002, *http://archives.cnn.com/2002/ WORLD/europe/08/20/germany.iraq*; and *Police end siege at Iraqi Embassy in Berlin, five detained*, Stephen Graham, the Associated Press, 20 August 2002.

17 My resourceful local journalist in Basra was a friend named Fakher Haider al-Tamimi. He was an extraordinary man, a wiry thirty-eight-year-old former factory worker, who only started working in journalism after the war and became addicted to it. He drove around the city in a battered old sports car which had several mobile telephones recharging in the cigarette lighter and

chased after the news with an extraordinary commitment. He worked with me on several stories in the city and for journalists from the *New York Times*. When I last saw him he told me how he'd just made his break into television reporting. Late on the night of Sunday 18 September 2005, two cars, one with police markings, pulled up outside his apartment in Basra. Gunmen dragged Fakher away, saying they wanted him for questioning. His body was found the next morning, his hands cuffed together and a bag over his head. He had been severely beaten and shot in the head. Fakher, who left behind a wife and three children, was the thirty-sixth Iraqi journalist to be killed since the war.

18 See 'Baghdad's Tale of Two Councils', Dan Murphy, *Christian Science Monitor*, 29 October 2003.

19 When the Baghdad City Council was first established, in July 2003, the Coalition Provisional Authority hailed it as a democratic breakthrough. 'This will mean that Baghdad city officials will be accountable to the people they serve for the first time since before the regime of Saddam Hussein.' It would give Baghdad's residents 'a mechanism for active participation in the rebuilding of their city's infrastructure and institutions.' But the council's powers were extremely limited and the power to take decisions and implement and pay for projects remained with the Americans and what was called the Municipal Executive Committee – in other words government officials and ministers. In small type, in a brief footnote to the announcement, the CPA said: 'The interim advisory councils are not responsible for the delivery of services to the community (e.g., police, electricity, sewage, medical, etc.). That remains the responsibility of the Interim Baghdad Municipality Executive Committee in co-ordination with the CPA.' See Coalition Provisional Authority Press Release, Date: 7 July, PR No. 0012, *Baghdad Interim Advisory Council Established*.

20 Brigadier General Mark Kimmitt, Coalition Provisional Authority briefing, Thursday 12 February 2004, Baghdad. See: *http://www.defense.gov/transcripts/2004/tr20040212-0441.html*.

21 For a good, detailed account of this incident see: Human Rights Watch, *Violent Response – The US Army in al-Falluja* (Human Rights Watch, June 2003).

22   Much later the Pentagon itself finally appreciated how serious this breakdown of trust had become. In a report in 2004, the Defense Science Board, which advises the Pentagon, said this: 'The information campaign – or as some still would have it, "the war of ideas", or the struggle for "hearts and minds" – is important to every war effort. In this war it is an essential objective, because the larger goals of U.S. strategy depend on separating the vast majority of non-violent Muslims from the radical-militant Islamist-Jihadists. But American efforts have not only failed in this respect: they may also have achieved the opposite of what they intended.' *Report of the Defense Science Board Task Force on Strategic Communication, September 2004* (Office of the Under Secretary of Defense for Acquisition, Technology, and Logistics, Washington DC), pp.39–40.

23   See Paragraph 87 in Case number CO/2242/2004, High Court of Justice, Queen's Bench Division, Divisional Court, Before the Right Honourable Lord Justice Rix and the Honourable Mr Justice Forbes, Between The Queen on the application of Mazin Jumaa Gatten al Skeini and others and the Secretary of State for Defence and the Redress Trust, 14 December 2004. The full judgment can be found at: *http://www.hmcourts-service.gov.uk/judgmentsfiles/j2980/al_skeini-v-ssfd.htm.*

24   See Paragraph 344 in Case number CO/2242/2004 as before.

25   See Paragraphs 330 and 345 in Case number CO/2242/2004 as before. The judgment was largely upheld at the Court of Appeal a year later, on 21 December 2005, in Case number: C1/2005/0461, C1/2005/0461B. Lord Justice Brooke, the most senior of the three appeal court judges, ruled that indeed the soldiers were bound by the Human Rights Act from the moment they arrested an Iraqi, though he also said that it was at that stage too early to determine whether a proper investigation had been carried out into the death of Baha Mousa. He also said that the military needed a major reform to the way it carried out investigations into deaths like this and that in future the chain of command should not be involved and the job should be left to the Royal Military Police. The Court of Appeal judgment can be found at: *http://www.bailii.org/ew/cases/EWCA/Civ/2005/1609.html#para 205.*

26 Brigadier General Mark Kimmitt, Coalition Provisional Authority briefing, Wednesday 31 March 2004, Baghdad. See: *http://www.defense.gov/transcripts/2004/tr20040331-0574.html.*

27 US Secretary of Defence Donald Rumsfeld, Media Availability with Jay Garner, Wednesday 18 June 2003, Washington. See: *http://www.defense.gov/transcripts/2003/tr20030618secdef0282.html.*

28 One of the best recent translations of *Gilgamesh* is by Andrew George, *The Epic of Gilgamesh* (London, Penguin Classics, 2003). This quote is from p.20.

29 *The Epic of Gilgamesh*, p.124.

30 Uta-Napishti was the first Noah – he survived a great flood – and was rewarded for it with immortality by one of the gods.

31 It's hard to find many English translations of modern Iraqi poetry. This poem was mentioned by several internet bloggers in the months after the war and they found the original Arabic version at this web address: *http://www.nizarkabbani.com/KASAEED/ 1710-sabbagu-alahzia-alsiaaf.htm.* You can find a couple more poems by Badr Shakir al-Sayyab in Daniel Weissbort and Saadi A. Simawe (eds.), *Iraqi Poetry Today* (King's College London, London, 2003), which has a lot about love and a little about politics and includes Sayyab's poem 'Love Me', which begins: 'I never deny my past, but all those I loved before you, never loved me back.'

32 Bernard Lewis, a Princeton University professor and scholar of the Arab world whose work has been openly admired by George W. Bush's administration, describes Gailani as 'notorious' and a 'proto-Ba'athist' and his brief government as 'a pro-Nazi regime'. See: Bernard Lewis, 'Freedom and Justice in the Modern Middle East', *Foreign Affairs*, May/June 2005. But Charles Tripp, a British historian of Iraq at SOAS in London, takes a more nuanced approach and says Gailani and other Arab nationalists thought the Axis Powers would win the war and so thought it important not to provoke them by being too pro-British. 'The British were still a power to be reckoned with in Iraq, whatever set-backs they were experiencing elsewhere. Consequently [Gailani] advocated a studied neutrality, although his justifications for this position meant that he became increasingly associated with the more

openly pro-Axis sentiments of the Golden Square.' (The Golden Square were four influential Arab nationalist pro-German Iraqi army colonels.) Tripp downplays the fact that Germany and Italy sent materiel to help Gailani and says 'they played a negligible part in the campaign'. See: Charles Tripp, *A History of Iraq* (Cambridge, Cambridge University Press, 2002), pp. 101–7.

33 See Olivier Roy, *Globalised Islam: The Search for a New Ummah* (London, Hurst & Co., 2004), pp.232–4.

34 See Sir Aylmer Haldane, *The Insurrection in Mesopotamia 1920* (the Imperial War Museum/The Battery Press, 2005), p.89: 'Like all semi-savages, they had shown themselves particularly bold when following up a retiring force, and were to be trusted to display marked skill in taking immediate advantage of a fault in dispositions.' Elsewhere he uses words like 'scheming' and 'cunning' to describe the Arab fighters and agrees with one sheikh who tells him: 'The Arab is a slave, and requires a hard master; give him the stick first, then the sugar.'

Sir Aylmer Haldane was made commander of British forces in Iraq in early 1920, three years after the British had captured Baghdad and just a few months before the country rose up in rebellion against them. In the months before he arrived his fellow officers had no sense of the imminent crisis: 'The country at this time was to outward appearances quiet, and that a little more than a year later it would become unsafe throughout its length and breath was not foreseen.' He did inform his readers though, that early on he noted the 'fundamental unsuitability of Mesopotamia as a place of residence for white women and children. The country, unlike India, is devoid of all the ordinary amenities of life, and possesses no hill-station – unless by the favour of the Shah of Persia.' The similarities between the 1920 uprising he describes in such detail and that which began in 2003 are remarkable – clashes in the same towns, the same shortage of troops on the ground, the same misunderstandings, the same arrogance of occupation. Looking back in 1922 after quelling the rebellion, at least in the short term, he wrote: 'We lived on the edge of a precipice where the least slip might have led to a catastrophe.'

35 This group went through various name changes. At first it called

itself *Jama'at at-Tawhid wal-Jihad*, the movement for monotheism and holy war. In the autumn of 2004 Zarqawi announced his allegiance to Osama bin Laden's al-Qaida and started to call his group *Al-Qaa'idatu fii bilaadi r-raafidayn*, al-Qaida in the Land of Two Rivers, sometimes known as al-Qaida in Mesopotamia or al-Qaida in Iraq. Zarqawi, whose real name is Ahmed Fadil al-Khalaylah, is a Jordanian Islamic militant, born in 1966, who travelled to Afghanistan towards the end of the Soviet occupation. He was later jailed in Jordan for five years for plotting against the monarchy and trying to install an Islamic state. After he was released he returned to Afghanistan where he set up a small militant training camp and operated, it is thought, largely independently of bin Laden. He was wounded while fighting in Afghanistan during the American attack after September 11, 2001. He fled to Iran then to northern Iraq. He was convicted in absentia and sentenced to death in Jordan for organising the assassination of an American diplomat, Laurence Foley, in October 2002. The US Secretary of State Colin Powell, in his speech to the UN in February 2003, named Zarqawi as running a 'deadly terrorist network' in Iraq and said he was a bin Laden collaborator. It was proof, he said, of a nexus of terrorism between Saddam and al-Qaida. This has since proved incorrect. Zarqawi was not then working for bin Laden, nor was there any substantial co-operation between Zarqawi and Saddam or al-Qaida and Saddam, nor was Zarqawi a Palestinian, as Powell stated. In the months that followed, though, Zarqawi did become one of the most important figures in the Iraqi insurgency, responsible for arranging suicide bombings, sectarian attacks, kidnaps and executions and by late 2004 he did indeed appear to have forged a relationship with bin Laden. For some time it was thought he had only one leg and wore a prosthetic limb, though American officials later said that was incorrect. For details on Zarqawi and one of the best accounts of al-Qaida and modern Islamic militancy see Jason Burke, *Al-Qaeda – The True Story of Radical Islam* (London, Penguin, 2004).

36 J. M. Rodwell (trans.), *The Koran* (London, Everyman, 1994), p.71.

37 This list was not an idle boast. The names mentioned in this list were people who were indeed attacked, although not all died:

Abdul Zarar, also known as Izzedine Salim, was killed in a suicide car bomb blast on 17 May 2004, as he drove into the Green Zone where he worked as president of the Governing Council; the deputy interior minister, Abdul Jabbar Yousif al-Sheikhli, was injured (he was not killed though at least five others nearby did die) when a car bomb exploded outside his house in Baghdad on 22 May 2004; the justice minister, Malik Duhan al-Hasan, survived a car bomb attack on his convoy which killed five of his bodyguards on 17 July 2004; the governor of Mosul, Usama Kachmula, was killed in an attack on his convoy on 14 July 2004; and five days later on 19 July, the governor of Anbar and the man shown in the film, Abdul Karim Birji, was indeed kidnapped.

38 The sculpture was at the time downstairs in the British Museum in Room 89 and was titled: *Installation of a new Elamite king*. You can read more about it in: Julian Reade, *Assyrian Sculpture* (London, the British Museum Press, 2004) pp.80–4.

39 E. M. Forster, *A Passage to India* (London, Penguin, 1979), pp.287–8.

40 In the January election, the Shia alliance won 48 per cent of the vote and took 140 seats in the 275-seat National Assembly. An alliance of the main Kurdish parties took 75 seats and a list led by Ayad Allawi, the former Prime Minister, won 40 seats. The next largest party was the list headed by the former President Ghazi al-Yawar and which included Hajim al-Hassani. Their party won five seats.

Bibliography

Aburish, Said K., *Saddam Hussein: The Politics of Revenge* (London, Bloomsbury, 2001)

Ajami, Fouad, *The Dream Palace of The Arabs* (New York, Vintage Books, 1999)

Ali, Tariq, *Bush in Babylon: The Recolonisation of Iraq* (London, Verso, 2003)

Anderson, Jon Lee, *The Fall of Baghdad* (London, Little, Brown, 2005)

Batatu, Hanna, *The Old Social Classes and the Revolutionary Movements of Iraq* (London, Saqi Books, 2004)

Bell, Gertrude, *The Letters of Gertrude Bell* (New York, Boni and Liveright, 1927)

Burke, Jason, *Al-Qaeda The True Story of Radical Islam* (London, Penguin, 2004)

Cockburn, Andrew, and Patrick Cockburn, *Saddam Hussein: An American Obsession* (London, Verso, 2000)

Cole, Juan, *Sacred Space and Holy War: The Politics, Culture and History of Shi'ite Islam* (London, I. B. Tauris, 2002)

Committee Against Repression and for Democratic Rights in Iraq (eds.), *Saddam's Iraq: Revolution or Reaction?* (London, Zed Books, 1990)

Dodge, Toby, *Inventing Iraq: The Failure of Nation Building and a History Denied* (London, Hurst, 2003)

Fenton, James, *All the Wrong Places* (London, Granta Books, 2005)

Forster, E. M., *A Passage to India* (London, Penguin, 1979)

Garton Ash, Timothy, *History of the Present* (London, Allen Lane, 1999)

Gellhorn, Martha, *The Face of War* (London, Granta Books, 1993)

George, Andrew (trans.), *The Epic of Gilgamesh* (London, Penguin, 2003)

Haldane, Lieutenant-General Sir Aylmer, *The Insurrection in Mesopotamia 1920* (the Imperial War Museum/The Battery Press, 2005)

Hourani, Albert, *A History of the Arab Peoples* (London, Faber and Faber, 1992)

Human Rights Watch, *Endless Torment: The 1991 Uprising in Iraq and its Aftermath* (1992); *Bureaucracy of Repression: The Iraqi Government in its Own Words* (1994); *The Mass Graves of al-Mahawil: The Truth Uncovered* (2003); *Violent Response – The US Army in al-Falluja* (2003)

Iraqi State Organisation for Tourism, *Iraq: A Tourist Guide* (Baghdad, 1982)

Jabar, Faleh A., *The Shi'ite Movement in Iraq* (London, Saqi Books, 2003)

Jabar, Faleh A., and Dawod, Hosham (eds.), *Tribes and Power: Nationalism and Ethnicity in the Middle East* (London, Saqi Books, 2003)

Hiro, Dilip, *Iraq in the Eye of the Storm* (New York, Thunder's Mouth Press/Nation Books, 2002)

Kepel, Gilles, *The War for Muslim Minds* (Cambridge, Belkhap Press, 2004)

Lawrence, T. E., *The Seven Pillars of Wisdom* (London, Penguin, 2000)

Lewis, Bernard, 'Freedom and Justice in the Modern Middle East' (*Foreign Affairs*, May/June 2005)

Makiya, Kanan, *The Monument: Art and Vulgarity in Saddam*

Hussein's Iraq (New York, I. B. Tauris, 2004)

Mansfield, Peter, *The Arabs* (London, Penguin, 1992)

Nakash, Yitzhak, *The Shi'is of Iraq* (Princeton University Press, 1994)

Nicholson, Reynold, *A Literary History of the Arabs* (London, Cambridge University Press, 1966)

Reade, Julian, *Assyrian Sculpture* (London, The British Museum Press, 2004)

Rodwell, J. M. (trans.), *The Koran* (London, Everyman, 1994)

Roy, Olivier, *The Failure of Political Islam* (London, I. B. Tauris, 1999); *Globalised Islam: the Search for a New Ummah* (London, Hurst & Co., 2004)

Sifry, Micah L., and Christopher Cerf (eds.), *The Iraq War Reader: History, Documents, Opinions* (New York, Touchstone, 2003)

Tripp, Charles, *A History of Iraq* (Cambridge, Cambridge University Press, 2002)

Weissbort, Daniel, and Saadi A. Simawe (eds.), *Iraqi Poetry Today* (London, King's College London, 2003)

Acknowledgements

I am most indebted to those people I have hardly mentioned: the Iraqis who worked with me as interpreters, drivers, guides and friends, at considerable risk to their own lives: Qais, Safa'a, Osama, Omar, Asa'ad, Wisam and Dr Ali. (I omit their family names for their own protection.) Without their help, bravery, patience and dedication none of this would have been possible. I also thank the men and women who are the main characters of this book, for so trustingly letting a stranger into their lives and for sharing their most personal stories at such a difficult time. Thanks to my colleagues at the *Guardian*, particularly Harriet Sherwood, Nick Hopkins, Dave Munk, David Hearst, Heather Mercer, Chris Elliott and Alan Rusbridger. Many thanks to Lisa Darnell at Guardian Books and Rebecca Carter at Chatto and Windus, who had faith in the idea of this book from the outset and who helped bring it to life.

There are many friends who were with me in Baghdad who gave generously of their contacts, advice, friendship and support. Thanks to Stephen Farrell and Ghaith Abdul-Ahad, who both led me into plenty of trouble and then led me out again. Thanks to Wendell Steavenson, Richard Lloyd Parry, Jason Burke, Sam Kiley, Ewen MacAskill, Jonathan Steele, Luke Harding, Michael Howard, Rory Carroll, Kim Sengupta, Patrick Cockburn, Patrick Graham, Farnaz Fassihi, Babak Dehghanpisheh, Toby Harnden, Anthony Loyd, James Hider, Lourdes Garcia-Navarro, Jack Fairweather, Christina Asquith,

Molly Bingham, Steve Connors, Colin Freeman, Stephen Grey, Tara Sutton, Hala Jaber and Tarek Ben Halim. Thanks to Mohammad Shaboot, the last optimist in Iraq, who always insisted I should look for the brighter side. Thanks to Piers Benatar for his advice and relentless humour, and to Andrew Kaye, for his encouragement and perceptive reading of the manuscript. Thanks to Omar Mahdawi for his talents with a videocamera. Thanks to those Iraqis I knew in Baghdad and Beirut for their unstinting kindness, good food and hospitality; Suad and Naira al-Radi, the late Nuha al-Radi, and Wess Tchorbachi. Thanks to Haitham al-Zubaidi for letting me borrow the title of his poem for this book.

Many tens of thousands of people have died in Iraq since the war began. I remember in particular my friends Marla Ruzicka, Faiz Ali Salim and Fakher Haider al-Tamimi. May they rest in peace.

Thanks to my parents, my brother Hugh and sister Kate. And thank you to my partner Juliette Seibold, who put up with my long absences, who came to visit me in Baghdad despite all the risks, who read every word of this book several times over, and who is always my light in the darkness.

Index

319

Mahdi, Imam (Mohammad al-Mahdi), 236–7
al-Majid, Ali Hassan (Chemical Ali), 78
al-Maliki, Sheikh Ahmed Jassim, 74–7
Mansour, Baghdad, 89, 103, 119, 278
Mansour Melia hotel, Baghdad, 10
Marsh Arabs, 306n9
Matrud, Hanan Saleh, 149–50
Mattis, Major-General James, 150
Maude, General, 49, 251
Mello, Sergio Vieira de, 301
Milewicz, Waldemar, 167–8
Ministry of Agriculture, 84, 95, 261–2
Ministry of Defence (Britain), 149
Ministry of Defence (Iraq), 61
Ministry of Education, 77, 209
Ministry of Human Rights, 197
Ministry of Industry, 215, 216, 217, 271
Ministry of Information, 9, 42, 43, 47, 61
Ministry of Planning, 42, 47
Mohammad, Prophet, 12, 243
Mohammad (television cameraman), 154–5
Mohammed, Shamil, 65
Mohsin (al-Taie's assistant), 43, 44
Mohsin, Syed Jabbar Syed, 24
Mongols, 40
Moore, Brigadier William Hewitt, 144
Mossad, 134, 212
Mosul, 51, 77, 159, 160, 208, 269, 301
    governor of, 249, 314n37
Mousa, Ala'a, 148
Mousa, Baha, 143–4, 145, 146–7, 148, 149, 302, 310n25
Mousa, Daoud, 144–5, 148, 149
Movement for a Democratic Society, 289
Muawiyah, Caliph, 12
Mukaradeeb, 150
Mukhabarat, 46, 49
Munif, Abdul Rahman, 281
Museum of the Martyrs of Hostile Persian Shelling, Basra, 29

Musharraf, General, 8
Muslim Clerics Association, 270
Mustafa, Abu, 60
Mustansiriya University, 114, 118, 279–82
Mutannabi, 176

Nabi, Ala Mohammad Abdul, 72
Nabi, Mohammad Abdul, 72–3, 76, 78
Najaf, 4, 37, 39, 105, 220, 222–40, 276, 301–2, 303
    cemetery of the Valley of Peace, 4, 225; the Hawza, 226
Nasb al-Hurriyya (Freedom Monument), Baghdad, 53–4, 307–8n11
National Assembly
    under Ba'ath Party, 41;
    dissolved, 61; after elections, 288, 295, 296, 314n40
National Security Directorate (Amn al-'Am), 21–2, 85–6, 202
National Theatre, 169–70
Nazis, 64, 69, 207–8, 209
an-Neifus, Mohammad Jawad, 28, 33–6
New Zealand, 60
1920 uprising, 30, 312n34
1941 coup, 207–9
1958 coup, 48–9, 134, 251
1991 uprising, 5, 7–8, 14, 15, 16–17, 21, 22, 26, 27–8, 29, 187–8, 193, 199, 200, 202, 203, 305n1 and n2 see also Mahawil killings
Nineveh, 40

Olympic Committee, 61
Omar, Ali Salim, 217–18
Omar, Taiseer, 131–2
Operation Vigilant Resolve, 156
Osama bin Zayed primary school, Falluja, 132–3
Ottomans, 40, 51

Pakistan, 8
Palestine Hotel, Baghdad, 166
Paradise Square, Baghdad, 50, 85
Paris, 42, 43, 48